PRIVATE GARDENS
of
AUSTRALIA

PRIVATE GARDENS
of
AUSTRALIA

TEXT BY *Sarah Guest*

PHOTOGRAPHS BY *Jerry Harpur*

HARMONY BOOKS/NEW YORK

THIS BOOK IS DEDICATED TO RICHARD JAMES CHESTER GUEST

SG

FOR MARJORIE, NICHOLAS, ROBERT AND MARIAN, MARCUS
AND DANIEL   JH

Copyright © 1990 by Sarah Guest
Photographs copyright © 1990 by Jerry Harpur

Published by Harmony Books, a division of Crown Publishers, Inc.,
201 East 50th Street, New York, New York 10022
Published in Great Britain by George Weidenfeld & Nicolson Limited in
1990.
HARMONY and ◢⟨⟩◣ are trademarks of Crown Publishers, Inc.

Manufactured in Italy.

Library of Congress Cataloging-in-Publication Data is available upon
request.

ISBN 0-517-58002-0
10 9 8 7 6 5 4 3 2 1

First American Edition

CONTENTS

TASMANIA

SOUTH AUSTRALIA

WESTERN AUSTRALIA

Author's Acknowledgements

I would like to thank all those who have helped in the preparation of this book, in particular Barbara Maund, Sam Daniell, John Patrick, Percy Pleskus and Trevor Nottle. The generosity of the garden owners has made the research and writing a very pleasurable experience and convinces me that the fine art of gardening is an integral part of the art of living. Above all I would like to express my gratitude to my husband, James, without whose assistance and patience this book would never have been completed.

Photographer's Acknowledgements

Photography took place over a period of eighteen months and I am very grateful indeed for all the help, advice and kindness of many people, not only of all the garden owners, but particularly the following:

John Osborne of the Toowoomba Tourist Board and Janet Langley (Queensland); Peter Valder and Allan McNeish, Geoffrey and Mary Ashton, and Julie Keegan (New South Wales); John and Beth Henwood, James and Sarah Guest, Pat Fraser, Ron and Jenny Phillips, and Kevin O'Neill and John Graham (Victoria); Peter and Prue Jackson, and Peter and Ann Cripps (Tasmania); Jerry and Kath Trethewey, and Dr Brian Morley (South Australia); Liz Adams (Western Australia) and Rosemary Verey, whose experience there did much to encourage me to take up Michael Dover's invitation to photograph this book.

Bob Ansett of Budget helped greatly with the cost of car hire; Ceta W1, London, processed the colour film; and Downtown Darkroom made the black-and-white prints.

I have thoroughly enjoyed liaising with Colin Grant and Coralie Hepburn of Weidenfeld and Nicolson through the various stages of this book and with Lindsey Rhodes, whose layout has done so much to embellish the photographs.

Finally, I am very grateful for the support of my wife Marjorie.

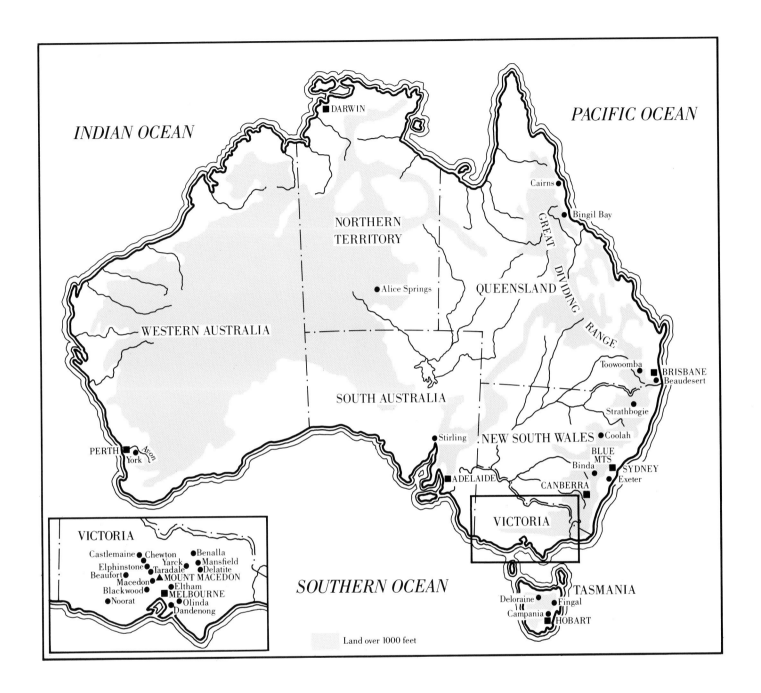

INDIAN OCEAN

PACIFIC OCEAN

■ DARWIN

NORTHERN
TERRITORY

● Alice Springs

QUEENSLAND

● Cairns

● Bingil Bay

GREAT DIVIDING RANGE

WESTERN AUSTRALIA

SOUTH AUSTRALIA

Toowoomba ● ■ BRISBANE
● Beaudesert

● Strathbogie

● Stirling   NEW SOUTH WALES   ● Coolah

BLUE
MTS

Binda ●   ■ SYDNEY
● Exeter

PERTH ■
● York   Avon

■ ADELAIDE

CANBERRA ■

VICTORIA

SOUTHERN OCEAN

TASMANIA

Deloraine ●   ● Fingal
Campania ●   ■ HOBART

VICTORIA

Castlemaine ● ● Chewton   ● Benalla
Elphinstone ● ● Yarck   ● Mansfield
Beaufort ● ● Taradale   ● Delatite
● Macedon ▲ MOUNT MACEDON
Blackwood ● ● Eltham
● Noorat   ■ MELBOURNE
● Olinda
Dandenong

Land over 1000 feet

A map to show the
states, the main towns
and the locations of
the gardens referred to
in the text.

INTRODUCTION

*A*USTRALIA – THE OLDEST of the world's continents and the only island continent – extends from the cold southern latitudes to the northern tropics. Its gardens, including those described in this book, reflect the differences to be found in the landscape of a huge continent and the wide variations in the climate.

The first human inhabitants are known to have had a solid practical knowledge of indigenous plants but there is little evidence of Aborigines cultivating the ground; for them nature itself was a garden, which they understood well. Australia's first European visitors saw the place as a botanic treasury and eagerly helped themselves. It is of interest to note that in early nineteenth-century Europe enthusiasm for plants was so intense and so universal that Josephine, Empress of France, was able to acquire the seeds of indigenous Australian plants from British sources at a time when Britain and France were at war. When the French ship the *Naturaliste*, carrying botanical specimens from Africa and Australia, was intercepted by British ships in the Channel, it was released on the express order of the Admiralty. This was in 1803 when the first European inhabitants of Australia were probably more interested in gardening as a means of survival than in the ornamental plant collections of Europe. In the early days of settlement the plants collected so avidly by Europeans were regarded with interest but seldom given a place in Australian domestic gardens. Such records as remain indicate that the first settlers from Europe, whose long and dangerous sea journey took about five months, looked back nostalgically to the land they had left and in their gardens hoped to create reminders of it. For them the ornamental garden was a place to collect and nurture familiar plants that were grown in Britain. The arrival, on the Sydney wharf, of the first wild British primrose (*Primula vulgaris*) to reach the antipodes is said to have caused a stampede among those desperate to catch a glimpse of this nostalgic symbol.

The climate these first gardeners struggled with was markedly different to the one they had left. The poet Mary Gilmore speaks of the courage of early Australian gardeners who faced drought, flood, bushfire, heatwave and even snow, possibly all in one season. When I first came to Australia I was told that it was a land with no climate, only weather. In fact it is a land of many different climates and many different extremes of weather – perhaps the only universal factor is that it is, almost without exception, a place of climatic extremes. To the hazards listed by Mary Gilmore can be added cyclones, dust storms and earthquakes.

The British were later joined by settlers from other parts of the globe, who brought with them their cultural preferences, including traditions of garden design and an attachment to particular plants. Chinese goldseekers, for example, brought with them a knowledge of meticulous plant craft. From the early days of settlement Australians of European descent visited the Orient and were often influenced by what they saw. Other influences came from the Mediterranean countries and this was reflected in formal designs and superb stonework. As the land became settled, the affluent established great gardens that imitated recognized styles or drew on the traditions of various cultures.

Although it was not a universal practice, many of these gardens were enclosed and the natural scenery screened from view. The rich created lush green gardens, secluded and safe, where the realities of a tough and sometimes dangerous world could be forgotten. The garden became a refuge, where the luxuries of a leisurely, cultured life could be enjoyed, and the harsh landscape, which some early settlers considered ugly, was shut out. However, as Australians have grown away from their diverse cultural origins, they have learnt to love the landscape, with its soft colouring, huge skies, wide horizons, harsh light and wide spaces. Today many old country gardens which began as enclosed spaces have been opened to views of the landscape beyond the garden's boundary. As the colours and forms of the natural

A simple picket gate leads to the house at Nooroo, New South Wales, where great tree ferns tower over wisteria and azaleas.

world came to be included in the garden's atmosphere, so an interest in native plants developed and the land itself influenced the design of the garden. One garden enthusiast, whose garden sits happily in the Australian landscape, told me he disliked the flat rectangular lawns he had seen in Europe, describing them as being 'against nature' and 'claustrophobic'. Today many Australian gardeners think twice before enclosing space or altering the natural fall of the land.

In many cases what makes a garden peculiarly Australian is a matter of detail. Sometimes it is the use of colours or forms which stand up to or are enhanced by the harsh light; sometimes it is the extensive use of white flowers, so that the garden will retain its decorative effects at night. Some of the rockwork depicted in this book is distinctively Australian, bearing little resemblance to the dainty effects often created by British gardeners. Even gardens that at a cursory glance might be situated anywhere in the English-speaking world, on closer inspection reveal specifically Australian characteristics. A grand avenue of the kind that elsewhere in the world might frame an imposing statue or an extensive sheet of water, in Australia might form a vista to a few trees planted in a natural way round a small pond. What the visitor may fail to appreciate is that those few trees have symbolic significance for Australians. To those with a different vision of pastoral paradise it might be difficult to realize that it was sights such as this, with their promise of water, which lured the early settlers out into the bush, leading to the opening up of the country. An imposing avenue of evergreens framing a marble monument in the formal Italian style might have its symmetry broken to dramatic effect by the presence of a single eucalypt which no one had the resolve to remove when the avenue was planted. Details such as these may be no more than local variations on standard themes but they give many gardens an undeniably Australian character.

Gardening in Australia calls for a knowledge of its particular conditions. The hazards of the climate necessitate the constant close observation of plant behaviour. In temperate areas the addition of water and fertilizers produces a growth rate which would be the envy of many gardeners in the northern hemisphere. But this rate of growth often produces as many problems as it solves. While it is possible to have a mature-looking garden in a few years it is also possible to lose it in a very brief period of neglect. Moreover, the ultimate life span of exotic trees which have grown faster than would be normal in their native habitat remains, in many cases, unknown. The long summers mean that plants, particularly those required in a flowering border, must perform for several months. Gardeners designing such borders must know which of their plants can be relied on to bloom continuously for months and which can be successfully encouraged to bloom several times during the season. Much of this vital information is only acquired by gardeners through trial and error and yet many of the borders described in this book are kept in flower for up to six months.

One factor, common to almost all Australian gardens, is the attention given to native birds, whose presence is encouraged and often influences plant choice, garden design and the use of colour. Almost without exception the gardens depicted in this book contain some plants chosen by their owners with the express intention of nourishing particular birds. Even in the smallest gardens water is invariably provided for birds, and the owners are rewarded with flashes of brilliant colour which no flower can match. Some gardeners go so far as to design and plant their gardens primarily to attract and display wild birds.

If some of the older gardens are only distinctively Australian in matters of detail, other more recent gardens, are consciously Australian in every aspect. Not only are natural forms copied in the layout of these gardens, but the plants grown are confined to those which are indigenous to the continent, or even to the specific area. Here, as in other gardens, much of the skill comes in learning about plants and in finding out how they will behave in a particular garden. With native plants there is even more to discover. As an added excitement there is the thrill of using plants which have never been incorporated into ornamental gardens before, noting their behaviour, needs and potential for creating decorative effects. The pioneer plantsmen and plantswomen who have used native plants extensively have created gardens that are unlike any to be found elsewhere in the world.

Fashion here as anywhere else plays a big part in garden design. A book written ten years from now will certainly reveal new trends in garden design and a different emphasis in plant choice. But it is the gardens of today this book is about and I am indebted to the owners of these gardens for their generosity in sharing their gardens, their knowledge and their thoughts with the readers of this book. I hope the book expresses my gratitude for their hospitality and patience and adequately reflects my admiration for their vision and skill.

QUEENSLAND

Manutara

CAIRNS

Kay Purvis

THE GARDEN OF Manutara stands on a hillside overlooking the wide valley which holds the city of Cairns and its harbour. The harbour can be seen from the garden but the dominant feature is the hills which surround the valley and overlook the garden. These North Queensland hills – ever changing in colour but always impressively strong in outline – are typical of the area and retain much of their dense indigenous rainforest. Kay Purvis, who has spent many years in the Centre, has made a garden wherever she has lived. She even introduced daffodils to Alice Springs, and says that, after some experimentation, they grew as well as they would in England, and clumped up nicely. When she came to Manutara thirteen years ago she began, once more, to make a garden – this time a garden with a spectacular view.

As the drive climbs the hill it is bordered on one side with a bank of Singapore daisy (*Wedelia trilobata*) and on the other with a wall of bamboo. Elegant spider hibiscus (*Hibiscus rosa-sinensis*) grows with the bamboo and hangs its scarlet, upturned petals over the driveway. Through the bamboo climbs the clock vine (*Thunbergia grandiflora*) and hangs its dreamy lavender-blue flowers from the wall of greenery for most of the year. The area where the drive opens out near to the garage is surrounded by a fairly dense planting and gives the impression of a jungle glade. To one side a specimen of the rain tree (*Samanea saman*) reaches a height of 100 feet (30 m) and in typical tropical style is a garden in itself, the massive branches supporting a village of vegetation. A variety of ferns display a dense mass of greenery from the heart of the tree and native tongue orchids (*Dendrobium lingui-forme*) spray their delicate white blooms

Left The house seen through the trunks of the golden-cane palms. The natural rainforest rises in the distance.

Right At dawn, *Coreopsis lanceolata* and bougainvillea pick up the light under the golden-cane palms by the swimming pool.

from the massive boughs. High above, the tree displays its own many-stamened flowers, which resemble pink powder puffs, but it is the dramatic torrents of *Bougainvillea × buttiana* 'Brilliant' which first catch the eye. Like many of the bougainvillea cultivars, 'Brilliant' displays bracts in various colours; they open out a coppery-orange and mature to a shade of bright cerise. The effect from the ground is of an apricot-coloured waterfall, which is made all the more dramatic by the height and the backdrop of blue sky. Also edging the glade are an African tulip tree (*Spathodea campanulata*), which is 80 feet (24 m) high, and avocado trees. Over the garage, mounted on the building itself, are ferns whose long fronds hang down over the entrance, making it look more like the entrance to a

cave than a man-made structure.

To one side of the glade is a gate from which steps lead up to the house. *Otacanthus* 'Little Blue Boy' hangs over the steps, providing a continuous display of soft blue flowers and the fragrant *Hoya australis* is trained round the retaining walls. As one reaches the top of the steps the full drama of the garden unfolds. The garden is planned round a swimming pool, and the whole site is perched on level ground on the hillside, with a view over the city to the hills beyond. The pool itself is lined with beige pebbles and surrounded by brown slate. Piles of dark brown rocks are used to give the area form and to one side these rocks have been used to create a waterfall. Arranged in a natural style, the rocks continue over the side of the pool and into the water itself, allowing the viewer to enjoy all their shapes and colours magnified and clarified by clear water. The area was designed to resemble a natural water hole and the highly reflective clear water takes on a soft green tint which, in the company of the brown slates and rocks, makes a simple, restful background for the brilliant colours of the garden.

Although the garden is beautiful and dramatic from all angles, to appreciate its full glory you need to be swimming in the pool. The view in one direction is through a fringe of flowers to the hills on the far side of the valley – it is like swimming into distant mountains. In the other direction there are the majestic hills behind the house, with their clothing of rainforest. To one side the trees from the glade breaking the sky are bright with the torrent of bougainvillea growing over the rain tree and the great orange flames of flower from the African tulip tree. Lying in the water you can watch the huge electric-blue Ulysses butterflies against the glowing bougainvillea or study the birdlife in the African tulip tree. The brilliant buds of this tree, which squirt water when pinched or pressed, attract the constant attention of the rainforest birds.

The view from the house over the pool to the hills on the other side of the valley is framed by palms. A group of golden cane palms (*Chrysalidocarpus lutescens*) overhang the pool and direct the eye across the valley. To one side *Bougainvillea × buttiana* 'Surprise'

Left With the flowers and the long leaves of the ginger lily in the foreground, the garden behind the house is designed to merge with the rainforest.

Seen past the heart-shaped leaves of *Syngonium podophyllum*, the waterfall torrent helps to create a natural effect.

fluffs its chimera of large clustered bracts. Some of its bracts are totally white, others are a bright magenta, and others a mixture of the two. At ground level *Coreopsis lanceolata* fringes the pool, its serrated petals making an interesting reflection in the water when contrasted with the strong lines of palm leaves. The gout plant (*Jatropha podagrica*) adds its striking orange heads of flower to the flowery display and its interesting gout-like swollen form to the reflections in the water. In the evenings the still water is broken by the visiting rainbow bird, whose iridescent-green feathers coupled with its gleaming copper underwing add flashes of electric colour to the garden. The sprightly little kingfisher, smaller than a sparrow and brilliantly clothed in gleaming blue-green feathers, also mistakes the pool for a water hole.

On one side of the pool, using a wall of the house which is closely covered with *Ficus pumila* 'Minima' as a backdrop, stones are arranged to flow through the plants and symbolize a dry riverbed. The arrangement is bordered with large rosettes of arching wine-coloured leaves provided by *Aechmea* 'Foster's Favorite' and a mat of grey-green leaves provided by *Raoulia australis*. On the

A visit to Easter Island was the inspiration for this guardian of the drive.

stony 'riverbed', held in a scooped-out rock, lie two egg-shaped stones which were once used by the Aborigines as grinding stones. The wonderful fossilized remains of an ancient tree trunk lie in the 'river' too. Beyond the 'riverbed' the emphasis is again on flowers and the building is draped with pink and white chains-of-love (*Antigonon leptopus*). Below this vigorous scrambler the clear blue flowers of *Evolvulus pilosus* 'Blue Sapphire' open their flowers each morning with the daylight. The corner of the house is marked with the spectacular indigenous cycad (*Lepidozamia hopei*), whose annual new growth has an almost luminous glow.

A little garden within a garden makes a private area in front of a bedroom door. It consists of a shady terrace bordered by a little fresh-water pond. The pond is covered with the aquatic fern *Salvinia molesta* and looks as if it was covered with deeply-cut damask encased in a dense border of green lace-like ground ferns. A stone in the centre of the pond supports a small statue of Diana. Above it hangs a sandpaper vine (*Petrea volubilis*), which hangs its bluish-violet sprays of flowers over the water and terrace, giving this charming little garden its private secluded atmosphere.

At one point the garden opens out and a teahouse is placed against the hill to overlook the swimming pool. Over the teahouse grows an abundance of fragrant, white *Stephanotis floribunda*. The beds here contain a selection of *Hippeastrum* cultivars and a collection of the plants usually referred to as ginger plants. Among them are found the plumes of red ginger (*Alpinia purpurata*), the red torch ginger (*Nicolaia elatior*) and the showy pinky-white heads of shell ginger (*Alpinia zerumbet*).

In this hillside garden man-made features have been carefully integrated with natural elements to take full advantage of the tropical setting and the dramatic views. The owner's joy in decorative colour is never allowed to override her respect and feeling for natural forms and shapes. A combination of gentle design and the glory of tropical flowers creates the magic of a garden in which, appropriately for such a dry continent, water plays an important role.

A Rainforest Garden

BINGIL BAY

Helen & Steve Wiltshire

THE GARDEN CREATED by Helen and Steve Wiltshire lies on the tropical coast of North Queensland, where the natural vegetation was impenetrable rainforest. The rainfall exceeds 172 inches (4300 mm) a year and the air is constantly hot and steamy. However, the first white settlers in the area were not daunted in their agricultural enthusiasm and clear felled the land in an attempt to establish coffee, tea and mango plantations.

The area is subject to periodic cyclone damage. In 1986 the garden was totally defoliated by a cyclone but the growth rate is such that today there is no evidence of the extensive damage. Immediately following the cyclone plants which enjoy sunlight thrived in the undergrowth but as the upper storey of foliage regenerated the forest garden has returned to its former character, with shade-loving plants thriving under the canopy and establishing themselves on the wood of living trees.

In its design the garden today owes little to European influences apart from following the European tradition of decorating an area close to a dwelling with edible and ornamental plants. The range of plants grown goes beyond those indigenous to the area but the atmosphere is that of natural rainforest altered only in order to make it accessible to man. There are no open lawns, no views over the countryside or coastline, no flowering borders, no elaborate statuary, no clipped hedges and no contrived vistas. Here even the distinction between garden and house is somewhat blurred. The main living area has a roof and a floor but there are no doors, windows or walls to separate it from the garden – people and animals can move from house to garden without the usual impediments.

The drive to the house resembles a simple forest track. Tall, slender Alexandra palms (*Archontophoenix alexandrae*), which are indigenous to the area, hang above the undergrowth. Their greenish-grey trunks rise to a height of about 100 feet (30 m) and their single-stemmed leaves are particularly graceful. The undergrowth glows with red crab claws (*Heliconia*), whose huge glowing red bracts light the lower storey of the forest and whose large solid paddle-shaped leaves make an interesting comparison with the feathery fronds of the ferns and tree ferns which surround them. As the driveway approaches the house it is bordered on one side by black fishtail palms (*Caryota rumphiana*), which are indigenous to the area. There are few palms with more decorative foliage. The grey trunks taper upwards to a height of about 33 feet (10 m) and the great fans of bipinnate leaves, which give the palm its common name, some reaching widths of 10 feet (3 m) and lengths of 23 feet (7 m), arch outwards, spreading widely from the central trunk. The other side of the drive is decorated with the classic beauty of coconut palms (*Cocos nucifera*), which have naturalized along the tropical coast of northern Australia. The exact origin of these well-known palms remains unknown but they are common to coastlands throughout the Pacific. To one side stands an African tulip tree (*Spathodea campanulata*), which carries huge brilliant orange-red blossom throughout the year.

A bridge links the driveway, which lies in a dry gully, to the house, which is at a higher level. The path structure is made out

of wire netting which is moulded into the required shape, covered with hessian and reinforced with concrete – the result is a natural-looking structure with the appearance of having been formed from a single piece of weathered stone. The structure widens as it crosses the gully and the area supports an open studio thatched with palm fronds. From this raised position at the middle level of the rainforest one can enjoy a closer view than is usual of the plants in the upper storey. The bridge also gives a view down on the lower storey, revealing the full expanse of the tracery of leaves – a view which is rarely available to the earth-bound human. The strange hanging wine-purple flowers of the banana trees (*Musa × sapientum*), which discard one petal each day, and each day produce one new petal, can be closely and easily examined. The deep maroon-red bananas pick up the colouring of the dramatic deep reds of the torch ginger (*Nicolaia elatior*), whose waxy blooms, the shape of their common name, rise from groups of paddle-shaped green leaves that are 6 feet (2 m) long. Looking down onto the gully the full lace-like drama of the foliage of young fishtail palms can be appreciated. Passionfruit vines (*Passiflora edulis*) and the glossy-leaved pink-flowering *Mandevilla sanderi* climb over the structure and, like so many tropical plants, can be relied on to provide their decorative flowers throughout the year. Close to the front door stands a golden guinea tree (*Dillenia alata*), which provides dense shade. It has a warm-brown bark which peels off in translucent papery flakes. It too flowers throughout the year. In the undergrowth close to the door chenille plants (*Acalypha hispida*) display their curious long velvety tails of dusty-red flowers against their lovely dark-green veined and pointed leaves.

The living area of the house looks directly into the lower storey of the rainforest. Raked gravel paths, speckled with soft shafts of the sunlight which penetrates the upper canopy of leaf, lead the eye through the forest. The pole-like trunks of the Alexandra palms, the clumps of slender-stemmed *Hydriastele wendlandiana*, and a variety of indigenous pandanus, with their interesting exposed upper roots, can be seen from within the house. These three groupings form the backbone of the garden. The roof line forces the eye down to examine the detail of the forest floor and the lower level of the rainforest. Growing beneath and up the trees are

Previous page No walls, windows or doors divide the living room from the garden in this house.

The drive, bordered on one side by ferns and on the other side mainly by banana palms, leads under the recently constructed bridge to the house.

a wide variety of plants and it is their contrasts of colour, shape and texture, enhanced by the constant flicker of the soft shafts of sunlight, that give the garden its fascinating detail. There are the large leaves and strong forms of *Bromelia humilis* and the bird's-nest fern (*Asplenium nidus*) at ground level and a little higher, as both often establish themselves on the trunks of the trees. The pale lettuce-green leaves of *Caladium bicolor* contrast with the veined rich-greens of *Maranta leuconeura massangeana*. The small electric fern (*Selaginella willdenovii*) produces its odd shimmering electric-blue foliage supported on stiff stilt-like roots from the ground beneath the trees. The native military fern (*Pteris ensiformis*), which takes its common name from its erect habit, displays its short branching dark-green fronds and *Dracaena sanderiana* contrasts its spiky dark form with the soft greens of the ferns.

Some flowers, like those on a low-growing scarlet bilbergia, are to be found at ground level but much of the floral glory in this garden comes from the creepers which climb through the upper storey of the trees. As one walks through the garden one becomes aware that there are other 'gardens' above one's head. The fragrant *Quisqualis indica*, whose petals change from white to red, flourishes in the trees and the cerise bracts of bougainvillea glow in the light shade. The brilliant Papua New Guinean flame-of-the-forest vine (*Mucuna bennettii*), with huge scarlet flowers resembling the upturned beaks of parrots, drapes its flowering vines through the trees and flashes its dramatic colour through the trees in early spring. As the forest recovers from the cyclone the ferns which prefer a higher altitude have regrown and today pour their greenery from the upper canopy. Delicate ribbon ferns (*Vittaria elongata*) once more hang from the trunks and the South American staghorn (*Platycerium andinum*) displays a mass of its curious pendulous fronds. High above, the canopy of palm foliage shields the garden and the visitor from the sun and gives the secluded garden its cool feeling and its fragmented pools of flickering light.

Nectar- and insect-feeding birds and

Right Lit by bright sunlight, which streams through a break in the canopy, the open air studio stands on a bridge spanning one of the gullies.

reptiles frequent the garden. The little emerald green tree snake adds his brilliant colouring to the greens of the forest. The large iridescent-blue Ulysses butterfly flaps through the garden. Emerald doves live on the forest floor and yellow-breasted sunbirds hang their long tapering nests from the vines. The spiky echidna waddles down the garden paths but perhaps the strangest visitor of all is the huge flightless cassowary, which can reach a height of 6 feet (1.8 m). Having no natural predators, these birds are without fear of the human race and occasionally enter the living room at meal times to check the plates. However, most of their time spent within the house is employed inspecting their own images in a looking-glass.

The gravel paths are linked and lead towards a wooden table with chairs set at the top of a deep gully which borders the garden. Arching over the table is the giant or king fern (*Angiopteris evecta*), which is indigenous to the area. It has a thickly grooved trunk and immense fronds. Nearby an angel's-trumpet tree (*Datura × candida*) hangs its dramatic long white trumpet-like flowers and, in the evenings, gives off an exotic musky scent. A bridge leads over the gully and from its edge the plants which line its steep banks can be inspected. There is water at the base of the gully but this is hidden, as it usually is in a rainforest, by the thick vegetation which overlaps the gully's floor. Coffee, tea and mango trees dating from the land's short career as a productive unit survive and have reached impressive sizes. The native, fern-like *Bowenia spectabilis* clothes the gully's steep sides and, making a strong contrast, elephants' ears (*Alocasia macrorrhiza*) spread their broad arrow-shaped glossy leaves through the under-growth. The lawyer's cane (*Calamus austra-lis*), which is used to make baskets and cane furniture, strings its slender, flexible stems from tree to tree, decorating each with its fern-like foliage. The vine gains its odd common name (in addition to lawyer's cane it is also known as the wait-a-while vine and hairy-mary) from its sharp reddish-brown spines which cling tenaciously to clothing. The matchbox vine (*Entada phaseoloides*) climbs through the dense vegetation and produces its large flattened dark-brown seeds. In the last century, these strange

Right A walk through this garden involves pushing aside the tropical vegetation.

Below The flame-of-the-forest vine, *Mucuna bennettii*, climbs spectacularly through the trees by the path leading to the house.

seeds, which gleam like polished walnut, were decorated with ornate silver filigree-work and used to hold tapers for the fire.

This garden shows such imagination that it is no surprise to discover that Helen Wilt-shire is one of northern Queensland's best-known artists. Instead of drawing on European traditions, the design is an enthu-siastic response to the tropical climate and vegetation, and shows its owners' know-ledge and enthusiasm for the plants which thrive in this environment. Perhaps the most interesting aspect of the garden is the way it lets one observe rainforest plants, many of them indigenous to the area, at different levels, something that is not possible on a casual visit to natural rain-forest. It is a place in which the play of light and shadow are as important as the fasci-nating contrasts between the shapes and colours of the leaves but, above all, it is a garden that explores every level of the rain-forest.

Greenlaw

TOOWOOMBA

Mr & Mrs Dennis Hill

MR HILL called his garden Greenlaw after his Yorkshire home. His enthusiasm for plants began when, as a child, he was given a small glass frame and a few cacti. By the time he was eight he was a member of the British Cactus Society. Since then his interests have broadened to encompass a huge range of plants, many of which he has the opportunity to grow in semi-tropical Queensland. The garden he has created covers 2.5 acres (a hectare) and has been developed from what was a bare site nineteen years ago.

Greenlaw stands in a leafy suburban street. Little of its botanical treasury can be seen from the street, which is screened by a curtain of weeping fig (*Ficus benjamina*), but on entering the drive the eye is immediately caught by four huge cycads (*Macrozamia riedlei*). Sometimes called Zamia palms, these cycads have a thick trunk (some of which is underground) and a dramatic fern-like canopy composed of many narrow leaflets. Indigenous to west Australia, these cycads have been transported and transplanted as mature specimens. These particular specimens are thought to be over a thousand years old. Whatever their age, they have tremendous stage presence.

A path leads under the cycads and through a rainforest garden to the rear of the house. Bangalow palms, (*Archontophoenix cunninghamiana*) tall, single-stemmed, feather-leafed palms, which are indigenous to the area, provide the upper canopy. The plants which grow with them in this garden come from all corners of the globe and a group of three pony-tail trees (*Beaucarnea recurvata*, also known as *Nolina recurvata*) from Mexico, with their short trunks and interest-

ing long, grass-like leaves, have been successfully established at the edge of the forest. The lower storey is filled with a selection of ferns – including the native *Adiantum hispidulum* and tree ferns – a variety of cycads and fishtail palms (*Caryota rumphiana*). Each trunk or log is a garden in itself and is hung with orchids and ferns. Staghorn ferns (*Platycerium superbum*) and elkhorn ferns (*Platycerium bifurcatum*) hang down their impressive greenery from above head height,

Right Cycads add their strong sculptural shapes to the drive.

Above Beyond the tarn, the hills on the far side of the valley add their magic to the garden's atmosphere.

Right The cactus garden is planted either side of the hill-side stream, with the tall cactus *Pilosocereus palmeri* dwarfing smaller cacti and succulents.

Below An antique statue of a boy stands in the rainforest.

while the finer leaves of the filmy maiden-hair fern (*Adiantum diaphanum*) cling to wet rocks. Orchids, including the Cooktown orchid (*Dendrobium bigibbum*), the tongue orchid (*Dendrobium linguiforme*), the deep mauve *Dendrobium phalaenopsis* and the golden shower of *Dendrobium speciosum* (all of which are native to Australia) spray from the trees in the company of the delicate soft mauve blooms of *Dendrobium pierardii* from India and a collection of the epiphytic *Cattleya* orchids. Dramatic *Vanda* orchids which flower in shades of blue, mauve, pink and maroon and are sometimes borne on stems 6 feet (1.8 m) long, grow from the tree ferns and there are also the *Brassocattleya* hybrids, which are sometimes described as the most beautiful orchids. The range of orchids ensures that the forest displays bloom from early winter until mid-summer, after which twining plants of *Hoya carnosa*, *Hoya bella* and *Stephanotis floribunda* add their charms to the floral display. Beneath the trees, edging the paths and rocks, are carpets of the native ivy-leaved violets (*Viola hederacea*) and the mauve cutleaf daisy (*Brachycome multifida*), both of which bloom continuously.

In the middle of the forest stands the lead statue of a boy holding an eel. The statue, dating from 1740, came from another English garden which Mr Hill had known well and been inspired by in his childhood. Today it takes pride of place in a rainforest and introduces the torrents of water which pour through the garden at the touch of a switch. Water is stored in an underground tank and is channelled through the garden at the rate of 1000 gallons (4546 litres) a minute. The shafts of light which penetrate the upper canopy and the glittering water, which flows over and under massive blocks of sandstone, give this shadowy forest garden a strongly theatrical atmosphere.

The garden's full drama, however, is only seen when one emerges from the flickering light of the forest to the open garden which lies on a northern slope behind the house. A wide lawn slopes gently down the hill and a glorious view to the tree-clad hills of the Great Divide on the farther side of the valley unfolds. Immediately below the garden is a sheer drop of almost 2000 feet (600 m).

From the garden itself all that can be seen are the many distant hills and the bird's-eye view of the mists which swirl through the valley floor. A tarn (Dennis Hill uses the word of his homeland to describe this mountain lake) lies at the garden's boundary. At its edge a selection of plants with sculptural forms are silhouetted against the theatrical backdrop. Queen palms (*Arecastrum romanzoffianum*), a group of three blackboys (*Xanthorrhoea hastilis*) and a selection of yucca varieties display their distinctive shapes against the mists of the valley and the soft shades of the surrounding hills. The tarn itself has been given an orange and white flowery border with the orange colour provided by the Colombian browallia (*Streptosolen jamesonii*) and the white by a mist of spiraea.

The fast-flowing stream vanishes underground at the edge of the rainforest garden to reappear just above the tarn, where it flows through a miniature sandstone chasm. Sandstone has been transported to the site and is used to link the various distinctively different areas in the garden. As sandstone is found in Europe, South America and Australia it is used throughout the garden to create a natural harmony between the diverse plantings. (The only exception is an isolated, highly formal area at the front of the house where English Portland stone has been used to create a formal effect.) The sandstone has been laid with great care and the rocky outcrops give the impression of coming from one great seam of rock.

Here, above the tarn, the sandstone is used to provide a natural-looking background to an extensive collection of cacti and succulents. Tall ribbed single spikes of the blue-green *Pilosocereus palmeri*, which produces tubular pink flowers with cream anthers at night, dominate the scene and rise to a height of 6 feet (2 m). The golden barrel cactus (*Echinocactus grusonii*) forms a perfect hemispherical dark shape with contrasting bright golden spines. The slow-growing columnar old man cactus (*Cephalocereus senilis*) wears a beard of long white hairs. *Aloe ferox* displays its orange-scarlet flowers from the centre of its branching rosette of blue-green fleshy leaves while the partridge-breasted aloe (*Aloe variegata*) produces its deep glossy green white-marked leaves and pinkish-red flowers. The royal agave (*Agave victoriae-reginae*) has frosted rosettes of white striped spineless dark green leaves and a variety of pincushion cactus (*Mammillaria*) forms spiny clumps and produces large cream and magenta flowers. Three different shades of bunny ears (*Opuntia microdasys*), white, yellow and orange, spread their circular forms against the angular shapes of the rocks. *Kalanchoe beharensis* makes an odd contrast in colour: the brown downy covering of its lance-shaped olive-green leaves gives the impression of them being mahogany-brown with silvery undersides. The combination of the varied shapes and colours of the plants makes an interesting study with the rock and the rushing water. What surprises those who are only accustomed to seeing such plants on windowsills is not only the variety of shapes, colours, textures and forms but also the abundance and delicacy of the flowers.

Greenlaw's garden is a plant collector's garden but it is also a designer's garden. Here great attention is paid to giving the various groups of plants the right setting, to grouping them in a natural manner, and to imitating natural formations of rock. Above all the garden has a great sense of theatre and makes full use of its spectacular site.

Nindooinbah House

BEAUDESERT

Mr & Mrs Patrick Hockey

MOST OF the garden at Nindooinbah probably dates from 1909 when Mrs Hockey's grandparents, Mr and Mrs William Collins, celebrated the birth of their son by enlarging an already imposing homestead and laying out a garden appropriate to its grandeur. The family had lived in the district since 1844 and Mr William Collins was the first white child to be born in the Albert River district. The house itself dates from the 1850s, only a decade after white settlement in Queensland began so the sophistication of its large rooms, wide verandahs and their elaborate but sturdy wooden chinoiserie is somewhat surprising. One factor dictating the choice of site was probably the presence of good timber; the elaborate woodwork is made from trees which grew on the property, chiefly Australian cedar (*Toona australis*). Mr and Mrs William Collins moved to Nindooinbah in 1900 and made it their main residence. Later, when the imposing house was extended under the direction of the architect Robin Dods (whose designs are thought to have included the garden), the chinoiserie was retained and new verandahs decorated to match the earlier elaborate tracery. Mr and Mrs William Collins had spent some time in Japan while on their honeymoon and when adding a grand entry pergola they adopted a modified Japanese style which harmonizes well with the chinoiserie on the house. The first kitchen, which like those in many other early homesteads was originally housed in a separate building, was moved to become a gatehouse. The gatehouse and the long verandahs which border the large house are still there. So are the gates and the pergola. The rich soil and

The boughs of the frangipani tree are seen against the elaborate woodwork of the verandah.

plentiful water which produced the strong wood now supports a large, elaborate and flourishing garden.

The house, which looks out over a wide valley, takes its name from a local aboriginal word, Nindooinbah, meaning 'the place of ashes'. In the valley quite close to the edge of the garden lies a long lagoon fed by a natural spring. Here the local Aboriginal people camped and made their fires and it is now assumed that the mounds of ash left by their fires gave the place its name. Today wood duck and geese swim on the lagoon. The view over the water and valley – on a clear day you can see for sixty miles (110 km) – is an important part of the garden's atmosphere. It is a scene which changes constantly with the light and with

Yellow Singapore daisies and *Iris kaempferi* edge the water in this view of the teahouse, beyond which rises Nindooinbah House.

Right At dawn a fountain plays amid irises near the front door, backed by palms and a bunya pine.

the movement of the layers of mist which roll through the valley. Beyond lie hills, the largest of which is called Biningera (meaning 'turtle') with a curious outline like the hump on a turtle's back. The indigenous people told a story of the great battle between the land animals and the sea animals. The land animals, with the turtle as their leader, were victorious but the great turtle died of wounds received in battle. It is his mountain which looks down on the garden at Nindooinbah and here that the little mistletoe bird who tried to staunch his wounds gained his red feathers. Nindooinbah as it is today bears evidence of both European and oriental civilizations but its past lies with the dreamtime.

The house is approached through an avenue of *Jacaranda mimosifolia* and camphor laurel (*Cinnamomum camphora*), which were planted early this century. The main drive leads through one of several gates designed in the Japanese manner and trimmed, as they always have been, in a glowing shade of lacquer-red. When a teahouse was added to the garden recently the shade was used once more. To one side of the gate stands a magnificent planting of bamboo, which reaches a height of 110 feet (35 m). On the other side stands a new plantation of bamboo; here Chinese bamboo with a green and yellow striped stem has been chosen to give height and the garden is edged with a mixture of shrubs and trees. These include a traveller's tree (*Ravenala madagascariensis*), which obligingly holds its great fan of foliage in line with the boundary fence. Large clumps of white and yellow ginger (*Hedychium coronarium* and *H. gardnerianum*) are planted with the shrubs. Close to the front door the house is bordered by huge summer-scented frangipani trees (*Plumeria rubra*) in a fruit salad of shades. Their stout fleshy forms look curiously correct with the strong lines of the chinoiserie behind them. The pergola, from which hangs an old Japanese lantern, supports grape vines, which were grown from a cutting taken many years ago at Hampton Court in England. The edges are bordered with flowering bulbs; jonquils, freesias and Ifafa lilies (*Cyrtanthus mackenii*) bloom in winter and spring, followed by clivias in early summer.

The garden opposite the main entrance has been redesigned in recent years and today a fountain, formed from a Colebrookdale urn, plays from the centre of a circular pool. The water in the pool is broken with Japanese irises (*I. kaempferi*) and waterlilies. Beyond this structured formality lies the old arboretum, which extends the impression of formal design with its well-grown well-placed old trees. The trees and grass are arranged so that they, in conjunction with a spectacular bougainvillea hedge, screen the main house and the formal elements of its surroundings from the other buildings on the property and link the garden to the productive land beyond. To one side stands a hoop pine (*Araucaria cunninghamii*) with an old Australian statue of an Aboriginal boy depicted in the 'noble savage' manner and holding his stone axe and woomera. Here too are found bunya pines (*Araucaria bidwil-*

lii), which are often regarded as Australia's answer to the monkey puzzle popular in European gardens of the same date. Bunya pines are known to have been thought of as friendly trees and their massive nuts regarded as a delicacy by the indigenous people. To the rear of the arboretum stands a superb bottle tree (*Brachychiton rupestris*) with its enormous swollen bottle-shaped trunk. It makes an unusual but compatible companion to an equally well-grown English oak (*Quercus robur*). Bottle trees are rare in this part of Queensland but this one was brought from one of the first Collins properties in the far west.

Recently the view between a side entry to the house and a magnificent cathedral-like woolshed (which has not seen sheep since the 1860s) has been opened up and given emphasis by extending and controlling the arboretum. A broad grassed pathway flanked on each side by high curtains of tropical greenery now gives the building the importance it deserves. To give these curtains uniformity pink pepper trees have been used at regular intervals but the main impression given is of walking between high green curtains of leaf. The impression is gained by the dense plantings of a selection of glossy-leaved trees and flowering shrubs which combine to give the one area of the garden which is not exposed to the drama of the view over the valley its own dramatic strength. Tamarinds (*Tamarindus indica*), silky oaks (*Grevillea hilliana*), weeping figs, both the native *Ficus hillii* and the Indian *Ficus benjamina*, leopard trees (*Ficus collina*), bauhinias and macadamia trees (*Macadamia tetraphylla*) all combine to make these walls of greenery a fascinating study in leaf and shape contrasts.

The trees of the arboretum are of interest and have reached impressive sizes in an area not noted for its tree growth but the trees in this garden which catch the imagination are the tall slender palms which wave high above the house and garden. The house, with its long stretches of ornate verandah, follows the Queensland tradition of being raised from the ground in order to allow the air to circulate beneath the floors and cool the dwelling, and it stands well above the garden. It is an imposing building sur-

rounded by rolling lawns but it is dwarfed by the elegance of the tall slender queen palms (*Arecastrum romanzoffianum*), which wave above the garden, decorating the skyline wherever one looks and dwarfing the world beneath their elegant foliage. Two great palm avenues fan out from the house. One extends from the steps leading down from the main verandah into the garden and was clearly intended to give the garden its chief axis. The other lies to one side of the house and picks up the line from some steps in what is known as the nursery wing and takes a great curving path through the extensive lawns. The lawns themselves are dotted with trees, garden ornaments and beds containing mixed plantings. A Moreton Bay fig (*Ficus macrophylla*), once described by Baron von Mueller as the grandest of Australia's avenue trees, stands in the mown grass and is planted with king orchids (*Dendrobium speciosum*). These grow around the tree and from the trunk itself, so that they seem to spray their spectacular blooms from its heart. An old circular rose bed has become a thick forest of canna lilies. The mown grass incorporates a grass tennis court and the netting surrounding it supports a variety of flourishing roses. One end of the court is adorned with the life-size figures of Adonis and Il Pitori. These traditional figures were commissioned in Italy by Patrick Hockey.

In front of the house a path runs parallel to the verandah. On each side of the path wide borders separate the house from the lawns. Hibiscus, abutilons, gardenias, camellias, hydrangeas, roses and golden marguerite daisies (*Anthemis tinctoria*) form the backbone of these plantings and a wealth of smaller perennials and annuals add colour throughout the year. In line with some steps, shaded by *Quisqualis indica* and a double cream honeysuckle, a path links the house by way of an elaborate circular arrangement of beds, known to the family as the Roundabout, to the major palm avenue. The beds of the Roundabout are planted with roses and a large Australian urn, dating from the Edwardian era, stands in the centre. The roses are underplanted with perennials, bulbs and annuals and the beds that border the path also include old Ed-

wardian favourites. Snapdragons, salvias, phlox, calendulas, marigolds and larkspurs mix informally with the plants favoured by the present generation of Australian gardeners. Among these are daylilies, nicotianas, petunias, verbenas, dimorphothecas, hippeastrums, Madonna lilies (*Lilium candidum*), November lilies (*Lilium longiflorum*) and watsonias. The garden is noted for its pink and white Shirley poppies, which billow through the flower beds. Sometimes as many as 20,000 flowering plants are established in a season and the flowery triumph is misted with clumps of fennel and Queen Anne's lace. Below the palm avenue and beyond the garden in line with the steps the slender spire of a flagpole stands against the magnificent view to the rolling country. To one side of the pole (and screened by shrubs from the view down the axial path) Patrick Hockey has built his studio using an unaffected simple early Australian style.

One side of the rolling lawn is bordered with a barrier of shrubs through which grow white and yellow Banksian roses. A stand of elegant Chinese tallow trees (*Sapium sebiferum*) display their soft heart-shaped leaves and catkins and an old wisteria is trained to tree-like proportions over a metal frame. A gap in the greenery reveals a gleam of water and an exotic teahouse, which appears to float on the water. Designed by Patrick Hockey, it resembles the structure depicted on willow-pattern china and reflects the mood of Nindooinbah where successive designs have picked up the oriental influence evident in the first design. This upper stretch of water, a recent addition, gives no impression of raw modernity and already has a deep collar of greenery provided by iris in shades of blue and mauve, papyrus and yellow-flowering Singapore daisy (*Wedelia trilobata*). Here one can enjoy the tranquillity that water brings. The lake has three fountains, simple jets of water whose plumbing and nozzles are below the surface of the water. A well-shaped jacaranda stands on the bank, made twice as magnificent when in bloom by its reflection in the water. The lagoon is separated from the lake by a sloping paddock, in which stands a magnificent and massive bunya pine. The two elongated strips of water lying at different levels, each enhancing the other, take up the horizontal lines made by the distant hills.

The folly garden which borders the lake contains a formal rose and lavender garden (the lavender blooms picking up the colour from the jacaranda which stands on the bank). To one side stands a shade house which, clothed in weather-worn lattice, looks as if it dates from the early garden. In fact it is a recent addition and is densely covered with the Alister Clark roses 'Lorraine Lee' and 'Black Boy', which cascade over the structure. On the outside the walls are bordered with grape ginger (*Alpinia caerulea*) and within lies a tropical fernery.

An old bush house which houses another lush glowing tropical setting stands at the back of the folly garden. Here bird's-nest ferns, tree ferns, maidenhair ferns and hydrangeas are used to provide a green and shadowy setting for an Edwardian four-seasons statue. The bush house opens into a space which was once occupied by a glasshouse and today links the garden to one end of the verandah. The low walls of the greenhouse remain and give definition to a small herb garden made all the more charming by the contrast in scale with the rest of the expansive garden. One wall is topped with a solid arrangement of terracotta pots holding a collection of pelargoniums. Planted on the other side of the wall and overhanging the pelargoniums grows a dramatic yellow hibiscus. The other low wall is covered by cascading nasturtiums. The beds within the enclosure are delicately planted with herbs, low-growing scented plants and old-fashioned roses.

The garden at Nindooinbah remains in good hands and within the family whose inspiration gave it birth. Nothing has been done to destroy the essentially Edwardian character of the garden and such changes and additions as are made are in keeping with the strong oriental influence of the 1909 garden. Nindooinbah is lucky to be served by the creative talent of Patrick Hockey, who is one of Australia's best-known artists, and by Margaret, who has the energy and knowledge to preserve and enhance a remarkable historic legacy.

Oleanders and shasta daisies (*Chrysanthemum × superbum*), frame this view through the garden to the hills beyond.

NEW SOUTH WALES

Coolah Creek

COOLAH

Mr & Mrs Donald Arnott

*T*HE PROPERTY of Coolah Creek lies in the Coolaburragundy valley some 250 miles (400 kms) to the north-west of Sydney. The lovely valley has a park-like appearance with tall, graceful trees, yellow box (*Eucalyptus melliodora*) and kurrajong (*Brachychiton populneus*) scattered through the paddocks. The Coolaburragundy River runs through the valley and supplements the garden's annual rainfall of 32 inches (810 mm). The homestead and its garden lie some 2,200 feet (670 m) above sea level at the head of the valley surrounded by the high country of the Liverpool Ranges. The winters here are cold with heavy frosts and the summers are described as 'usually mild'.

The garden is the creation of three generations of the Arnott family. It began in 1928 when Colonel and Mrs J. M. Arnott built the house, laid out a garden and, in the paddocks close to the homestead, added elms, oaks, chestnuts and ash to the indigenous trees. The garden of today follows the lines of the original plan but Mr Donald Arnott attributes the bones of the present garden to his parents, Mr and Mrs Pat Arnott. Mr and Mrs Donald Arnott moved to Coolah in 1970 and during their tenure the garden has been maintained, extended and, when necessary, replanted with enthusiasm and knowledge. The most noticeable additions made in recent years are the spectacular flower borders.

The road to Coolah Creek runs along the valley floor – it is as if the valley itself forms a part of the garden. When the drive enters the garden it swings to one side of the house, providing tantalizing glimpses along the lawns and into the greenery of the garden. Much of the atmosphere and colouring in this garden derives from the hills which surround it. The colours of the hills change constantly with the weather and time of day and, in consequence, the light within the garden itself alters quite dramatically from time to time. Many of the colours used in the garden are chosen from a pale palette with whites, creams, soft pinks, and blues predominating and echoing the misty shades of the surrounding hills. Occasionally a brightly coloured flower joins the soft display to add focus to the soft colouring of the natural environment or to bring emphasis to a particular part of the garden.

A wide band of lawn lies parallel to the north face of the house. Below it, on land which slopes gently away from the house, lie another two tiers of mown grass. At the centre of the northern aspect of the house lies a courtyard and the garden takes as its main vista a line running between this central courtyard and a gate which allows access to the home paddocks. From the courtyard the eye is led down the three tiers of lawn to the gate. The three expanses of lawn are separated by mixed plantings of trees and shrubs. Each area has its own character and individual details, and each

Left The house from the herbaceous border, framed by the foliage of *Acer negundo.*

33

The main vista framed
by the twisted
columns of the
northern courtyard.

provides charming views which cut across the major vista and add a pleasant sense of exploration to a garden tour.

The northern courtyard is surrounded by tiled covered walkways. These are sufficiently wide to allow for chairs and potted shrubs and, on three sides, they connect the house to the courtyard. The fourth side exposes the view over the garden and centrally placed steps allow access from the courtyard to the garden. The courtyard's central square is open to the sky and here a circular pond is embedded in neatly clipped ivy. A small lead statue of a boy playing the pipes is used as a fountain. The courtyard affords shelter to tender plants and as rain water is used on the container-grown plants the area is reserved for those enjoying acid conditions. In early winter *Rhododendron* 'Christmas Cheer' displays its blush-pink flowers. This decorative bloom is followed in mid-winter and late spring with the flowers of azaleas and camellias. In early spring the pink buds of *Jasminum polyanthum* break into a torrent of white star-like flowers, which scent the courtyard with their enchanting fragrance. In summer there are the creamy flowers and scent of gardenias and the colours of pelargoniums, and in autumn these are followed by fuchsias. The northern courtyard has the formal atmosphere needed in an area which is almost incorporated into the imposing house. It makes an interesting contrast with the garden beyond its strongly delineated boundaries, where the well-grown trees and shrubs give the garden an informal relaxed atmosphere. There is a southern courtyard, where similar plants are used and the pale blue *Plumbago auriculata* is trained against a sheltering wall.

The first broad stretch of lawn is bordered on one side by the house which, covered with Virginia creeper (*Parthenocissus quinquefolia*), provides a wall of greenery. Along the wall there are specimens of container-grown conifers. On the other side of the grass a low wall separates this higher stretch of lawn from the lower level. The wall itself is almost invisible behind a dense flowery planting of shrubs and roses. The rose 'Baby Darling', the highly fragrant mock orange (*Philadelphus coronarius*), the rose-pink *Spiraea* 'Anthony Waterer', and two plants with soft pink flowers, *Abelia schumannii* and *Weigela* 'Apple Blossom', hang over the low wall shaded by the large trees dating from the first plantings. Pink and white flowering hawthorns (*Crataegus laevigata* cultivars) are used throughout the garden and today display well-formed shapes, rough furrowed bark and thickly massed bloom. The central path is guarded by buns of spiraea and by two well-grown specimens of *Acer negundo*. Standing on this top lawn is a strikingly beautiful ghost tree (*Acer negundo* 'Variegatum') and visitors get their first glimpse of the garden through the branches of this elegant silvery tree.

The second tier of lawn lies directly below the first tier. The open space is bordered by informal plantings of trees and shrubs, with a few trees standing on the grass as isolated specimens. The area has the feeling of a woodland glade – a glade which is given excitement by Judy Arnott's wide flower borders. These borders, which are invisible from the house, lie below the low wall which separates the two lawns and take as a backdrop the shrubs and trees from the higher level. Early in the year there are great clumps of creamy-yellow Louisiana hybrid irises set off with foaming mounds of catmint (*Nepeta* × *faassenii*). When the flowers of the early irises fade, the spikes of their

Right The top lawn seen from beneath the boughs of *Acer negundo* 'Variegatum'.

Below A view over the herbaceous borders from the top lawn.

foliage remain, contrasting with the soft mounds of the catmint, which mists the border with its mauve-blue flowers and lace-like grey foliage until late in the autumn. Clumps of softly coloured apricot foxgloves stand beneath the trees. The dancing heads of apricot-pink aquilegias extend the soft colouring, which is brought into focus by a soft yellow marguerite daisy (*Chrysanthemum frutescens*), which flowers throughout the season and retains its mounding form. As the foxgloves and aquilegias die back, leaving the interesting contrast of their leaf forms, pink daylilies (*Hemerocallis* hybrids), pink bearded irises, white *Nicotiana affinis* and white shasta daisies come into bloom. White and pink dianthus are used in the foreground with clumps of *Pyrethrum parthenium* 'Aureum', whose little white flowers provide a wealth of bloom and whose sharp yellow leaves reflect the colour found in the flowers of the marguerite daisies. The rose 'Honey Flow' tumbles through the border and standard forms of two other roses, 'Apricot Nectar' and 'Peace', bloom with the perennials. Spikes of blue are provided by *Campanula rapunculoides*, delphiniums and veronicas. Pineapple sage (*Salvia rutilans*) speckles the border with its small scarlet heads of flower and provides mounds of soft-green leaves. The border is well thought out and the flower display lasts for a good six

35

months of the year. Mounding bun-like plant forms contrast with spiky leaves, and the backdrop of the low wall is softened by the shrubs which pour over it. The effect is of soft colouring used to extend a feeling of woodland tranquillity.

This second tier of the garden contains two ponds. The first lies in the lee of the low wall and is hidden from the open garden by the trees which border the lawn. The water is surrounded by flowers and more flowers pour from the top of the wall. These include the rose 'Sea Foam', *Convolvulus mauritanicus* and *C. cneorum*, a blue-mauve verbena, berberis and lots of the white form of *Centranthus ruber*. *Malus* 'Eleyi', which carries deep wine-coloured blossom and later displays a crop of apple-shaped fruits and red autumn foliage, stands by the pond and nearby is a pink hawthorn and the purple-leaved *Prunus cerasifera* 'Nigra'. Beneath their branches are dramatic clumps of white arum lilies (*Zantedeschia aethiopica*) and white and blue agapanthus. Deep blue Pacific irises stand on the banks with *Bergenia cordifolia* and pink crinum lilies (*Crinum moorei*) and from the water itself rise

Left A small lead statue of a boy playing the pipes stands as a fountain beneath the open sky in the courtyard.

Very early light on the pond with pickerel weed, arum lilies, blue irises and pink and white *Centranthus ruber* framed by a cordyline on the right.

conjunction with the autumn foliage in the woodland glade, are spectacular and remain to decorate the garden with a flash of scarlet through much of the winter.

The third tier of lawn sweeps round the lower garden in a shallow curve. An avenue of poplars has been planted to emphasize the curve and the area is known as the Poplar Walk. On one side the park-like paddocks can be seen through the trunks of the poplars. On the other side the walk is edged with the well-grown trees which border the woodland glade. Among these trees many roses have been established; the garden contains over one hundred different varieties. Some climb through the trees themselves; others, like 'New Dawn', have been trained over huge frames, which drip with blossom against the woodland backdrop.

Coolah Creek is a relaxed country garden that enjoys a dramatic setting. The formality of the courtyard and the area close to the house merge imperceptibly with the informal lawns and woodland plantings which, in turn, strike a compatible note with the park-like paddocks close to the garden. Above all, the garden has been planted by a great colourist who has taken the colours of the surrounding countryside as her palette.

the magical blue spikes of the Asian water hyacinth (*Eichhornia crassipes*).

The second pond, which lies to one side of a woodland glade, has a different character. The water is clearly visible from the open lawn and the small expanse of water is used to emphasize the sense of space and distance as one looks over the pond through the branches of a weeping willow and a fringe of pampas grass (*Cortaderia selloana*) to the hills. A few large rocks, which look as if they had been placed on the banks by nature itself, bring the pond into focus. Trees planted informally on the lawn include a grove of silver birches; liquidambars, with their striking red autumn foliage; claret ash (*Fraxinus oxycarpa* 'Raywood') and desert ash (*Fraxinus oxycarpa*); the West Australian *Astartea fascicularis*; and the elm-like nettle tree (*Celtis australis*). The second tier of lawn is divided from the third lawn by a clipped hedge of cotoneaster. Its white flowers add to spring's drama and its red berries, seen in

Above Rocks are used to give focus to the pond set at one side of the lawn. The water itself draws attention to the view of the countryside beyond the formal garden.

A gate at the far end of the main vista allows access to the park-like paddocks.

A North Shore Garden

SYDNEY

Mr & Mrs E. Georg Herda

MR AND MRS HERDA bought the old orchard of an established garden sixteen years ago. Three large trees, some Kentia palms and several camellia bushes were retained in the irregular block. The large trees were incorporated in the design of the new garden, which combines geometric straight lines and soft curves, the formal and the informal. The palms were moved to the vicinity of the swimming pool and the camellias were used with other evergreen shrubs to screen the view of neighbouring houses. An old spreading maple surrounded by a curving low wall now stands in the courtyard in front of the elegant house. Behind the house a great redwood and a large pin oak (*Quercus palustris*) add their presence to a strongly designed garden. Today the garden is fully established and the trees planted by Mrs Herda are well grown, so that it is impossible to guess which trees were there before the modern garden.

This is, in essence, a suburban garden but it is a garden which has lost the rigidity imposed by the strong territorial boundaries of well-fenced Australian suburbia. The garden borders are planted to screen unwanted views and to merge into the foliage of neighbouring gardens. Fences are clothed in closely clipped ivies and evergreen jasmines and resemble thick green hedges. However, within the garden the spaces are strongly controlled and it is these defined spaces which attract the eye and lead to the enjoyment and examination of scale, plant and flower.

The driveway curves gently through dense banks of shrubs. Each side is edged with clipped evergreen azaleas which bear large single white flowers in spring and autumn. These thick small-leaved shrubs merge together and have been clipped to resemble a soft swell of sea which is broken with crests of white flower through late winter and spring. Behind the swell of azaleas stands a solid wall of camellias. The gleaming leaves of *C. sasanqua* 'Mine-no-yuki', which bears its double white flowers in autumn, are used here to great effect. The two thick bands of greenery, the azaleas dull green and camellias a glossy bright green, one clipped to give emphasis to the horizontal line, the other to provide vertical strength, give the curving driveway its dramatic form. However, the disciplined treatment is neither sterile nor dull and *Freesia refracta* 'Alba' has been allowed to add its less than neat grass tufts to the scene. Content with their situation, these freesias have seeded themselves through the azaleas and along the base of the low brick wall which borders the higher side of the shrub-planted driveway. The creamy flowers peep at irregular intervals from the gravel surface and spice the early spring air with their clear scent.

On the lower side of the driveway the shrubs are pierced by a row of liquidambars (*L. styraciflua*) which have been stripped of their lower branches and only allowed to spread their horizontal elegance high over the driveway. The treatment gives the bands of evergreen shrubbery beneath their branches sufficient protection from the summer glare while allowing the shrubs the light needed to maintain their thick well-foliaged appearance. The fence, resembling a dense green hedge, has orange jessamine (*Murraya exotica*) trained and clipped

against it. The heavily perfumed creamy-white jessamine flowers, in spite of heavy clipping, decorate the summer scene for several months at least. This driveway is almost never without a lavish trim of white or cream flower but it is the strong use and control of foliage which gives the entry its constant grace and form.

The driveway leads on one side to the garage and on the other through low walls, where the rose 'Clair Matin' winds round the gate lights, into a raked gravel courtyard in front of the house. The area is defined by the walls of the house, by the low walls which separate the courtyard from the driveway and by a bank of plants. Immediately inside the courtyard stands the old spreading maple. The ground beneath the maple is planted with *Trachelospermum jasminoides* 'Variegatum', which bears decorative pink and white new foliage as well as carrying scented white flowers for many months. The plants are clipped low to the ground, making a decorative carpet throughout the year. Opposite the maple stands a gleditsia with an interesting under-planting of the rose 'Blanc Double de Coubert'. The graft is well covered by a thick layer of mulch, encouraging the production of suckers, which are clipped back almost to the ground each winter. The result is a foaming horizontal layer of rich green foliage and masses of scented blooms. There are none of the vertical divisions which are normally visible between rose bushes grown in a more conventional manner. The borders of the gravelled space are edged with low thick geometrically trimmed box hedges which continue around the central space to the front door. These box hedges and a white *Camellia sasanqua* 'Mine-no-yuki' espaliered against one wall give an architectural quality to this elegant area. The rose 'New Dawn' is grown against the front of the house and on either side of the front door stand matched clipped bay trees. In the beds in this area a shell-pink Japanese anemone is used extensively for its soft blooms and carpet of fresh green leaves and against one fence pear trees have been espaliered. The courtyard has the strongly formal character appropriate to the fore-court of an imposing house but is made in-

Geometric shapes are made with stone, brick and clipped box making the soft shapes of the foaming roses all the more dramatic.

Previous page The yellow-green foliage of *Gleditsia triacanthos* 'Sunburst' hangs over the courtyard at the front of the house.

teresting with the unusual and successful choice and treatment of the plants, in particular the training and cutting of groups of similar plants to form soft horizontal planes of greenery and flower.

The garden behind the house has a strongly controlled design with formal geometric elements near the house, merging imperceptibly with the less structured planting on the periphery. The house itself is hung with the rose 'New Dawn' and *Rosa laevigata*, and is bordered with huge tubs of holly. A stone and brick terrace, decorated with containers filled with topiary and flowering plants, runs the length of the house. The terrace is bordered by two impressive rectangular formal gardens, a herb garden and a rose garden. Wide formal stone steps, decorated with superb topiary, lead down to the mown grass of the less formal area. Here the beds have gently curving outlines, the plants are allowed to spread themselves and lawn rather than stone paving is used to define the two major

spaces. The garden in this section (furthest from the house) is on two levels and a curving sunken wall, which runs approximately at right angles to the house, divides the two levels. Steps set into the wall link the two informal garden spaces. A great redwood underplanted with Japanese maples guards the far end of the garden. The beds here are planted with white hydrangeas and white Japanese anemones standing before a hedge of *Camellia sasanqua* 'Pure Silk'. In autumn a planting of rain lilies (*Zephyranthes candida*) adds a wide ribbon of crocus-like flower. The pin oak, underplanted appropriately with oak-leaved hydrangeas, stands to one side of the upper garden. Pillars of evergreen conifers, topiary and flowering trees, the chief of which are a single pink weeping cherry and a *Magnolia × soulangiana*, separate the two levels in the informal garden.

The rectangular herb garden bordering the terrace, edged with dwarf peach trees, strawberries and apple-scented pelar-

the topiary and hedging in this garden, has been clipped constantly and systematically over the years so that it has an impenetrable solid appearance. The garden has a simple rectangular design and within the box outline stand three huge standard weeping 'Sea Foam' roses. Their trunks are now thick and the well-pruned canopy of leaf and flower billows out over a large area so that they look more like perfectly shaped trees than rose bushes. It might be thought that a rose garden containing only three rose plants would not qualify as a rose garden but this example is spectacularly dramatic because of the simplicity and discipline of its design, and its superbly grown plants, not because of the number of specimens. The ground beneath the rose trees is planted with mind-your-own-business (*Helxine soleirolii*), each trunk rising from a rectangular mat of fresh green velour, which is controlled to cover the exact area of earth deeply shaded by the rose. Where more light penetrates the canopy, low-growing white fibrous-rooted wax begonias provide small clusters of flowers and decorative leaf for nine months of the year.

Wide stone steps bordered by perfect

The herb garden borders one of the entrances to the garden by the kitchen door.

Right Standard roses 'Sea Foam' in the formal rose garden are underplanted with white *Begonia semperflorens* and the mossy ground cover of *Soleirolia soleirolii.*

goniums, contains a series of small beds in which golden marjoram is used to provide a central golden cushion. The other beds contain mats of golden thyme and santolina. The low matting foliage contrasts well with the small triangular beds of blue-grey spear-like foliage and purple flowers provided by dwarf iris. At one end of the herb garden stands a simple stone bench enveloped in clipped box. Behind the bench curves a hedge of clipped Mexican orange (*Choisya ternata*) and above that is a bank of mixed evergreen shrubs clipped to form a wall of flowering greenery. Once again the clever combination of horizontal and vertical lines pleases the eye. In this case the device also performs the practical tasks of providing a dramatic backdrop to the garden, forcing the eye down to the herb garden and providing privacy for the household.

The dramatic rose garden, separated from the herb garden by the grass of the informal garden, is edged in neat box, which, like all

cones of box lead down from the terrace to the grass. A swimming pool lies at one end of the terrace but at a lower level so that if one looks along the terrace the water is unseen and the eye rests on a summer-house placed at the far side of the pool on the main axis to the terrace. As the land drops away the stone of the terrace and the stone of the retaining wall which border the pool are separated by a clipped hedge of var-iegated golden euonymus. This is cut to the same level as the upper stonework and curves round to border the steps which lead down to the grass. The pool itself is sur-rounded by white azaleas, camellias and *Gardenia jasminoides* 'Radicans' and the fence clothed with well-trained *Mandevilla laxa*.

Informal garden beds curve round the trees and border the lawns in the part of the garden farthest from the house. Shrubs screen the garden, and the beds are densely planted with flowering perennials and annuals. Despite an effect of random charm, the plants are carefully placed for harmoni-ous colour groupings and interesting leaf shapes and contrasts. On the far side of the garden the low curving wall is screened during the summer months by a wisteria-like fall of pink *Indigofera decora*. The dainty shrub is planted with the white form of valerian (*Centranthus ruber*). The silvery leaves of helichrysum are mixed with the pink forget-me-not 'Carmine King'. Pale blue lace-cap hydrangeas are situated under

A seat is edged with clipped box at one end of the herb garden.

a golden ash. Blue pansies and blue-toned true geraniums make good contrasts of plant shapes and bloom together. In places the ground is thickly greened with the leaves and white flowers of an oxalis cultivar. *Parochetus communis*, which makes a green clover-like carpet of leaves and has gentian-blue pea-shaped flowers, is used in a similar fashion. In the shade a soft pink salvia, columbines and irises display their complementary colour and leaf forms. Jeru-salem sage (*Phlomis fruticosa*) is used to fill the ground space round two columnar conifers, completely hiding the somewhat dusty bare nether parts of the trees, which rise from the grey collar of foliage. The creamy white *Rosa bracteata* winds round a simple wooden support in front of the two evergreens. The dull dark leaves of the conifers provide the perfect backdrop to the shiny leaves and glowing new growth of the rose. This study in yellows and greens is completed with fresh-green clumps of feverfew foliage with its yellow daisy-like flowers. Daylilies, blue iris and true gerani-ums are particular favourites in this area. As elsewhere in the garden, the colours are mainly confined to pastels. Pale blues, creams, soft yellows, pinks and mauves are chosen in preference to strong reds and oranges. The garden gains its spectacular effects from good grooming and the abun-dance of flowers and flourishing growth rather than from brilliant colour.

The imaginative combination of the formal and informal has produced impres-sive results in this garden. There are flowers right up to the windows for much of the year and when, in winter, there are fewer flowers, the perfect proportions of the hedging and topiary remain to decorate the scene and please the eye with their perfect symmetry. This is a garden which combines the best of most gardening worlds. It is well designed, well planted and well maintained and, for the most part, it is the work of one woman, Mrs Herda. All the pruning and clipping are done by her and she estimates that most of the topiary and extensive hedging is clipped at least five times every two years. All garden rubbish is recycled to provide the rich mulch needed for healthy thick growth in this climate.

Greenwood

SYDNEY

Mrs Elisabeth Longhurst

GREENWOOD, AN OLD sandstone house built in a simple classical design, lies in the northern suburbs of Sydney. What began in the 1870s as the cottage of a rural timber-getter is now a charming family house bordered by one of the city's busiest roads. In spite of the road it retains the feeling of a country garden and a far-away-from-everything atmosphere which derives in part from the adjoining Dalrymple Hay Nature Reserve. The 40 acre (sixteen hectare) forest which sweeps round two sides of the garden is the last surviving stand of vegetation native to the area. The great pole-like trunks of blackbutt (*Eucalyptus pilularis*) and Sydney blue gum (*Eucalyptus saligna*) rise to 215 feet (65 m), forming a dramatic backdrop to the garden. In the formal parts of the garden the strong vertical lines, made by the trunks of the gums, force the eye down to the detail below. But to the rear of the property, in a part of the garden which is more informal in its design, the trunks themselves play a major part in the visual drama of the garden. From time to time the odd bush turkey drifts into the garden, bandicoots are inclined to forage in the lawn and each

A view from the house.

evening the sky is darkened by the flying foxes as they leave their day-time forest roost on their nocturnal hunt for food.

When Mrs Longhurst's parents, Mr and Mrs Brian Canny, acquired the house in 1945 the bones of the garden were already there as it had been the home and plant nursery of Jocelyn Brown, a noted Sydney landscape gardener. The garden is generally regarded as among the best of her work to survive; however, much of its present form and plant groupings are a tribute to the late Mrs Canny and her daughter, Mrs Longhurst, who maintains the garden today. The front door is set in what appears to be a simple one-storey cottage but the land slopes away sharply from the road and at the back the house rises to two storeys. When the Canny family went to live at Greenwood the road was bordered by a noted pear walk, composed of very old trees, and the front path was bordered by deep flower borders in a traditional cottage-garden style. As a result of road widening in 1975 both of these features were tragically lost. Today both house and garden are protected by the National Trust of Australia.

The front garden, which lies between the busy road and the front door, now has a totally different character, having been transformed into a formally designed stone-paved forecourt. The stone used for the house and paving is the delicately hued local sandstone, which acquires a soft golden glow as it ages. A thick high wall built in the same stone gives protection from the road. Against it, facing the house, the double white *Camellia sasanqua* 'Mine-no-yuki' has been espaliered with great success. The dark green shiny leaves contrast well with the soft rough glow of stone and the plant has been superbly trained into strong horizontal lines and to frame a stone bench which stands beneath the wall. Another strong green horizontal line is added with a carpet of native Australian violets (*Viola hederacea*), which separates the stone of the wall from the stone of the paving. Two containers holding large formally clipped Chinese hawthorns (*Photinia serrulata*) guard the front door. Their leathery oblong-elliptic leaves with saw-like edges have the architectural distinction needed in this

somewhat severe setting. In summer the plants display trusses of white blossom, which is followed by red berries (great favourites with the birds), but many think that the most decorative moment in the Chinese hawthorn's seasonal cycle is spring, when the terminal growths are a rich bronze. The courtyard also displays the less regular but highly decorative shape of a *Magnolia × soulangiana*. The unbroken lines of greenery and stone give the area a strongly formal character. This is totally different to the rest of the garden, where, although the spaces are clearly defined, the greenery of shrubs and the colour of flowering plants exuberantly overflow.

The garden to the south side of the house and below the stone courtyard is composed of three vistas running parallel and at right angles to the house. The entire area has

Various forms of contrasting greenery are used to define a vista.

well-defined boundaries. Opposite the house stand the forest trees, one side is bordered by the stone wall which separates the garden from the road and the other side is curtained with bamboo rising 100 feet (30 m) above the garden. The dense barrier of bamboo leaf divides the geometric formal spaces from the less controlled, more open spaces, to the rear of the house. The plantings in this area with its three distinct divisions have been carefully controlled and mix strongly clipped formal shrubs with plants which are allowed to display their naturally irregular shapes. The larger shrubs are carefully placed, usually in pairs, and trained so that the slope of the land is not obvious.

Perhaps the most romantic of the three vistas is the sunken garden. It is paved in hand-made bricks, now mossy with age, of which several are imprinted with shallow heart-shaped indentations. A bird bath rising from a bed of ivy and stone stands at the head of the sunken space and the garden itself is entered by way of narrow steps and swells out into a wide paved area surrounded by low walls composed of sandstone bricks. Pergola posts looped with chains to support roses also define the space. At one end of the sunken garden lies a circular lily pond guarded by a large brown china frog and beyond the pond narrow steps lead the eye on to the far view of

conifers and camellias which stand against the vertical pole-like trunks of the forest trees. The occasional brick is missing from the paving and these intentional spaces are filled with small ground-covering plants. A white form of mondo grass (*Ophiopogon japonicus*) makes attractive mounds on the flat paving. Roses clothe the poles and a variety of Banksian roses flower abundantly in the light shade. Whenever the vista narrows, strong green forms on either side force the eye to follow the line of the path. This garden designer's trick, cleverly used throughout the side garden, has the effect of making the vistas appear longer than they really are. Several clipped shrubs are used in this manner and in the sunken garden a pair of *Strelitzia reginae*, with strong spear-like leaves, are used at the far end.

Today the sunken garden, its strong form almost obscured by the well-grown trees and shrubs, is a shady place. Form rather than flower is the chief consideration to the owner. However, there remains a strong core of shade-tolerant flowering plants. Camellias, particularly C. 'Lady Loch', and the white japonica (*Chaenomeles speciosa* 'Nivalis') provide their decorative trim in winter and early spring. Abutilons and the hybrid fuchsia 'Tom Thumb' bloom constantly and in summer and autumn are joined by the flowers of *Heliotropium*

Below left Camellia *sasanqua* 'Mine-no-yuki' frames a bench and plate against the stone wall.

Below Beneath the balcony an urn of echeverias stands in front of the topiary, backed by an effective screen of bamboo.

This view towards 'The Lady' is one example of Greenwood's many parallel and crossing vistas.

arborescens. The beds contain clumps of pink and white belladonna lilies (*Amaryllis belladonna*) and Japanese anemones (*Anemone × hybrida*) grow thickly. Several species of *Berberis* and *Ochna serrulata* add their flower, leaf and decorative berries to this romantic and charming area.

The second vista, on a lower level than the sunken garden, follows, by comparison, a simple design and the shrubs are set off with mown grass. In this part, too, evergreens have been trimmed into simple formal shapes. White azaleas, white marguerite daisy bushes (*Chrysanthemum frutescens*) and clipped nandinas (*Nandina domestica*) decorate the area, which is overhung by a jacaranda tree. This tree has the curious habit of displaying decorative dying yellow leaves in early spring, then in early summer displaying its spectacular bluebell-blue floss of flower before the green leaves reappear. Here strong clumps of green flax give the vista its elongated form.

Below lies a third vista which follows the line of the old driveway and, close to the house, opens out to join the lawn to the rear of the house. When the driveway was blocked off a gazebo was added to give the vista depth and a focal point. The great curtain of bamboo lends one side of the walk its dramatic form and against it, with two very large cumquat trees standing guard at each end, a seat has been placed. On the other side *Philadelphus coronarius*, *Weigela florida* 'Variegata' and the port-wine magnolia (*Michelia figo*) are underplanted with hostas and arum lilies. There is a persimmon tree (*Diospyros kaki*) and a Mexican tree daisy (*Montanoa grandiflora*), which produces its white flowers in autumn and follows the display with clumps of green bobble-like pods. Gardenias are clipped to outline the path. Another Mexican shrub, the tree fuchsia (*Fuchsia arborescens*), is used to mark the curve of the old lawn, displaying in winter its reddish-purple flowers. *Clivia miniata* blooms in the light shade and adds its strong shapes to the decorative romantic scenery.

As the side gardens became more heavily shaded and when the old pear trees, which had added their scale to the area, were removed it was decided to open the long vistas and Mrs Longhurst created a new vista, which cuts across them. It is bordered at each intersection with well-pruned citrus trees and takes its direction from a statue (known to the family as 'The Lady') placed against the stone wall.

Steps, outlined with a rim of ribbon grass (*Phalaris arundinacea* 'Picta') curve down round the high dense curtain of bamboo. At the bottom of the steps the character of the garden changes dramatically. The heavily planted and strongly designed spaces change to open spaces and the dramatic view into the forest dominates the scene. The bottom lawn, a favourite place for family entertaining, is shaded by a well-grown Chinese oak (*Quercus acutissima*), a tree rare in Australia. It stands in company with a Portugal laurel (*Prunus lusitanica*) and a *Gordonia axillaris*. A wide semi-circle marked by clumps of ginger plant (*Hedychium*) and blue and white agapanthus separates the oak lawn from the paddock which slopes down to the forest edge. A few trees stand on the sloping mown grass of the paddock, among them a nettle tree (*Celtis australis*), a lemon-scented myrtle (*Backhousia citriodora*) and an Indian hawthorn (*Raphiolepis indica*). A splash of orange-yellow from browallia (*Streptosolen jamesonii*), which is almost always in bloom, adds a brilliance to the quiet scene.

On the northern (sunny) side of the house the original design of the patio survives, with brick piers and beams defining the space. Today the area is shaded by a huge linden tree and the silver-grey native plant *Plectranthus argentatus* is trained against the piers. The swimming pool is screened from view by a fragrant murraya hedge.

In essence the garden of Greenwood is a family garden. The romantic atmosphere introduced by Jocelyn Brown has been consciously retained and enhanced first by Mrs Canny and now by her daughter, Mrs Longhurst, both of whom have had the vision and energy needed to maintain the early design as the plants (as all plants do) attempt to outgrow the scale of the garden. It remains a romantic place where the eye is guided from view to vista, from stone to plant, from plant to tree and from ornamental tree to the forest beyond.

Wentworth

SYDNEY

Mrs Bernard Riley

MRS RILEY'S GARDEN on Sydney's North Shore has evolved over sixty years. The house was built for her mother, a young widow. It was the beautiful outlook over a gully which influenced her to buy the steeply sloping rocky block with heavy clay soil. The architect, with great foresight, designed a series of stone walls, pleasant paths and terraces which minimized the slope, and the well-weathered stone remains a feature today. The house, which sits well below the level of the road, looks from the gate to have only one storey but the slope is so steep that, at the rear, the building has three storeys. The garden continues to slope downwards until far below the street level it terminates in a tree-filled creek bed.

On the grass verge bordering the street in front of the house a flowerbed runs the full length of the land. In this open position there is always some flower to be found and the bed is filled with what are often regarded today as the old-fashioned flowers. There are daisies (*Bellis perennis*), alpine forget-me-not (*Myosotis alpestris*), love-in-a-mist (*Nigella damascena*), little wax begonias (*B. semperflorens* hybrids), the flowers-of-the-

Far left An effective swag of ivy and clipped shrubs frame one of the front windows.

Left The garden hose, not usually regarded as decorative, is given elegance and style.

47

The front garden
showing the strong
design which disguises
the slope on the land.

west-wind (*Zephyranthes candida*), veronica, dianthus, iris, true geraniums and many others. The plants are limited to those bearing blue, pink and white blooms and there is extensive use of grey foliage. Mrs Riley uses Jerusalem sage (*Phlomis fruticosa*) for its silver-grey leaves and structure and removes the yellow heads of flower. 'The Fairy' and 'China Doll', both low-growing roses, bloom for months in this open sunny position and the floral abundance attracts the attention of all who pass. The fence, its white railing gleaming above what has become a hedge of severely clipped ivy, makes a backdrop for the border. A few well-controlled evergreen shrubs are used to give the bed form and define the space. Steps lead down through the flowery bed to the neat white gate and a sloping paved path ends at the front door. A green handrail beside the steps hints at the change of character within

the garden. The green colouring is provided by the rigorous training and clipping of the ivy which completely masks the structure itself but leaves its outline distinct and its purpose clear.

Within the front gate the character of the garden changes dramatically. Clipped evergreen shrubs are used to give the area its strong forms and the garden is bathed in a green glow from their healthy gleaming leaves. To emphasize important boundaries the use of *Murraya paniculata* and *Buxus sempervirens* are particularly striking. Sometimes as many as three layers of clipped contrasting evergreens are used to give the area its strong shapes. Strong lines distract the eye from the slope of the land and enlarge the somewhat limited space. A narrow sloping stretch of groomed grass lies on either side of the front path and is bordered with more severely controlled greenery. Box hedging is looped round shrubs clipped to maintain soft rounded forms or round ornamental urns planted with contrasting leaf shapes and shades. These deep dark green loops of hedging lie immediately under the front fence and mask a front boundary which runs on a diagonal line to the house it borders. Opposite the loops of box and parallel with the front of the house a straight line of box is used. To one side of the front door, the clipped box hedge encloses a bed which contains a row of identical circular mounds of clipped box. The effect of this treatment is to make the garden and house look wider than they are and minimizes the slope of the land.

On the other side of the door and under a window the shrubs are contained with swags of ivy, clipped ivy enveloping the vertical posts and the chains which sag between them. The result is a perfect eighteenth-century hanging swag of ivy forming a garland at the base of a shuttered window. Ivy is used extensively in the garden but only allowed to enjoy its natural sprawl if a soft line is required to counterbalance the strong upright spiky forms of other plants. Mrs Riley says, 'I am not kind to plants. They must do what I want.' True to her conviction, she uses plants as an embroiderer uses threads of silk. Seen from the garden

each window is elegantly framed with trained plants and the garden itself is arranged so that the view from each window reveals a vista terminated by an architectural object. Frequently an urn planted with grey-green or rosy-pink tipped succulents provides the focal point. Mrs Riley describes her glowing mounds of succulents as looking like green roses but, despite this striking simile, within the garden's boundaries flowers are subsidiary to the use of texture and greenery. Plants bearing noticeable flowers are chosen for their ability to provide leaf contrast and to fill the strong shapes made by the hedging with a variety of contrasting shapes and greens. No time in the year is 'the worst time to see the garden' and the garden never displays the empty spaces found in many gardens as the seasons change. There are no weeds because there is no space for weeds. Each bed, clearly defined by clipped greenery, is well filled with more clipped shrubs and flowering perennials. White irises are used as much for their grey-green spikes of foliage as for the elegance of their bloom. 'Green Goddess' arum lilies display their fresh green pointed leaves and flowers above the topiary and, where low growth is required, the beds are carpeted with the fibrous-rooted wax begonias (*B. semperflorens*

The contrast between the clipped foliage, including that of camellias in a line of identical pots, and the natural shapes of palms and tree ferns beyond, gives strong definition to the terrace and lawn below the house.

The terrace at the back of the house.

curve to this garden of greens and curves. (The vine is pruned by the simple expedient of unhooking the swag from each post, laying it down on the carport floor and re-shaping the branches.) Below the carport steep steps lead to the back terrace. Ficus is trained to cover the drop on each step and the wall supporting the carport sports another elegant swag of evergreen. Here, cat's-claw vine (*Doxantha unguis-cati*), often thought of as a rampant menace, is perfectly controlled and adds a yellow silken swag of flower to the summer garden.

The steeply sloping garden behind the house is viewed from three levels, making a total of four levels to be taken into consideration if one counts the terrace which runs along the back of the house a few steps below the ground floor. Placed along the terrace are identical tubs of viburnums with white ivy-leafed pelargoniums making a frothy underskirt. Trained against the walls of the house are pink hibiscus, the pink *Camellia sasanqua* 'Plantation Pink' and two lemon trees which are trained to frame a window. Mrs Riley makes the point that these plants are not espaliered, but tied and clipped close to the wall to provide a textured flowering and fruiting wall. When seen from the garden below, the skirt of greenery at the base of the tall house serves to minimize the height of the house and stops it from looking too heavy. Steps from a garden room to the terrace support 'a herb garden', where mint and chives are grown in matching pots and a wide border of well-grown parsley flourishes. Here, in a slight change of the colour rhythm, terracotta is used for the containers but elsewhere in the rear garden colour is confined to the shades provided by plants and stone. A neighbour has recently added a glass wall in line with the terrace. Rather than masking the window with a shrub, Mrs Riley has framed it, using her favourite ivy clipped and trained over an arbour. The result is a decorative focal point at the end of the terrace and at night the framed light from the neighbour's window is much appreciated.

Steps lead from the terrace to the lawn below and are lined with helxine and wild strawberry but apart from these small green details (which are not permitted to follow

hybrids). These provide a flowering garland around the fat circular mounds of clipped box. Glossy gardenias are shaped and used to extend the flowering greenery and scent the summer months. Elegant tubs designed by Mrs Riley's father, an architect, are placed either side of the front door and planted with an old camellia cultivar, 'William Bull'. The plants bloom throughout the winter months but after some weeks Mrs Riley is likely to remove the flowers, saying they remind her of the currants in a bun.

To one side of the house lies a carport and here again Mrs Riley's ability to make plants follow her wishes is demonstrated. An ornamental grape vine is trained so that it is looped between the posts until each space is hung with a leafy garland resembling the elaborate swags of curtain used in the eighteenth century. The new growth of the vine adds an almost transparent pinky green their usual habit and spread about) the back garden has a carefully controlled formal appearance. Stepping stones through the grass align with the steps and terminate in a curve of stone on which a bird bath has been given a central position. Mrs Riley has observed that if a red camellia is placed to float on the water the currawongs will remove it and, if she persists with this colour scheme, take the offending flowers and place them, in protest, by the back door. Other shades of petal or leaf are tolerated. Behind the focal curve of stone a band of stone paving lies against a low stone wall topped with clipped privet. Immediately behind the bird bath, in a central position, is a stone bench bordered on each side with four impressive stone tubs containing camellias. Great attention is given to the height of these visually important shrubs; the containers stand on the decorative bases of old stone pillars. Seen from the verandah on the second floor they appear to be aligned with the top of the clipped privet hedge which separates the formal garden from the steep drop into the creek bed below. But when viewed at eye level the leaves can be seen to rise well above the height of the hedge. The camellias have been chosen and arranged in matched pairs to provide a long flowering display but once more Mrs Riley's chief aim is to make the picture with clipped greenery and she is likely to remove the flowers before they finish. A yellow variegated euonymus is much valued in this area for its ability to

display lime-green, not yellow, leaves when grown in shade. One side of the lawn is bordered by a clipped hedge; the other is planted with a variety of shrubs and hydrangeas, which are successfully used to veil the view of a neighbouring house.

Behind the stone wall and in strong contrast to the formal garden which it borders is the creek bed where the tall trees of the natural rainforest remain to break the skyline. Tree ferns have been encouraged to hold their horizontal ferny fronds at the same level as the top of the privet hedge; when viewed from above, they mask the sharp drop in the level of the land. Ferns are used extensively as ground cover, and the native blue gums (*Eucalyptus saligna*) and turpentine trees (*Syncarpia glomulifera*) hang high above. The middle ground in this green textured backdrop, which adds such drama to the formal rear garden, is taken up by the highly decorative boughs and leaves of Japanese maples. The native plants and trees provide their year-round structures and greenery while the changing seasons are reflected in the colours and shapes displayed by the maples.

The garden is constantly fed, watered, clipped and mulched. The lawns were the pride of Mrs Riley's late husband and she says they do not look the same now that they are in her care. However, to the casual onlooker the lawns look beautifully maintained, as does the whole garden. The plants used are those Mrs Riley knows she can grow well in her conditions and she knows every part of her terrain intimately, being able to recognize exactly which areas will receive sun in a particular season and which areas are prone to waterlogging or drought. Today she is assisted by young students, whom she values for their willingness to work and to meet her exacting standards with intelligence.

Although evergreen shrubs and clipped hedging feature prominently at Wentworth, their use has little in common with the current revival of parterre and knot gardens. Here the clipped greenery does not force the design. It is the site itself which is the primary consideration to an owner and designer whose chief effects are achieved by a skilful manipulation of scale and proportion.

The varying uses of plants in classical containers along the front of the house, including ivy in a topiary shape, typify the character of this garden.

Nooroo

THE BLUE MOUNTAINS

The Valder Family

*T*HE PROPERTY of Nooroo, an Aboriginal word meaning shady place, was purchased in 1917 by the grandfather of Dr Peter Valder, who maintains the garden today. It lies 3,300 feet (1000 m) above sea level in the Blue Mountains 80 miles (125 km) to the north-west of Sydney, where rich soil, adequate rainfall and cool summers led to the development of the area as a summer retreat in the 1870s. The low house built of pit-sawn timber with tall chimneys in local sandstone was built in 1880. Large trees, which date from the period of the first owner, remain, give the garden its mature form and define the principal spaces and vistas.

To celebrate the centenary of the house in 1980 a summerhouse, with wooden details matching those on the main house, was added to the garden. However, to quote Dr Valder, 'Urns, steps, balustrades, columns, statues, lead cisterns, sundials, Japanese lanterns and other artefacts of a foreign nature have been avoided and any constructions in the garden have been confined to objects made of wood and the local basalt.' This policy is felt to be in keeping 'with the modest wooden house and an Australian attitude to what is a simple composition based, not surprisingly considering the time of its establishment, on English antecedents.'

Mr and Mrs George Valder, Junior, the parents of Dr Valder, extended the garden and introduced plants from Britain, Holland, Japan, New Zealand and the United States. Dr Valder has continued the family tradition of plant collecting and added a great variety of plants, many of them acquired on expeditions to Burma, China, Hong Kong, Indonesia, Malaysia and Thailand. During his stewardship Dr Valder has been keen to avoid garden clichés. As he says, 'There are daffodils and bluebells under the oaks and chestnuts but herbaceous borders, laburnum tunnels, all-white gardens and over-

Left Evening rain drifting over the great eucalypts gives a romantic look to this view of the summerhouse, which is framed by *Wisteria floribunda* 'Longissima', a red maple, rhododendrons and azaleas.

Right From the shade of the verandah, stone steps, bordered with rhododendrons and azaleas, lead to the summerhouse.

The house, dwarfed by
the surrounding trees
and tall tree ferns.

careful colour schemes and so on have been
eschewed as not reflecting the Australian
culture and temperament.' As the plants
have grown and, on occasion, outgrown
their allotted space, Dr Valder has opened up
views and vistas, extending the garden to
include park-like paddocks, added the spoils
of his expeditions to the mature plantings
and created an unusual and impressive
wisteria garden. Some of the original native
vegetation remains on the site and has
become a part of the garden. However, in
spite of the fact that Dr Valder is a recognized expert in Australian flora, such plants
are rarely added to the garden as they are
considered to be a fire hazard in an area
which is prone to bush fire.

There is little evidence of the garden
beyond when one enters the poplar-guarded
gates at Nooroo. To one side of the simple
drive lies a neat stone-edged lawn and to the
other two well-grown white-flowering magnolias rise from a bed of low flowering
shrubs. The raked gravel leads directly to

the shrub-bordered low house but it is not
until the driveway turns towards the front
door that the lure of the garden is felt. Over
the door on a horizontal support wide
enough to park a car beneath its spread
hangs a fifty-year-old mauve wisteria
(*W. floribunda* 'Longissima'). Opposite the
front door lies a garden composed of stone
paths and ponds dominated by an impressive stand of rough tree ferns (*Cyathea australis*) which are thought to be at least two
hundred years old. The pole-like trunks give
this part of the garden a form which could
only be found in Australia and add their
strong vertical lines to the mounds of exotic
shrubs and intricate stone paths. One of
them makes a solid support to a white
wisteria while others are wreathed with
Clematis montana. Beneath them the beds
are planted with a selection of flowering
bulbs; many, including *Narcissus bulbocodium* and *N. triandrus*, have been grown
from seed imported some years ago. All are
now thriving and multiplying with little at-

tention. Lily-of-the-valley and old-fashioned double columbines (grown from seed purchased in a French market town) have also naturalized in the area. Dr Valder describes these beds as having reached an 'ecological balance between weeds and bulbs' but, to the uninformed eye, the beds look neat, tidy and bright with flowers, some of which are rarely seen in Australian gardens.

From beneath the canopy of wisteria by the front door the eye is attracted into the garden by the charming presence of the simple summerhouse, which lies above the house in line with the wisteria-clad portico. Stone steps edged with clumps of *Nerine flexuosa* 'Alba' (which bloom in autumn as the leaves of the many maples display their autumn colour) lead up to the lawn on which the summerhouse stands. To one side of the summerhouse is a dark solid pyramid of holly in sharp contrast to the fragmented airy forms of Japanese maples which form the background. Both the orange-scarlet 'Osakazuki' maple and the yellow 'Aoyagi' have been used in this position. The borders of this lawn are edged with yellow deciduous azaleas which bloom in spring at the same time as a carpet of blue forget-me-nots and bluebells.

To one side and at a higher level than the summerhouse is an upper lawn or woodland glade surrounded with maples, rhododendrons, crab apples (grown from seed collected in the college gardens of Cambridge University) and a pink horse chestnut (grown from seed collected at Wynstay, one of the original gardens on Mt Wilson). The trees are underplanted with *Viburnum plicatum tomentosum* 'Lanarth', and corylopsis and mahonia species.

These two upper lawns merge with the woodland which rises high above the house. Here some of the original vegetation remains. Huge gums (*Eucalyptus viminalis* and *E. blaxlandii*) tower above the scene making the maples and rhododendrons (many of which have reached what is probably the maximum height for their type) look small and frail. The maples are selected from seedlings raised from 'Osakazuki' and chosen for their contrasting autumn colours. In autumn the soft mists pierced by the massive pole-like trunks and

flickering with the brilliant leaf shades have both mystery and majesty.

The summerhouse occupies a key spot: it lies in line with the view from the front door and well above the house but it also lies on an axis with a great oak, which stands in the company of other well-grown oaks and chestnuts at the far end of a long sweep of lawn which terminates well below the house. This stretch of mown grass forms the main vista in a garden that is well endowed with informal but well-considered vistas (each thoughtfully provided with seating of some sort) which lead the eye and feet through the garden. The house itself, set at an angle to this major sweep of lawn, shares with the summerhouse the view down to the oak wood. The long grassy vista is defined with mixed plantings of trees and shrubs. Once more maples are used extensively and combined with other trees noted for their autumn foliage such as witch hazel (*Hamamelis mollis*) and *Parrotia persica*, which add their yellow finery to the reds of the maples. Two magnolias, *M. sprengeri* and *M. sargentiana robusta*, grown from seed sent from Caerhays Castle in Cornwall, also lend their spectacular flowers to this decorative planting. Definition is given in winter by the green of rhododendrons, Portugal laurels

The old tennis court has now become a wisteria garden. Here flourish twenty-eight wisterias, with clematis and pots of rhododendrons and azaleas filling out this October scene.

and hollies. At the bottom of the lawn where the great oaks and chestnuts of the first planting stand, the ground is covered with a vast planting of daffodils and bluebells. The blue, white and mauve shades of the Spanish bluebell (*Hyacinthoides hispanica*) are used extensively and the planting contains a drift of English bluebells (*Hyacinthoides non-scriptus*); once again the plants have been raised from imported seed.

To one side of the grand sweep of lawn, and contained behind a wall of greenery, lies a remarkable wisteria garden of formal design, established on what was once a tennis court. A pair of yellow rhododendrons stand at each side of the simple entry. Within the hidden garden are rows of standard wisterias. In all there are twenty-eight plants of twelve different varieties. Today the tall umbrella-shaped plants have great stature and one can walk with ease between their thick trunks and through the tunnels formed by their well-pruned branches. The wisterias have been planted directly into the court and now rise from a bed of raked gravel. Under their branches, maintaining the theme of plants originating in China and Japan, are simply designed pots containing a selection of azaleas and small rhododendrons. In spring this garden is a foaming mass of blossom in all the soft colours of an ice-cream display set off with specks of mint green as the new growth breaks through the canopy of flower. Down one side of the courtyard clematis (*C. armandii, C. chrysocoma* and a number of large-flowered hybrids) have been added to grow up simple supports made from iron piping. When the clematis are not in bloom the unobtrusive supports merge with the background of greenery but when in flower they add to an already lavish spectacle.

On the opposite side of the main vista beyond the oak wood is a newly established informal garden. Three seats have been placed against a curved planting of the dwarf rhododendron (*R. yakushimanum*) backed with *Forsythia × intermedia* 'Lynwood', which adds its yellow bloom to that of the late daffodils and its yellow autumn foliage to a garden already rich in autumn colours. The seats lie in a line between a huge gum (*Eucalyptus* sp.) which breaks the

skyline behind them and a gate in the park-like paddock which lies below the garden. Behind the curve of shrubs stands a selection of well-grown older plants which include a collection of rhododendron hybrids, a Himalayan spruce (*Picea smithiana*) and a Serbian spruce (*P. omorika*) and two shrubs of Chilean origin, *Embothrium lanceolatum* and *Eucryphia cordifolia*. From the seats the eye is naturally led over the stream of mown grass to the gate leading into the drive beyond the sheep paddock. A new planting opposite the oak wood defines the far side of the vista. It is an interesting vista, given strength by the line formed by the gum, the seats and the gate, but with a border which changes shape with the changing seasons. In spring and early summer the thick planting of daffodils outlines the curves of mown grass but in late summer and autumn, when the daffodils have died down and the woodland

The Japanese maples in this garden are selected for colour and shape from seedlings grown by the owner.

Sheep graze in the paddocks at the end of this view from the north end of the garden.

is mown, the swell of lawn extends over a larger area.

The garden also contains an extensive area where plant breeding, propagation and experimentation are carried out. Over the years wisterias have been imported from many parts of the world and a large number of other plants and trees have been grown from imported seed and nurtured in this area before transfer to their permanent homes in the garden. Here *Prunus sargentii* was grown from seed collected beside Lake Chuzenji in Japan, Italian cypresses from seeds taken from trees growing amongst the ruins of Hadrian's Villa near Rome, *Magnolia grandiflora* raised from seed collected from trees beside the steps of the Capitol in Washington and a Cedar of Lebanon from seed sent from Lebanon. At present the breeding of *Camellia reticulata* is occupying space. Dr Valder finds the predominating reds and bright pinks of these camellias hard to ac-

commodate and is hoping to produce some softer shades.

Nooroo has a large garden and a small house but with the skilful manipulation of space the two maintain a pleasing relationship. Such focal points as have been added in recent times have a low-key presence and are in harmony with the surrounding countryside. With the exception of the enclosed wisteria garden, no attempt has been made to formalize the layout or make dramatic changes to the natural fall of the land. However, great attention has been paid to scale, perspective and to enhancing the spirit of the place, which has been home to three generations of plant collectors. The garden finds its antecedents in a British inheritance but today its character derives from an Australian attitude and the eucalypts and tree ferns form an unmistakably Australian background to the exotic plantings.

Sheep graze in the paddocks at the end of this view from the north end of the garden.

Hillview

EXETER

Mr Dean Havelberg & Mr Douglas Smith

TWELVE YEARS AGO there was no garden at Hillview, just a simple somewhat rundown weatherboard house, typical of many to be found in rural Australia, standing on a hill beside a country road. Two well-grown deodar cedars (*Cedrus deodara*) stood on the hillside but otherwise the 'garden' was devoted to rough grass. Rare in some parts of Australia, in New South Wales the deodar is frequently the only survivor in neglected gardens as it can withstand the dry heat typical of inland areas and is sought after for its shade in the heat of summer and its ability to add its gently weeping dark green form to the barest of winter scenes. Today the garden looks mature; the young trees are well grown, the stonework weathered and there are flowers everywhere. What began twelve years ago as a weekend hobby has developed into a remarkable plant collection.

The hill, which looks out over rolling paddocks where the gums hang their fragmented tracery of leaf, is covered in a rich basalt red soil. The winters are cold, with heavy frosts and a sporadic sprinkling of snow; but only the occasional thunderstorm relieves the dry dusty conditions of summer. The annual rainfall is 40 inches (102 cm) and most precipitation occurs in spring and autumn. Some of the stone used in the garden was obtained on the site when the borders were being dug, the rest came from a local quarry. All the stone now has the pleasant harmonious look which only local stone can impart. The major part of the ornamental garden slopes down from the house to the road, which lies hidden behind a stout prickly hedge of berberis. To one side of the block a straight driveway, lost in the greenery of the garden, leads up to the house. The garden itself descends from the house in a flow of lawn bordered by a series of informal interrelated circular beds. Throughout the garden there are well-clipped cones of evergreens. The specimens are mainly variegated box but to one side of the garden the striking silhouette is echoed in a clipped cone of hornbeam.

Immediately in front of the verandah lies a level circle of stone paving where, for many months, little stone is visible between the clumps of low-growing plants. Fat cushions of the sharp-emerald *Scleranthus biflorus* flow round and over the stone,

The view over the front hedge with a mass of irises in the foreground.

58

white wisteria trained and grown as a standard and by an airy mound of white broom, under which flourish strong clumps of *Helleborus lividus* and *H. l. corsicus*.

Steps curve down round the circular terrace to the mown grass. Below the stone wall which supports the terrace lies a second level stone circle, which has a more formal character. Cotoneaster and lithospermum hang over the wall masking the stone and displaying their scarlet berries or clear blue flowers in season. A white weeping cherry (*Prunus subhirtella* 'Pendula') is placed in the centre and in the cracks and crevices of the stone paving *Cyclamen hederifolium* has established well. It now carpets the shady circle beneath the boughs of the cherry tree with its marbled leaves and adds a myriad of flowers to a highly decorative late summer garden. In late winter there are hundreds of *Crocus tomasinianus* in flower.

The two circles, one open and sunny, the other more enclosed and shady, form the essential elements in the upper part of the garden. The two areas, although clearly defined, are contained within a series of overlapping, also circular, informal plantings which set off the two important design elements and lead the eye on through the garden with their wealth of flower. Plants from all areas overlap their beds, softening the lines of the design and giving the garden a naturally harmonious atmosphere. These surrounding beds are densely planted with flowering shrubs, perennials and the bulbs for which this garden is noted. At the lower level the beds on one side of the garden billow out across the grass to surround a pond, which is centrally placed in line with the house.

On the side of the garden where the drive lies unobtrusively along the fence line stand the two deodars; one situated close to the house providing a green backdrop to the stone terrace. Other trees have since been added, the earliest plantings including different varieties of dogwoods and magnolias, two groups of plants that have become particular favourites. Today they overhang the beds, giving the garden height and form and providing enough shade for a collection of flowering shrubs, which include deciduous and Kurume azaleas and

making a strong contrast with the softly shaded foliage of armerias, alpine dianthus, the purple-leaved oxalis and thymes. The leaves add their decorative trim throughout the year and, as the seasons progress, the flowers appear and small flowering bulbs raise their heads from between the clumps of foliage. The garden contains a collection of *Rhodohypoxis baurii* and many of them bloom throughout the summer months on this sunny terrace. Dwarf varieties of *Babiana stricta*, *Freesia refracta* 'Alba' and *Cyclamen coum* all thrive here and provide masses of flower from late winter until early summer. The terrace is given height by a

Allium oreophilum, red dianthus and thrift (*Armeria maritima*) decorate the steps to the house, framed by azaleas.

small-leaved rhododendrons. The beds are heavily underplanted with primulas, narcissus, snowdrops, erythroniums, fritillarias, bulbinellas, ipheions, species tulips and crocuses. The wealth of flower produces some charming pictures. In one spot a glowing khaki-brown polyanthus blooms with cream freesias and together these provide the perfect foil for the emerging crimson growth of great clumps of peonies. In another the dainty pale cream and lemon-yellow *Narcissus cyclamineus* 'Dove Wings' picks up the colour in a lemon-yellow hose-in-hose primrose. The more brightly coloured narcissus bloom with the acid yellow and clear yellow of two different forms of cat's tails (*Bulbinella floribunda*) and the sharp acid yellows of *Euphorbia myrsinites*. The varied yellows paint a

pleasant picture with the milky-blue *Ipheion uniflorum* and the emerging grey leaves of the aquilegias. The ruby-red and silvery-mauve shades of a number of pasque flowers (*Pulsatilla vulgaris*) bloom at the same time as the cherry trees froth with pink and white flower. In this garden bulbs are often planted to grow through the lower branches of shrubs. The nodding brown heads of *Fritillaria gracilis* appear between the low bushes of a dwarf bronze-leafed mahonia. Nerines emerge from beneath the branches of a prostrate juniper, Kurume azaleas are underplanted with alliums and liliums, and there are pleiones edging a yellow-flowered rhododendron, *R. chrysomanicum*.

The mown grass pours down the hill like a stream held between banks of greenery and flower in this superbly flowery garden;

Below   White irises and viburnum frame the path down to a pool planted with *Iris laevigata* and *I. pseudacorus*.

The leaves of *Helleborus corsicus* and racemes of *Wisteria sinensis* frame this afternoon view of the thrift-covered terrace. On the left is the tea tree (*Leptospermum scoparium*) just coming into flower, backed by rhododendrons and azaleas.

even in mid-winter, when the bones of the garden are exposed, the ground is lit with clumps of flower. The hottest part of summer is the only time, Mr Havelberg says, when, apart from some flowering perennials, there is nothing much in the garden, just 'green on green'. To one side of the grass the trunk of the lower deodar is circled with the dark leaves of *Helleborus orientalis* and a ring of clipped dark green box hedging which terminates in cone-shaped finials of variegated box. The bed provides the contrast of geometric formality and the cool dark colour needed to emphasize the gently swirling forms of the less formal plantings without breaking the garden's theme of intersecting circles. On the other side, at a higher level, the same type of contrast is provided by a small space surrounded by

dark evergreen trees, the contrast in this area being provided by *Cupressus sempervirens* 'Swane's Golden' grown against a backdrop of smoky *Cryptomeria japonica* 'Elegans'. Within the space stands an urn containing houseleeks, and the dark surrounding trees are cleverly placed so that, when a theatrical shaft of sunlight penetrates the dark wall of foliage, it falls dramatically on the urn.

Below this evidence of Italian influence the beds resume their circular form and as their curves border the lawn emphasis is added with thick bands of white flowers; white polyanthus, single white anemones and different forms of white arabis are used to achieve this effect. These white bands give dramatic force to the collection of irises the bed contains. There are now over twenty-

Variegated box is used
to light the ground
and give form under
the weeping tip-foliage
of *Cedrus deodara*.

five different dwarf irises and an extensive collection of the more unusual taller varieties. The decorative period of the border is extended by allowing *Primula malacoides* to self-sow and bloom in late winter and early spring, well before the irises raise their heads. Later, after the iris display, herbaceous clematis (*C. integrifolia* and *C. × durandii*) and *Galtonia candicans* bloom until the heat of late summer cuts them back. This side border terminates in a striking planting of Spanish lavender (which blooms throughout the year), forming a strong background with its silvery leaves and mauve-topped branches to a group of dwarf lemon forsythia bushes, *Forsythia viridissima* 'Bronxensis'.

The lowest level of the garden contains the pond bordered with candelabra primulas and deciduous trees and shrubs. To one side *Corylopsis sinensis* and *Ribes sanguineum* have been clipped to form a flowering arch of dangling lemon-yellow and raspberry-pink sprays of flower. The water gleams between the branches of corkscrew willow (*Salix matsudana* 'Tortuosa'), *Garrya elliptica*, a dwarf weeping maple (*Prunus subhirtella* 'Autumnalis'), which blooms intermittently from autumn until spring, and the Cornelian cherry (*Cornus mas*), which presents its yellow pincushions of flower before the leaves appear in mid-winter. As the trees and shrubs spread their shade the character of these beds is changing. In the early days of the garden they were filled with a variety of sun-loving perennials; now they harbour plants which thrive in semi-shade. There are trilliums, geums, hostas, Solomon's seal (*Polygonatum*), the white form of *Dicentra spectabilis*, plume poppies (*Macleaya cordata*), lady's mantle (*Alchemilla mollis*), herbaceous and tree forms of peonies and many different aquilegias and lilies.

On one side of the house lies a silver birch grove heavily underplanted with bluebells, narcissus, grape hyacinth, star-of-Bethlehem (*Ornithogalum nutans*) and a creamy-lemon sparaxis cultivar with a dark red reverse to the petals. Beyond lies a wisteria walk which borders two sides of a rectangle of land bordering the house, which here is clothed in the rose 'Mermaid'. One side of the pergola is planted with white wisteria and the other with a mauve variety. The base of the walk is bordered with a thick band of *Colchicum autumnale* set against a hedge-like row of belladonna lilies. The late summer and autumn display is spectacular and the two plants combine to provide contrasting lush bands of greenery during the winter months. To one side of the wisteria walk stands a thick laurel hedge underplanted with a flourishing edge of *Narcissus tazetta* ssp. *italicus*; this divide separates the ornamental garden from the still decorative but more utilitarian part of the garden.

Behind the hedge lies an intensively cultivated vegetable garden, orchard and orchid house (where only species orchids are grown). In this area many of the bulbs are grown from seed and nurtured until they reach a state of maturity and can be added to the ornamental garden. Raised bulb beds, set in the open ground but given protection from the winds by an outer band of trees, contain an amazing variety of bulbs grown from seed which has been imported from all over the world. There are Oncocyclus irises from the Near East, Juno irises and *I. reticulata*, numerous tulips, including *T. humilis aucheriana*, *T. greigii* from central Asia, the lady tulip (*T. clusiana*) and *T. sylvestris*. A new lemon hoop petticoat narcissus hybrid blooms with different forms of *Anemone blanda*, a yellow pleione, and the wild form of *Cyclamen persicum*. The crown imperial (*Fritillaria imperialis*), which many Australian gardeners find a challenge, thrives here and is multiplied from seed collected in the garden. The seed boxes and bulb beds are always full of new arrivals, which are nurtured and assessed for performance and appearance. From this area has come a tiny clematis from New Zealand (*C. marmoraria*), foxtail lilies (*Eremurus*), crocus species including *C. etruscus*, *C. graveolens* and *C. banaticus*, *Meconopsis grandis* and a large number of species primula and interesting old cultivars.

The variety and health of the plants at Hillview are remarkable – even the rare white form of Chile's national flower *Lapageria rosea* (a plant that is the despair of many Australian gardeners) thrives here. The garden is the product of two men. Mr Havelberg was a plantsman who, when his life was restricted to city living, followed his interest in plants in a small orchid house. Mr Smith was primarily the garden's designer but, as in all such situations, the lines of demarcation have become blurred over the years and today's charming flowery garden is the result of the enthusiasm, skill and knowledge of two men who have shared the work and the pleasure a garden can bring.

An urn is lit by a shaft of light controlled by a pair of 'Swane's Golden' cypresses.

Markdale

BINDA

Mr & Mrs Geoffrey Ashton, Jr.

MR JAMES ASHTON built the existing Markdale homestead in 1921, choosing to site the house on a hill slope scattered with magnificent gums. His four sons gained world renown on the polo field. One of them, Mr Geoffrey Ashton, Senior, took over Markdale in 1935 and with his late wife, Janet, lived there until 1984. Post-war wool prices enabled considerable refurbishment and the improvements began with the garden in 1949. The landscape designer Edna Walling was employed to make suggestions and draw up plans. The following year Professor Leslie Wilkinson was engaged to improve the homestead. It is only at Markdale that the work of the renowned Melbourne land-scaper and the famous Sydney architect are to be found together.

At an early stage the hillside garden had been generously planted with thick windbreak hedges and trees typical of the era, mainly cypresses, both the golden and the dark-green varieties, and poplars. These additions to the original gums had been established, in the manner of the day, in strong straight lines. Early illustrations show only two curved lines in the early garden: the turning circle at the front of the house and a tiny circle of level mown grass below the tennis court. (This circle of ground corresponded exactly to the space allocated to polo ponies when on board ship.)

The Edna Walling design contains many of her trademarks. She proposed moving the neat circular driveway in front of the house to one side and transforming it into one of her typical irregular looped driveways,

bordered by woodland paths and more closely resembling a woodland track than an imposing geometric grand entry. Her suggestion was adopted, and a year later, when Professor Wilkinson became involved in work on the house, the visitor's entry was moved to the same side as the driveway. Today the driveway runs under the massive dark cypresses of the early planting (lit in winter by flashes of yellow self-sown wattle) out into the lighter, now mature, woodland glades of the Edna Walling planting. It was a logical change and the driveway is now

Left A eucalyptus overshadows the low stone wall and informal flower border in front of the house.

Below Wisteria *floribunda* and *Centranthus ruber* soften the strong shapes of stone in this view across the lawn.

necessary protection against bush fires and, curiously, providing a barrier against the plagues of grasshoppers which invade this part of New South Wales from time to time. The wall is intersected by naturalistic stone steps to the rough grass Edna Walling favoured and this is informally planted with trees, shrubs and bulbs. Immediately opposite the front of the house, where the informal garden is fairly shallow, a row of trees (mainly claret ash) and shrubs protect the house and inner garden from the winds which blow up the valley but it is still possible to get glimpses of the rolling hills on the horizon. On either side of this shallow band the rough grass streams down the hill at an angle. On one side stands a pergola and tennis court, on the other a gleaming dam.

Edna Walling followed here her usual practice of keeping and cherishing what was good but getting rid of what she considered was not worthwhile. Many of the windbreaks were retained, but the heavy straight hedges were taken out and in their place she introduced the soft lines of the hills to the garden. The gums remained, and more trees were added, many of them deciduous. The climate here is both cold and hot, with heavy frost and snow in winter and periods of scorching wind in summer. The soil is an uncompromising heavy clay so that pickaxes had to be used when planting trees. Workable soil was brought up from a creek and used in the flowerbeds and erosion held at bay by the use of the curving stone walls.

On one side of the rolling grass a long wide rustic pergola made from local timber leads by shallow steps to the tennis court. No one is quite certain when the pergola was erected but it is known to pre-date Edna Walling's involvement in the garden. Happily it was retained, its uprights harmonizing well with the vertical lines of the trees surrounding it, and it is still an important element in the garden's design. Her plan shows, on the other side of the grass, a naturalistic swimming pool typical of many in her country gardens. This pool was never installed but at a somewhat lower level she constructed what she came to describe as the best thing she did for the garden, the dam. A small creek had left a badly eroded

unobtrusively integrated with the well-treed garden and serves both the house and the stables. The stables can be seen from the house and in the early days the Ashton boys were directed to encourage their ponies to hang their heads over the stable doors.

Edna Walling's desire to extend the natural landscape was so strong at Markdale that she wanted to bring the rough turf right up to the house. The idea did not find favour with Mr and Mrs Geoffrey Ashton and wide lawn now rolls from the narrow informal flowery border immediately in front of the house (where flowers peer in through the windows and scent the air close to the house – a typical Walling touch) to a gently curving low stone wall. This lawn is now the only area to be watered in times of drought, cooling the house, providing the

Above left A central feature at Markdale is the long pergola walk, hung with roses and wisteria.

gash in the paddock just below the boundary with the early garden and this became a gleaming highly reflective stretch of water. Rough grass, planted with bulbs, flows from the house down the hill to the point where the early planting of poplars add their straight lines to the reflections in the gleaming water. The embankment was planted with soft smoky-blue cypresses, which lend their colour to the design in the bareness of winter and make a cooling contrasting background to the ornamental trees in the heat of a summer. Closer to the water, weeping willows were added to lend their graceful broken forms (one being established on the small island in the dam) and a neat row of flowering crab apples curves round one side of the upper bank. The contrasts in shape, form and colour of

the various trees is highly effective at all times of year. In spring the frill of pale pink crab-apple blossom is given emphasis by the insertion of an 'odd man out' in the shape of one which flowers in a deeper darker shade of pink.

When Mr and Mrs Geoffrey Ashton, Junior, took over the property in 1984 the garden was well established. The bones of the design were there, the trees were well grown and some of the ground-cover plants favoured by Edna Walling had developed into the 'sheets and sheets' of colour she favoured. In other places trees needed attention, plants had died, alterations had been made and the sheets of ground cover had overrun large stretches of garden. The family preoccupation with horses had faded somewhat and tennis and swimming had

An autumn view in late April from the bridge towards the house, with willows and poplars brilliant against a clear sky.

67

Above This sculpture on the lawn of a sheep shearer by Rix Wright reflects Markdale's function as a sheep station.

Below A stone path bordered with lavender and shasta daisies. Wisteria hangs from the pergola in the background.

taken their place. A decision had to be taken to let the garden run down or to make an effort to save it. Happily the decision was made to preserve and enhance the garden.

Mary and Geoffrey Ashton have given the past few years to restoration, replanting and planning. Markdale has always been an informal country garden in harmony with the surrounding countryside reflecting the interests and activities of life at the homestead and these essential characteristics remain.

The woodland paths which surround the driveway and give access to the stables have been cleared, the beds cleaned and many replanted. The light foliage of silver birches and gums predominates and the soft lines are given strength with an occasional column of evergreen. The largest of the woodland glades provides a turning circle in front of the main entrance. The now mature planting gives a peaceful natural impression. To one side, and overhung by trees, there is a life-size bronze of a shearer with his sheep by Rix Wright. The beds contain a mixture of shrubs with the soft foam of spiraeas delineating some paths. Mary Ashton has introduced many new shrubs here and elsewhere in the garden, including a collection of viburnums. She likes to add some evergreen to each shrubbery and often uses escallonias and iteas to add year-round form to these arrangements. The ground in this area is covered in late winter and early spring with sheets of bluebells and in autumn with yellow *Sternbergia lutea*. In this section of the garden there is a characteristic Edna Walling visual trick with the garden looking quite different when viewed from different angles. Without being too contrived, the trick encourages expectations that make the visitor want to explore the garden. A formal note is struck close to the front door and camellias are placed at regular intervals along the forecourt. The lattice design on their stone containers is matched to the weave of the baskets in the wool shed.

The old pergola carries a heavy load of mauve wisteria growing from a trunk now larger than the thick poles of the supporting columns. The edges of the path beneath are thickly planted with hellebores (*H. orientalis*), which bloom through the winter and last in bloom until early summer. Under each shallow step a fringe of grape hyacinth has established – a touch of charm in an imposing setting. Grape hyacinths and blue forget-me-nots have become naturalized under the trees so that in spring this area has a blue glow. Considerable work has been undertaken recently on either side of the pergola. The area still has the natural sweep and small glades of the Walling design but Mary Ashton has introduced a selection of the perennial border plants she enjoys. One side of the structure is reserved for plantings of pink, blue, mauve, silver and white. The other side, picking up the strong colours of a nearby golden elm, has a perennial border in yellows, reds, apricots and white. Golden Rod (*Solidago*), lady's mantle (*Alchemilla mollis*), geums (*G.* 'Mrs Bradshaw' and *G.* 'Lady Stratheden') and rudbeckia cultivars are used. The rose bed above picks up the yellows, apricots, whites and green (this last colour in the rose 'Viridiflora') of the border below. Mary Ashton prefers not to place pink and yellow flowers together but does use colour boldly. Each year spring is greeted with a central splash of brightly coloured anemones and ranunculus.

The garden is now full of pretty colour pictures. Pink tulips bloom with the same shade of pink tree peonies at the same moment as *Magnolia × soulangiana* unfolds its deep rose-pink buds above their heads. A bed of blue agapanthus is interspersed with an old floppy chrysanthemum cultivar in faded shades of cream and pink – the floppy plants held aloft by the strong spiky leaves of the agapanthus rather than by the rigid stakes most gardeners are forced to employ. Lilies (*Lilium longiflorum*, *L. regale* and *L. candidum*) bloom with rhododendrons, dogwoods with viburnums. Different types of white shasta daisy are used to prolong the flowering season and the rose 'Cécile Brunner' is used because it flowers at a time when the other roses are pausing for breath. The extensive introduction of roses has been effected with care and imagination. Roses in soft tones have been established and trained against the lower side of the wall dividing the lawn from the rough grass, with the result that during the warm months roses

and shiny green leaves froth along the top of the wall. In winter, the naked canes are out of view from the house. Iris, Solomon's seal, thalictrums, globe thistles, silver artichokes, nerines, dianthus and a lovely bed of day-lilies in soft apricot shades have been established in the company of freesias, thymes and *Erigeron karvinskianus*, the last three ground-cover plants much loved by Edna Walling.

The small circle of lawn below the tennis court has now had a small pavilion built on it. The pavilion, which is steeply roofed in the style of the first buildings in the neighbourhood, provides a sheltered space from which to watch tennis and a changing room for the pool which has been installed below the court. On the pool side, brick steps which lead down to the pool are large enough to sit or lie on. The pool itself is green and the surrounds are in a warm tone of brick. The two colours, red and green, are picked up by plantings of the evergreen cotoneasters, photinias and red grevilleas (G. 'Glen Pearl'). The cotoneasters are trained against the walls of the pavilion and the grevilleas and photinias form sheltering hedges to the pool. From the steps of the pavilion there is a view through a fringe of grevilleas into the orchard, where freesias

have naturalized in the grass.

Mary and Geoffrey Ashton have added another small, but highly effective, piece of architecture to the garden in the form of a small bridge which crosses the overspill at the far end of the lake. Once more the design echoes a plain early Australian style and the bridge has simple crossbanded panels. It is painted in the same pale smoky-blue gum colour as the house, a colour which reflects well in water. Looking at the dam from the house one sees the bridge and its reflection; looking from the bridge one sees the house and its reflection. These two small architectural additions to the garden, the bridge and the pavilion, have added form and individuality to the garden but neither interfere with the view to the hills.

No garden is ever static. Here the emphasis is on renewal, with trees and plants being added for future generations; among them *Eucalyptus nicholii* is a favourite. Meanwhile the banks of the dam are being planted with agapanthus, red hot pokers, and arum lilies. The garden has always enjoyed a harmonious relationship with nature and provided an elegant background to an energetic family. The present generation of four children expect to enjoy the garden for many years to come.

The highly effective focal point of the dam is the recently-placed bridge.

VICTORIA

A Garden of Trees

BENALLA

Mr & Mrs L. H. Ledger

THREE GREAT GARDENERS have contributed to the harmony existing between this suburban house and its garden in the Victorian country town of Benalla. Here a rectangular suburban block has become a flowing series of woodland glades. Bark and bough in all their hues and shapes give the garden its structure and, at first glance, there is no obvious design. It seems as though this is nature at her best – meandering, beckoning, exciting. A more penetrating look reveals the perfect placement of trees in relation to the curve of a path, the side of the house or a boundary fence. A fall of rocks is as easy to the eye as an outcrop from the surrounding countryside but is too well sited to have been there when the block was developed. The final confirmation of man's involvement comes from the extensive use of flowering shrubs.

The original plan, by the landscape designer Edna Walling, exquisitely executed in fluid watercolours on hand-made Whatman paper, hangs inside the house. The rocks may look as if the Creator himself had placed them, but their skilful arrangement is the work of Ellis Stones. This 'rockery', complete with lovely mounds of greenery and flower, is also a perfectly practical and easily negotiated flight of steps linking two levels in a fairly steep garden.

The third person to make a creative contribution to this tranquil setting is Mrs Ledger, who commissioned the work and implemented the design with her own hands. Over the years she has made occasional careful adjustments, nurtured the plants, chosen replacements when necessary, and filled the understorey with her collections of camellias and viburnums. One important high spot in the garden's terrain

Far left Daisies and daylilies frame the woodland glade beyond which the red bottlebrush *Callistemon rigidus* flowers by the verandah.

Left The path to the front door, lit by the sun of an October evening, runs through rhododendrons, ferns and silver birches.

has been brought into focus with the clever placement of the sculptural leaves of a huge bird's nest fern (*Asplenium australasicum*, also known as *A. nidus*). The trees, so essential to the garden's form and design, are pruned by her. Not one looks hacked about but every trunk and branch is perfectly placed to expose a new vista or frame an interesting detail.

A formal iron gate set in an ivy-draped brush fence leads to a wide curving trail of flagstones set in mown grass and bordered by trees and shrubs. The angle of the path has been changed slightly from the original plan, but the garden is still evocative of much of Edna Walling's work. Silver birches (placed to give the area width) and fairly dense underplantings give the impression of walking into dark woodland. A glade then opens out, light pours through a gap in the tree tops, the front door is revealed and a glint of silver water is seen.

The hint of water framed by trees lures one down into the back garden, where the slope is contained by a series of banks which surround level lozenge-shaped patches of lawn. There is a series of these gently curving small spaces, each with its perimeter

bordered by trees and shrubs, until the path curls back towards the house and into the largest of these woodland glades.

Here a huge honey locust (*Gleditsia triacanthos* 'Inermis') adds its canopy of elegant leaflets (which in autumn turn pleasantly yellow) to the drama of leaf and bark. This sunken grassy space, well below the level of the house, is contained by the Ellis Stones rockery, a dry stone wall and a sloping bed containing a froth of viburnums. From a chair in the sitting room one looks directly through the branches and tree trunks down into this glade, or, as some of the leaf canopy is at eye level, one can watch the birds playing and feeding in the trees. Honey-eaters feed in the tree tops, regularly checking the progress of each bud as it matures, black-crested shrike tits return each season and, from time to time, rosellas add their parrot colours to the scene.

Essentially this is a garden of trees. Bark and leaf contrasts are as important to Mrs Ledger as they were to Edna Walling. Silver birch trunks gleam throughout the year, their delicate leaves giving summer shade and their black twigs making a lacy pattern against the winter sky. The Chinese elm (*Ulmus parvifolia*), with warm brown mature bark, is almost evergreen in this climate and adds a touch of green in all seasons. Mrs Ledger's great favourite, *Cotinus obovatus* (syn. *Rhus cotinoides*), which has wonderful grooved bark, marks with its red autumn splendour and scarlet berries a pivotal spot where the garden drops to a lower level.

A maidenhair tree (*Ginkgo biloba*) adorns the canopy of leaf with its summer tracery of delicate green, which turns clear yellow in autumn. Next to this lacy tree, with leaves that seem to dance in the softest breeze, stands a stout dense evergreen lilly-pilly (*Acmena smithii*). The leaves are dark, the form solid, its habit immobile. These two trees make a sharp contrast and, when the maidenhair tree is bare in winter, showing only its strong yellow tufts of bud, the lilly-pilly is massed with waxy fat pink berries.

A grove of crape myrtles (*Lagerstroemia indica*) was established to replace an earlier planting of large trees whose size and roots had outgrown their situation. The bark of the crape myrtles glows in winter and in

Left Edna Walling's trademarks included details like the bird bath and mushroom which she made for this garden.

spring the new growth is tipped with red. Summer brings trusses of papery white flowers and, with autumn, come the well-known shades of fiery red and orange. Mrs Ledger has established scarlet nandinas to take up the red of the crape myrtles.

The garden trees merge visually with those beyond the boundaries and greatly extend the feeling of space in what is essentially a suburban garden. In summer, when this inland area is relentlessly hot and dry, the trees provide much-needed shade, reducing both the heat and the glare. Many of them have fine leaves which move with the slightest breeze, further reducing the oppressive heat. Odd shafts of sunlight penetrate the canopy of leaves and highlight the plantings beneath. Healthy camellias (cultivars of *C. japonica*, *C. sasanqua* and *C. reticulata*) flourish beneath the trees, decorating the winter garden with bright flower and matching their shades of pink to a winter-blooming Formosan cherry (*Prunus campanulata*). Their green glossy leaves look cool in the summer heat.

Hydrangeas, spiraeas and viburnums flourish and add their flower to a garden which is never without bloom or berry. It is a garden which, in spite of cold wet winters, never looks bleak, dreary or empty. Its fresh flowery winter appearance is, in part, due to the total absence of roses. Mrs Ledger does not regard rose bushes as good landscape plants. She attributes much of the success with the underplanting to the shade from the trees, water pumped throughout the summer from the lake beyond the garden, and the fact that fallen leaves stay on the ground. From time to time some rearrangement of the fallen leaves is needed to prevent small ground-cover plants from being smothered but, speaking generally, what comes down stays down and mulches the earth below.

Ground-cover plants have been chosen with an artist's eye and do far more for the garden than merely conserve water and smother weeds. The aquilegias, admired for both flower and leaf, are confined to a particular shade of blue, their fine leaves carpeting the earth for most of the year. A special miniature clear-blue forget-me-not nestles between the rocks and the purple-leaved ajuga is just the right shade of purple to enhance the shades found in wet rock. Other plants have also been chosen with great care. A primrose with just a tint of blue to its pink petals huddles beneath a rock with a touch of blue in its dark stone. Close by, the mauve-pink of the fairy primulas (*P. malacoides*) takes up the theme with their display of small upright whorls of colour. The golden gleam in the pronounced eyes of primroses breaks the blue-pink theme and lights up the tiny picture. Baby's tears (*Erigeron karvinskianus*), great favourites with Edna Walling, still peep their daisy-like faces from the corners and, when the wind ruffles them, display the port-wine undersides to their petals. There are no grand herbaceous borders in this garden but wherever and whenever you look there are charming details to catch the eye.

Still treasured in the garden are examples of Edna Walling's pottery. The steps from the verandah are bordered with a selection of her flower pots, simple honest shapes in natural earth colours. Their rough simplicity makes the perfect foil to the elegantly marbled leaves and dancing pink petals of *Cyclamen hederifolium*. A bird bath still gleams with water, flanked by two of her earth-coloured pottery toadstools. This arrangement may sound a little too charming but the texture of the pottery, the earthy colours, the natural setting, and the simplicity of the design save these artefacts from being cloyingly sentimental.

Here one can see Edna Walling's art at its best and enjoy one of her gardens in its maturity nurtured by one whose skills and taste rival those of its designer. It is a place of peace in a world of suburban activity.

Seaton Vale

YARCK

Mr & Mrs Ross Sutherland

*T*HE HOUSE AND GARDEN at Seaton Vale look out over a wide shallow valley, with its typically Australian tree-lined creek, to the foothills of the mounding Strathbogie Ranges. In early morning and late evening when all, gum and grass alike, are gilded with shafts of low-angled light, kangaroos feed in the paddocks. Mr Sutherland grew up on the property and when he and his wife moved into their present home in 1967, the garden consisted of no more than a few circular beds and some huge trees, many of which were past their prime. The driveway, leading nowhere in particular, cut across the front of the house, slicing the front garden in two. Since then the driveway has been diverted to the side of the house and visitors' cars no longer impede the view or damage the lawn. The fences dividing the garden from the paddocks have gone and in their place a stout wooden ha-ha, constructed from old bridge stringers, performs the useful job of keeping the Angus cattle (descendants of a herd established by the family in 1929) out of the garden.

Left   Roses frame the view over the valley.

Right   A pair of brolgas, created in copper by Cecil Norris, dance in the midday sun below the house.

Even when there are no black cattle in the rolling landscape a sculpture depicting a pair of life-sized dancing brolgas or Australian cranes provides a focus. Mrs Sutherland, who loves all native wildlife, commissioned the work from Cecil Norris, the South Australian sculptor, bullying and coaxing him into completing the commission. (He is reputed to have sold his tools on finishing this masterpiece.) The placement of these angular dark objects in the front paddock is an inspired touch. At noon, when the light is so harsh that the flowers lose their colours, the gums cast little shadow and the countryside takes on the appearance of a faded sepia photograph, these dark birds do not fade into the harsh light. They remain, their fanciful dance of delight visible in the midday sun. In summer when the crop is high the thin legs of the birds vanish from view and only the upper half of their angular wings can be seen in silhouette above the vegetation. When the seed crop is cut a circle of uncut greenery is left for the dancing brolgas so that these birds from the northern plains will look at ease in their southern home.

One of the most impressive traces of the first garden to remain is a row of immense cypresses, dusty, dark and huge, which shield the garden from the bitter south winds. Others have been removed, their stumps hollowed and left in the shrubberies to provide shady bird baths during the hot summer months. Beside the lower part of the driveway a well-placed row of magnificent southern mahogany gums (*Eucalyptus botryoides*), stand sentry. Their great straight mahogany-coloured trunks, more than 3 feet (1 m) thick, and spreading branches give great dignity to the approach.

The winters are cold here, with heavy frosts, but many members of the narcissus family bloom months before the advent of spring. In mid-winter the front paddock, just below the house and lawn, blazes with a trail of bright narcissi as if someone had purposely arranged the bulbs in the formation of a shooting star. In fact the plough was put through one of the old circular beds and a few bulbs followed the plough, taking root where they fell. The chance effect has great style and the flowers make happy colour companions to the winter-flowering Cootamundra wattle (*Acacia baileyana*).

After leaving the bright light of the open paddock the drive winds upward through a densely planted section of the garden. The house and lawns are hidden from view by trees and shrubs. Closer inspection reveals a maze of small paths heavily planted with trees, shrubs, perennials and bulbs. A grove of weeping she oaks (*Allocasuarina verticillata*, also known as *Casuarina stricta*) is cleverly carpeted with ajuga (*Ajuga reptans* 'Atropurpurea'). The dull grey-green shade of the fine foliage and dark grey of the furrowed bark of the elegant trees are shown to advantage against the metallic-blue carpet of ajuga leaves. Hidden in this secret garden are mounds of pineapple sage (*Salvia rutilans*) and the rare smoky-blue version of pride of Madeira (*Echium fastuosum*), whose silver-silk leaves hold through the depths of winter.

One area for bulbs is marked off with a great row of arum lilies (*Zantedeschia aethiopica*), the classic whites being mixed with the spectacular long-spathed 'Green Goddess'. The white rose campion (*Lychnis coronaria*)

Left A secret garden path, winding beneath an oak and silver birches, is carpeted either side with *Ajuga reptans* 'Atropurpurea'. Clumps of lychnis and iris provide differing textures.

is used extensively, the leaves adding their silver to the winter scene and their flowers starring the beds for months in spring and summer. A yellow-flowered Jerusalem sage (*Phlomis fruticosa*) with variegated leaves forms large bushes which give the plantings shape even in the depth of winter. There are apple trees here, too, decorating the garden with blossom in spring and fruit in autumn. The area contains in addition many favourite plants which have been collected over the years and many are in unusual shades or have uncommon leaf markings.

The drive swings round into the visitors' parking bay and a chain of paving stones leads across the lawn to the house. The wide informal entrance to the garden is flanked by a pair of Chinese elms (*Ulmus parvifolia*), which are being trained to form an arch. In time this will frame the house in one direction and the view across the valley in the other.

The low house now sits well on its site after some adjustments to levels. The blue-grey shade of its trim was arrived at by asking the painter to match the underside of the leaf from the silver-leaved pear trees (*Pyrus salicifolia*) which flank the garden. The colour of the paint is now complemented by the soft pink rose 'New Dawn', which grows up the house. Mrs Sutherland likes to repeat touches of silver throughout the garden, the intention being to lead the eye from one area to the next and to give the garden form at night when these silvery shades gleam in the moonlight.

The large lawn, sloping away from the house and down to the ha-ha, has been kept open. A group of prickly-leaved paperbarks (*Melaleuca styphelioides*) remains from the period before the construction of the ha-ha and changes to the levels. No one had the heart to remove these much-loved native trees and as the soil was banked up they began to look more like shrubs. Despite this treatment they never looked like dying and today the fine dark foliage bushes out down to ground level. The central tree has been trimmed of its branches on one side so that the group now forms a horse-shoe shape and a seat has been placed in this perfect arbour. Above it the exposed trunk of the central tree displays its peeling papery white

Right The weeping pear (*Pyrus salicifolia*) has acquired a wind-swept look on the lawn.

bark, a magical sight by moonlight. In summer the arbour is frosted with dense cylindrical spikes of creamy-white flower and at all times of the year native birds dash back and forth.

There is a low narrow planting of favourite flowers and small shrubs in front of the house so that, from inside, the view to the hills has a foreground of decorative flower. There are marguerite daisies, perennial ageratums, nicotianas, foxgloves, artemesias, miniature roses, lamb's ears, white nigellas, freesias, snow-in-summer, white honesty, campanulas and a small clear yellow wallflower. All are protected from the bitter frosts by the heat reflected from the walls of the house. Architectural points (steps and corners) are emphasized with strong low-growing evergreen shrubs. Lavenders and both the prostrate and upright forms of rosemary are used. At one corner a bush of mahonia thrives, scenting the garden in winter and providing leaves in summer for use as Christmas 'holly'.

The side of the lawn from which one enters the garden is planted with the willow-leaved silver pear and edged with flowering shrubs. Here a weeping *Camellia sasanqua* grows happily with torrents of roses, its shining green leaves, elegant form and white flowers making it especially valuable in winter.

On the far side of the lawn the dark dry old cypress trees shield the garden from the prevailing winds but give rise to problems which will be familiar to anyone who has tried to grow anything near or under them. Mrs Sutherland has been skilful and successful in choosing plants which are undaunted

by these greedy trees. The lower branches are now festooned with creepers: a yellow clematis (*C. tangutica*) thrives and blooms freely through the summer months while the potato vine (*Solanum jasminoides* 'Album') carries generous bunches of flower throughout the year. Below the cypresses, bushes of the Australian bluebell (*Sollya heterophylla*) have been thickly planted. Blue periwinkle (*Vinca minor*) carpets the ground and blue against green is used once again in a huge urn, from which torrents of the evergreen blue-flowered convolvulus (*C. sabatius*) cascade to the ground.

This grouping is typical of many in the garden where native and exotic plants are mixed together. The tennis court is planted with roses and wattle and in one corner of the garden *Clematis montana* winds its flowery way through the weeping foliage of a *Melaleuca incana*. These combinations may not please purists but they are interesting and attractive to those who like to paint with flowers and do not displease the local koalas, who are just as likely to be found dozing the day away in a birch as in a gum.

The silver birches are found behind the house where the atmosphere changes dramatically. Here the spaces are more rigidly defined. Beside the house, and at the same level, lies a flowery courtyard which is perfect for summer meals. Beyond, and on a slightly higher level, is a peaceful green yard bordered by low walls and planted with silver birches and *Melaleuca incana*. The walls of the yard, like most things in this garden, were constructed by members of the family using materials found on the property. A simple path of mown grass leads the eye and feet through this yard and to the trees and land beyond. The effect of this disciplined simplicity is tranquil, reminiscent of the stillness found in a Japanese garden. This generously sized yard provides the link needed to harmonize the gay colours in the courtyard with the bleached soft colouring of the landscape beyond.

A small wooden hut, constructed from massive hand-sawn logs by early settlers, was moved to the property some years ago (each log being carefully numbered so that it would be restored to its original position). The low hut now sits beneath a large maple and sets the scale for the courtyard. The courtyard is thickly and informally planted with flowering creepers, perennials and bulbs and is filled with flowers throughout the summer. Scented-leaved geraniums cling to the warm walls of the house in the company of the twining Chilean jasmine (*Mandevilla laxa*). Honeysuckles, white wisteria and roses pour from the cooler walls of the outbuildings. The beds contain a collection of irises and sisyrinchiums. The white buddleia 'White Bouquet' attracts the butterflies and honey-eaters and the paving is laced with the upturned cream trumpets of *Nierembergia repens*. At the far end of the courtyard stands a prunus with particularly deep purple foliage. Mrs Sutherland has cleverly combined the purple of the prunus with the clear yellow of the pillar rose 'Golden Showers'.

In bad weather Mrs Sutherland stays inside, spending her time drawing and embroidering flowers and planning the next step in the development of a large country garden. She hopes, one day, to flood some of the land near the creek to give the house a view of distant water and to provide shallow water for wading birds. I was asked not to use the word lake to describe this stretch of water but to use the correct Australian word, billabong.

Left The trunks of silver birches with grass cut at different levels make interesting textural contrasts and contribute to the peaceful atmosphere of the walled lawn.

Mawarra

OLINDA

Mr & Mrs F. H. Walker

MAWARRA, meaning 'a quiet resting place', lies in the heart of the Sherbrooke Forest deep in the Dandenong Ranges to the east of Melbourne. Here a damp misty cold-winter climate, combined with a lime-free humus-rich soil led to the establishment of several extensive estates where keen gardeners could indulge their enthusiasm for exotic plants. In 1932 Mrs McMillan and her two sisters, the Misses Marshall, commissioned the landscape designer Edna Walling to create a garden on a sloping 5-acre (2-hectare) site. In spite of her belief that the garden at Mawarra was her finest creation, Edna Walling had an argument with the owners and did not complete the supervision of her design. Happily, Eric Hammond, with whom she worked on many occasions, completed the job. As he is known to have been pleased with the work and to have been a loyal friend to Edna Walling, we can, with some certainty, conclude that her designs were carried out much as she would have desired. After Mr and Mrs Walker bought the property in the 1960s Edna Walling, who became a family friend, visited regularly and was often heard to murmur, 'Thank goodness you two have got it now.'

At Mawarra Edna Walling was able to exercise her talent for architectural symmetry and her enjoyment of well-cut and well-placed stone. It is of interest to note that all the stonework dating from her involvement in the garden was hand dressed without the help of modern machinery. Today, after fifty years of weather, the stones have a pleasantly matured appearance and their presence does much to enhance the informal display of leaf and flower and to control the erosion which would be inevitable if nature were left to take its course on the steeply sloping site. However, in spite of the strong design, in which the stonework is a predominating feature, the overwhelming impression given by the garden today is of nature at her artless best.

The Walling design is basically very simple. Faced, as she often was, with an imposing house standing on a bare site, she designed a garden from which maximum enjoyment could be derived from within the house. Five parallel paths run across the slope and, where they connect with the house, are carefully aligned with the windows so that from the house the eye is

A woodland path leading to the house, freely planted with rhododendrons and azaleas.

Stone steps, edged
with *Lamium
galeobdolon*
'Variegatum' and the
fern *Matteuccia
struthiopteris* on the
right, lead down past
the house into a
woodland glade, given
height by the Italian
cypress (*Cupressus
sempervirens*).

led naturally into the informal plantings of trees and shrubs. From the front face of the house a series of magnificent steps and terraces runs down the steep slope to terminate at an octagonal pond. It is sometimes said that Edna Walling's gardens are nothing more than poor imitations of the English countryside. Here, in what is known to have been her favourite garden, the most clearly discernible influence in the design is Italian and what remains of her planting shows the individuality which marks all her work. A *Fagus sylvatica* 'Tricolor', with leaf edges striped in pink and cream, now rises to 60 feet (18 m); the hornbeam (*Carpinus betulus*), displaying lovely autumn foliage and long chains of seeds through the cooler months, is now fully mature; the snowy mespilus (*Amelanchier canadensis*) from North America, which carries white spring-time flowers and striking red and yellow autumn foliage, now reaches a height of 25 feet (8 m). The oaks, maples, cornus and

birches found in many of her early gardens are there but so too is an indication of her growing interest in native flora. The house, when approached from the drive, is seen against the spreading branches of an impressive *Eucalyptus globulus* ssp. *bicostata* and no attempt has been made to screen the impressive view to the forest of eucalypts which shelters the garden. Indeed, it is well utilized as a backdrop to the ornamental garden.

In only one area did Edna Walling attempt to block out the landscape beyond the ornamental garden and this was in an area where future development might have proved a problem. Here she used a row of the native lilly pilly trees (*Acmena smithii*). At that time, when many gardens were encased in conifers and all glimpses of the Australian landscape carefully eliminated, the treatment was innovative. Today the lilly-pillies have gone, having outlived their purpose, but it is of historical interest that when a quick-growing screening plant was needed a native plant was chosen. As the owners were away while work at Mawarra was in progress it is most likely that many of the fundamental design and planting decisions would have been hers rather than theirs. It is recorded that, on their return from an extended English sojourn, the owners perceived little English charm in the design and complained that their well-built garden resembled a well-walled, well-known prison.

Today any feeling that the garden consists of unbending straight lines coupled with overpowering architectural stonework has vanished and the leafy walks and vistas have acquired a timeless quality. As Mrs Walker says, 'You can make straight paths but nature will soon add her curves and quirky bits.' Edna Walling often complained that her clients never had the courage to control the gardens that she purposely over-planted in order to achieve a quick effect. Here at Mawarra she had nothing but praise for Mrs Walker, who has, over the years, cut back and removed trees and shrubs in a manner which, she freely admits, some find a trifle savage. The proof of her wisdom can be seen throughout the garden, which has a well-grown woodland feeling but is never claustrophobic, as are so many heavily-planted gardens in a quick-growth climate. As natural attrition has left space, Mrs Walker has added some of her favourites, which include *Styrax japonica*, a tree of singular grace and beauty. A specimen has now reached a mature size and displays pendulous pure white thread-like flowers from the undersides of the branches.

In spite of the regular pruning and clearing, Mrs Walker describes the garden as 'a kind garden'. There is almost no weeding and the woodland setting can incorporate a few fallen leaves without giving the garden an unkempt appearance. Furthermore, the essential character of the garden happily incorporates many plants which some would describe as invasive. The ground under the shrubs and trees is carpeted with various forms of *Vinca minor*, including one in an unusual wine-purple shade and a double clear-blue variety. Shade-loving bulbs such as bluebells grow in drifts under the trees, clumps of daffodils grow where the light penetrates the leaf canopy and a variety of small-leaved violets creep through the undergrowth, often finding a satisfactory home on the edge of a pathway. Forget-me-nots add their mist of blue throughout the garden and the stone work is encrusted with Edna Walling's favourite, baby's tears (*Erigeron karvinskianus*). Hellebores flourish and display great clumps of their leathery leaves and flowers, and mats of shiny green foliage are provided by the curious mouse plant (*Arisarum proboscideum*) and epimediums.

To the side of the house, where long narrow paths make vistas in line with the windows, the area is densely planted with a selection of ornamental trees. *Prunus* 'Elvins' a variety which originated in Victoria in the early 1940s is planted with a wide selection of *Malus* and *Magnolia* species. The shrubs include many rhododendrons and Mrs Walker has added modern hybrids, some such as 'Kalimna' and 'Denise' bred at a local nursery, to the simpler forms of the early plantings. The garden also contains a range of azaleas, virburnums, forsythias, kerrias and kalmias. Until recently a massive oak shaded this area and its loss has changed its character, allowing more light

to reach the ground. In less than a year nature has filled the vacuum; trees previously dwarfed by the massive oak have filled out and the shrubs have gained stature and bloom more freely. The trunk of the oak remains and now supports a flourishing *Clematis armandii* 'Apple Blossom'. This evergreen climber comes from China and bears clusters of small whitish-pink flowers and displays a beautiful bronze tinge to the new foliage; when the foliage sometimes acquires a scorched brown appearance in summer the disfigurement is unnoticeable against the bark of the old tree. The woodland area, in spite of its simple geometric layout, is an excellent example of Edna Walling's ability to create mystery out of simplicity and it is easy to lose one's sense of direction while walking down a straight path.

One woodland pathway terminates in a miniature house known as the Children's House, which has its own small garden enclosed by stout high hedges of *Photinia glabra* 'Rubens'. Here, in a distinct change of character, brick is used to contain the small terraced beds; the red-orange shades in the brick are well matched with the autumn colour in a Canadian sugar maple (*Acer saccharum*), which shades the little house, and with the rich shades found in the new growth of photinias. Mobcaps of dark-green box mark steps and the beds are planted with a selection of old-fashioned perennials.

The small white flowers of *Nierembergia repens* delineate the paving on the top terrace.

Right The leaves of *Epimedium × youngianum* and the flowers of *Erigeron karvinskianus* soften the lines of the stone walls and steps which were designed by Edna Walling.

A kookaburra surveys Edna Walling's octagonal pond at the bottom of two long flights of stone steps.

A second straight woodland path has a bright border of 'Christmas Cheer', a Kurume azalea. A pair of tall column-shaped birches (*Betula pendula* 'Fastigiata') marks the point where the informal woodland area joins the more formal architectural arrangements which border the front of the house. This path leads straight across the front of the house, where, paved with stone and given form by mounds of variegated box, it forms a terrace overlooking the view to the octagonal pond. (Mrs Walker notes that *Buxus sempervirens* 'Variegata', which she established on the terrace, only needs cutting once a year in comparison to the plain-leaved varieties which, in this climate, require much more frequent attention.) Just below this terrace is a large specimen of the scented Japanese magnolia, *M. kobus*. Here, too, stand well-grown examples of *Pieris japonica* 'Chandleri', a variety bred in a nearby nursery, which displays attractive pink new growth.

Below the terrace which borders the house and intersected by the narrow vistas which run across the hill lies the major architectural feature of the garden. As the slope falls away from the front of the house it is contained by a series of stone steps and terraces. Simple broad stone steps, frilled with *Erigeron karvinskianus*, lead down from the house to the first terrace. A pair of large calico bushes (*Kalmia latifolia*) stand beneath the supporting walls. Below this terrace a pair of shallow-stepped ramps, consisting of raked gravel and low stone-edged steps curve downwards, their low retaining walls embracing an oval level garden, and linking the upper terrace to the lower terrace. The grassed oval glade-like terrace, its open space in sharp contrast to the woodland which surrounds it, is planted in a controlled formal manner. A raised pond has a stone border wide enough to sit on and has been cleverly surrounded with *Cotoneaster horizontalis*. The branches have been trained to spread out over the water, eliminating the need for the usual wire framework required to protect fish from the kookaburras which inhabit the garden. On each side of the pond large examples of *Camellia* 'Margaret Waterhouse' stand sentry. In the shallow curve of wall at either end of the oval garden stand fifty-year-old specimens of the Japanese flat-crowned cherry tree *Prunus serrulata* 'Shimidsu-sakura'. A low-growing spreading pair of *Juniperus communis* links the curving stone walls to the grassed entry to the oval garden. A focus for the formal design, achieved through impressive stone-work, perfect scale and the well-grown meticulously paired plants, is provided by a single small weeping maple. It has heavily dissected bronze leaves and overhangs the stone-bordered pond.

The stone terrace bordering the oval garden forms part of one of the narrow woodland vistas which lies across the slope. This one leads through the herbaceous borders, which, now that the huge oak no longer shades the area, are under recon-

A woodland glade seen from the house, a delightful setting for entertaining, decorated by an attractive bird bath.

struction. The planting plan bears little resemblance to the neatly clipped edges and carefully graded plant heights and colours of an English herbaceous border. Here the plants give a naturalistic impression as if they had arrived of their own accord and found a satisfactory home in a woodland glade. Trees and shrubs form the backdrop, and the straight narrow path which leads through the flowers resembles, as do all the paths in this area, a woodland track. In this instance the flowers, not the trees, break the strong line of the pathway, which serves merely as passage for the feet and to direct the eye from one area to the next.

From the terrace bordering the oval garden a flight of thirty stone steps, punctuated only by one stone terrace, descends the steep slope to the octagonal pond. The first steps are marked by a pair of *Fagus sylvatica* 'Riversii', with black-purple leaves, and thin columns of dark yew, which are repeated on the outer sides of the terraced beds, planted with trees and shrubs, which border the steps. It is a tribute to the craft of Edna Walling that this fall of steps is neither monotonous to look at nor tiring to negotiate. The pond itself is given emphasis with a simple central fountain and is surrounded by azaleas and overhung with trees. One further vista crosses the slope at this level and leads to what was once a much-photographed birch grove. The original trees, which gained much of their fame

through their random and naturalistic placement, have now died of fungal infection. (Edna Walling often gained her naturalistic effects by throwing potatoes from a bucket and establishing her trees where the potatoes fell.) Today new trees are growing to take the place of the early inhabitants and the site, no longer shaded by the lilly-pillies, receives more sun. It is hoped that this will prevent a further outbreak of the infection. In the place of the lilly-pillies there is a stout band of rhododendrons, forsythias and ginger plants (*Hedychium densiflorum*). From the silver birch grove the path leads back up the slope through open lawns punctuated by shade trees (under which seats are placed) to a photinia-bordered rectangle where Mrs Walker has designed and established a formal garden. A sundial stands in the centre and the beds are filled with roses and perennial herbaceous plants.

The garden at Mawarra today has a very particular character. The extensive use of exotic trees and shrubs (many Australian bred) give it a universal quality. The swirling mists which so often envelop the mountain, constantly changing the garden's appearance, create a mystical feeling. Many of the garden's characteristics could be found elsewhere in the world but the contrasts of colour and texture between exotic and native plants and such incidents as the flashes of brilliantly hued rosellas tie it firmly to its Australian inheritance.

Delatite Station

MANSFIELD

Mr & Mrs Geoffrey Ritchie

DELATITE STATION dates from 1860 when the building now used as an office and much of the present house were built. The Ritchie family have lived here since 1902. Three Ritchie women, all keen gardeners and married to successive generations of Ritchies, have designed, altered, planted, trimmed and nurtured their plants on this property. Mr and Mrs Geoffrey Ritchie now live at the big house. Mrs Ritchie, Senior, sister to another great gardener, Dame Elisabeth Murdoch, whose garden at Cruden Farm is to be found in this book, still lives close by and takes a great interest in the entire property. As it stands today, the form of this mature garden is largely the work of the senior Mrs Ritchie.

This is mountain country, snow country, and in its early days would have been very isolated. Delatite Station lies in the foothills of the Great Dividing Range and the Delatite River sings, as only mountain water can sing, as it pours through the valley. Magpies (whose song lives in the heart of all Australians) add their carolling warble to the river's song. It is a garden filled with music. Old

Approached by a wide, sweeping drive, the cream-coloured homestead is fronted by evergreen shrubs and its wide verandahs are trained with a muscatel grape vine.

Standard forms of 'Renae' give height in the rose garden where two varieties of box are used to emphasize the strong design.

pines, shaped by the mountain winds and with gnarled coppery bark, line the narrow approach, which opens into a wide circle in front of the house. The circle is filled with beautifully maintained mown turf with a central circle of segmented flowerbeds. In each bed there is a bush of *Berberis thunbergii* 'Little Favourite' to give the beds form and then the flowers are distributed in a more irregular fashion. They include pinks, iris, *Iberis sempervirens* 'Little Gem' and *Euphorbia epithymoides*.

The house, with its simple generous lines and the wide verandahs of an early-Australian homestead, sits low on the site. All the buildings are painted in a warm cream and trimmed in white so that even on the darkest of winter days they glow as if lit by sunlight. The front door is flanked by massive cumquat trees grown in containers under the shelter of the verandah. Their bright orange citrus fruits gleam against their dark shiny foliage, providing a formal touch in a classical setting. A muscatel grape vine is trained to grow along the perimeter of the verandah. In summer its fringe of wide leaves give shade. In autumn they turn to glowing shades of yellow and great

trusses of grapes hang down. In winter there is the grey bark to admire. The vine is old and over the years has been well pruned. Today its thick trunk runs up a verandah post and horizontally along the front of the house. This beam is now so wide that a portly tabby cat can snooze in comfort above the front door. The vineyards of Delatite and its wine are renowned.

The area immediately in front of the house used to be massed with summer flowers but this arrangement left the house looking exposed and bleak in winter. Now this edging bed is planted with a variety of low-growing evergreen shrubs. An interesting *Picea pungens* from the Koster's nursery has established well in the company of a garden variety of *Chamaecyparis lawsoniana*, *Berberis thunbergii* 'Little Favourite', *Lavandula angustifolia* 'Vera' and *Rosmarinus officinalis*. These contrasts of sculptural form, leaf and colour now soften the line of the house throughout the year.

The only problem remaining with this interesting planting is the problem familiar to most Australian gardeners – the growth rate. By many standards this is a harsh climate but the majority of cultivated plants grow with such energy and speed that so-called low-growing shrubs rapidly reach tree height and dwarf shrubs become tall and leggy. Rigorous attention is needed to keep these interesting sculptural forms from rising, blocking the view from the house, and exposing their leafless leggy nether parts to the world. The work is worthwhile and this effective grouping comes into its own in the bleak winter months, distracting the eye from the bare branches of the deciduous flowering shrubs which line the outer perimeter of the driveway. The ground under these shrubs is planted thickly with hellebores, providing winter flower and matching their dark green leathery leaves to the green of the low conifers. In summer nothing could distract the eye from the glory of the flowers which bloom with massed abundance in this mountain setting. The most dramatic of these shrubs is the rose 'Wedding Day'. Once an apple tree stood to one side of the driveway. When it died the rose was established in the traditional manner to grow through the dead branches. Soon extra supports were needed and the rose now climbs to 25 feet (7.6 m) and cascades downward in a spectacular pyramid of bright glossy green embroidered with great trusses of white flower.

When Mrs Ritchie began developing the garden she did not want to use roses as landscape plants. Later, she revised this view, and now believes that roses do better in the company of other plants. Today there are well-grown roses throughout the informal plantings, many of them grown on their own roots from cuttings thrust into the soil.

However, for her first rose garden Mrs Ritchie reserved a rectangle of land to one side of the house. It is backed by the house with its wide verandah and flanked by the low straight wall of the office building. The rose 'Fortune's Yellow', an old Chinese variety, was one of the early plantings. Now, growing from a massive trunk, its glossy foliage hangs along the verandah forming a dramatic backdrop to the formal rose garden.

The land was levelled and the rectangle bordered with a thick hedge of hardy dark-leaved English box. This outer hedge is now stout, a stalwart hip-high barrier against mountain winds. Narrow paths divide the generous rose beds which are bordered with more box. Here the less hardy Dutch box with lettuce-green leaves was used. These inner hedges are narrower and cut to a lower level than the outer hedges. The two varieties of box make a strong geometric planting, providing pleasant contrasts in their varied shades of foliage and saving the design from looking insignificant in this powerful landscape. Moreover, the scale of this design is in perfect proportion to the surrounding buildings. This successful planting bears no relationship to the charm school of gardening often associated with rose and box combinations. In the central beds are four tall standards of the rose 'Renae' and the beds are filled with a selection of favourite rose bushes. 'French Lace' has just been added to the collection. The combination of the solid dark hedging and the multicoloured roses which froth above the hedges is one of the summer's most

Right A pergola of softly-coloured climbing roses, backed by the dry hills beyond, covers a path which leads from a bed containing *Iris Kaempferi* and an abundant tea tree (*Leptospermum scoparium*).

area blooms for eight months of the year, and the climbing version of 'Iceberg' cover the supports. Beneath are plantings of blue irises, pink leptospermum and pink and white *Cyclamen hederifolium*. The progeny of the first three cyclamen corms now form large marbled mats of leaf and several have migrated to populate other gardens belonging to members of the Ritchie family.

When the Ritchies first came to Delatite the area to the rear of the house was reserved for orchards and poultry yards. Today the lawn rolls down through trees, shrubberies and flowering borders to a dry-stone ha-ha. It is an area both open and mysterious. The wide surge of grass circles trees, curving into bays and swelling into open spaces as it leads the eye down through the ornamental plants to the river below. Small paths lead into the thickly growing trees and shrubs. It is an area for exploration. Below the dark stone ha-ha, which is mossed with soft humps of aubrieta, lies a small wilderness sloping into the tumbling willow-edged river.

Three massive sugar pears (thought to have been planted when the house was built) now reach a height of 60 feet (18.3 m). They strike a strong note amid the gentler decorative elements of lawn and flower. Their huge black trunks of furrowed bark and lacework of twigs decorate the winter scene. In spring the trees are thickly snowed with blossom and in autumn there is the prolific brown fruit and yellow leaf to enjoy. The beds beside the lawn are filled with a mixture of perennials and annuals. Mrs Ritchie uses lots of whites in the borders to 'throw everything into focus' and loves to add cream and pale yellow. She almost never uses orange-coloured flowers. She says, 'This dream is often shattered, and while we aim at pastel colours, some monstrosity often appears.' At present a bright yellow achillea is being weeded out and a new lemon-yellow achillea is being encouraged. Each year the seeds of pastel zinnias, which are no longer available commercially, are carefully collected.

Over the steps which lead down to the wilderness hangs a well grown 'Mount Fuji' cherry. When it foams with flower in the early spring the steps are bordered with the

Left Jerusalem sage (*Phlomis fruticosa*) stands out from the low-growing evergreen shrubs in the verandah border.

dramatic sights. In winter the garden's strong architectural form distracts attention from the bare rose branches.

On the opposite side of the house beyond a grass tennis court lies a rose-covered pergola. Once it led to a nine-hole golf course but family interests have changed; now it leads straight into the fence which divides the garden from the paddock. A small statue (known to the family as Granny's G-nome) has now been placed at the far end of the walkway and clothed in a circular skirt of pale silvery ivy. It makes an arresting focal point which is given greater emphasis by the contrast provided by the addition of some dark evergreen columns and by raising the line of the fence behind the little statue. The statue is just outside the shade cast by the plants which cover the pergola, and the whitish ivy, catching both sunlight and moonlight, lures one through the flowery tunnel.

In summer this pergola is covered with pink and white roses. 'Pinkie', which in this massed flowers of two varieties of alpine phlox. One side of the steps glistens with white, picking up the white floss of the cherry blossom; the other throws the picture into sharp focus with a glow of clear sugar pink. In this garden the progress of the seasons brings a succession of new arrangements to delight the eye. Plants which through colour contrast or coordination enhance one another and bloom in the same season are arranged to make small 'floral paintings' within the larger scheme.

The side verandah, where the family entertains in summer, is shaded by an old wisteria, with a tree-sized trunk. As it comes into mauve bloom so do the lilacs. Once more the trick of bringing colour-matched flowers into focus by using contrast is employed successfully. In this instance the contrast is provided by *Euphorbia epithymoides*, which Mrs Ritchie describes as 'liquid sunshine'. In high summer the paving in the deep shade cast by the wisteria is starred with *Nierembergia repens*, which makes a full recovery from an onslaught of human feet within a matter of days.

The back of the house has been added to over the years and no longer has the simple symmetry of the entry. The irregularity has been carefully balanced with the placement of a simple circular flowerbed. The bed contains mixed herbaceous plants chosen for their ability to remain decorative in winter as well as for their summer display and a small stone minaret stands at the centre. In summer the stone is lost in the foliage and flower; in winter it reappears, bringing the house into balance with its garden setting. The summer display includes *Delphinium* 'Blue Heaven', white and purple phlox, the lemon-yellow achillea, penstemon, nicotianas and the graceful *Lilium regale*.

The wilderness was planted with a few narcissus bulbs when the Ritchie family came to Delatite and over the years many more have been added, predominantly in pale shades. Some, 'Cantatrice' and 'Moonstruck' among them, have been imported from Ireland. In winter and early spring the banks are thick with the flowers. Mrs Ritchie has never lifted or divided the bulbs and says, 'They have been all right for fifty years; something disastrous always happens if you move a daffodil or a tulip.' In a far corner of the garden a swing bridge, typical of those found in mountainous country, hangs over the river. The bridge was recently restalled by one of the first men to climb Mt Everest without oxygen, Sherpa Tensing.

This is a garden of flower and form. The elements of formality found in many traditional European gardens are here but this is no mere re-creation. The themes are adjusted and adapted, modified and embellished, to suit a different landscape and a different way of living. No attempt has been made to isolate this garden from its country setting through the creation of the heavily walled enclosed garden 'rooms' so popular in Britain. The garden falls naturally with the terrain, one section flowing easily into another without visual abruptness. It is a garden in harmony with its strong mountain setting, the creation of a family who live on their land and whose relationship with that land and the mountainous countryside beyond is more important than the shelter given by man-made walls.

Nierembergia repens encrusts the paving below the verandah.

Bolobek

MACEDON

Sir Robert & Lady Law-Smith

MAGNIFICENT OLD TREES, rich volcanic soil and an adequate rainfall were the attractions which led Sir Robert and Lady Law-Smith to Bolobek twenty years ago. The best of the trees remain but by a process of modification and addition the earlier garden has been transformed into a highly personal creation with a clear, strong design which achieves all the elegance that logical simplicity brings to a site.

The drive leads through an avenue of great mahogany gums (*Eucalyptus botryoides*). These trees have an annoying habit of unexpectedly dropping large branches but here they have achieved a primeval splendour. The foliage is long, glossy and deep green and the branching trunks, in some cases fire scarred, are massive and furrowed. Through the trees can be seen the open paddocks, dissected by the lines of pines which are typical of the area. Ancient volcanic mountains, of which Mount Macedon is one, overlook the gently rolling farmland. The garden and house are hidden from view by a low wall, large trees and well-controlled shrubs. There is a pleasant contrast between the busy life of the farm and the calm seclusion of the garden within the gates.

Within the garden a lawn lies to one side, with old oaks, elms and beeches standing on the closely mown grass. A band of low-growing shrubs defines the area and as the shrubs come into bloom they draw the eye to the spaces between the trees and the patterns their trunks and shadows make against the flat surface of mown grass. *Viburnum plicatum tomentosum* 'Mariesii', which smothers its horizontal branches with white blossom, lights one edge of the lawn and a pure white evergreen azalea stands on one corner. Close to the house itself is a rectangular pond where a small lead statue of a boy splashes water into water. The paved area close to the front door shelters containers planted with evergreen shrubs. Species camellias and simple forms of *C. sasanqua* are used in this garden in preference to the better-known eye-catching hybrids. Here, by the front door, *Camellia yunnanensis* from South China scents the air and displays its small, creamy flowers throughout the winter months. Elsewhere in the garden *Camellia lutchuensis*, from the south islands of Japan, with its small white single flowers and decorative russet-tipped foliage, spreads its delicate perfume. To one side of the house an old Japanese flowering crab (*Malus floribunda*) – the oldest of the ornamental crabs, its origin now unknown – displays, in spring, its crimson buds and prolific pale pink to white blossoms.

Left The apple walk in full blossom in early October. *Rhododendron* 'Pink Pearl' flows over the formal hedge to one side of the old stone statue.

The statue, given emphasis with a border of clipped hedging, is the focal point of this part of the garden.

A second, matching, crab stands within the woodland garden which lies to one side of the house. This side garden, overlooked by the living room, takes much of its atmosphere from these two spreading trees. It is sheltered from the mountain winds by towering holly hedges against which grow a few rhododendrons that have reached 60 feet (20 m). The wide variety of trees growing here creates the atmosphere of this garden. A New Zealand beech (*Nothofagus fusca*), its form as elegant as those of the silver birches which line one side of the area, lends its warm, brown bark, small leaves and autumn colour to the scene. A copper beech (*Fagus sylvatica purpurea*) and maples add their shapes, forms and colours to the tranquil setting. The light plays through the canopy of leaves constantly changing the lace-like patterns of shadow on the ground below. (Variegated leaves used elsewhere in the world to create this effect are eschewed at Bolobek. The light here is so strong that it penetrates the leafy canopy and there is no need to add to nature's moving tracery of deep shadow, shade and sunlight.)

Beneath the trees a few colourful shrubs light the late spring scene. The creams, yellows and soft oranges of the deciduous azaleas and the pinks of dogwoods glow in the shaded light. Here small pools rather than strong waves of colour pick up the flickering light and lead the eye gently through the delicate scene. White flowers are used more extensively and the greeny-whites of *Viburnum macrocephalum* and the Chinese pearl bush (*Exochorda racemosa*) snow the scene. The ground is given form and decoration with mounds of English primroses, spikes of foxglove and elegant stands of the great Solomon's seal (*Polygonatum commutatum*). The mown grass streams round the trees and shrubs as if following nature's path. The circular beds and geometric shapes of another era have gone (Lady Law-Smith says, 'Whenever I have simplified something it has been much better'). A woodland path curves through the garden and leads, at the far end, to the statue of a lady placed centrally upon a circle of bricks edged with clipped box. The bricks were obtained when an old chimney was taken down and are individually moulded to form a perfect circle. Behind the statue *Rhododendron* 'Pink Pearl' hangs her soft colours.

Masses of *Helleborus orientalis* and forget-me-nots border the paths under lines of silver birches either side of the main lawn. On the right is the lilac hedge at the entrance to the poplar walk.

At right angles to the woodland path is a paved path which leads through an avenue of crab apples. Here *Malus* 'Golden Hornet' displays its pink and white flowers in spring and, in autumn, golden fruit and decorative foliage. Beneath their boughs (which meet over the path) favourite plants are allowed to self-sow in an informal manner. There are great clumps of hostas, *Primula japonica* 'Postford White', white aquilegias, a simple, lemon-yellow polyanthus with an elegant form, wild English cowslips (*Primula veris*) and, in summer, the lime-green flowers of *Hydrangea arborescens*. At the far end of this shady path light shines on open lawn.

As the view opens it can be seen that the broad grassy path leads right across the main vista of the garden. To one side lies a rectangular lawn and on the other a long border of lilac grows from an extended low mound of clipped *Vinca minor*. Above the lawn stands the house, its verandah draped in a wisteria which carries long, white racemes of flower with just the most delicate hint of pink and mauve in the petals. The wisteria blooms at the same time as the lilac displays its mauve and white heads of flower, and the refreshing scent of the two wafts through the spring garden. On either side of the rectangular stretch of grass are straight rows of silver birch underplanted with a row of the rose 'Iceberg'. Rather surprisingly, the roses thrive in this shady position, producing flush after flush of white bloom through the summer months. Silver trunks and the tracery of dark twigs line the lawn in winter; in the warmer months a foam of white roses overhung by the small birch leaves delineates the lawn. On each side paths lead under the birches and beside the roses, linking the area near the house to the cross-axial grassy path. One of these side paths is edged with deep bands of white *Helleborus orientalis* which, in this climate, can be relied on to bloom all through the winter months. Retaining walls which link the house to the lawn at a lower level are covered with clipped ivy.

As one looks across the lawn from the front of the house the eye is caught by a gap in the wall of lilac, emphasized by a pair of box bushes clipped into simple shapes resembling cottage loaves. The gap, which is

in line with a sundial standing centrally in front of the house, opens up to a long avenue of tall poplars, which leads the eye down the hill towards a glint of water. The borders of the avenue are densely planted with the late-blooming fragrant *Narcissus poeticus*. When these finish their display the strong clumps planted behind them of the white-flowered watsonia present their elegant spikes of flower. A second cross-axial path intersects with the main vista, crossing the poplar avenue below the lilac hedge. These paths are at their most dramatic in spring when the lindens (*Tilia*) which overhang the area begin to unfold their leaves, and daffodils, chosen from a range with short corollas in pale colours, display a mass of gently shaded bloom. At the end of the grand avenue is a small lake bordered with silver birch, eucalypts and silver poplars. It is a peaceful stretch of water given drama by the sculptural shapes of tree trunks reflected in the clear stillness.

The grassy path which runs across the main vista and is bordered by the lilac hedge leads on to a pergola. Over this grows a white wisteria and the surrounding planting is restricted to white and green. The green arum lily (*Zantedeschia aethiopica* 'Green Goddess') stands in a damp spot, surrounded by white penstemons, white lupins, white perennial phlox and a white shasta daisy which bears very full fringed flowers. It was found some years ago in an old garden and has been treasured and propagated ever since. Double white violets carpet the ground. The path leads through the pergola

Pale, pendulant racemes of wisteria add their elegance to a pergola.

The lime walk, planted with daffodils either side, bisects the poplar avenue, itself bordered with the spikes of white watsonias, seen here in the foreground.

The ground beneath the roses contains a carefully chosen selection of small plants, their shades and forms selected to harmonize with the roses. Auriculas display deep purple-pink tones picking up the faded pink and purple hues found in the old roses and adding their deep silk-velvet texture to the lush texture of rose petals. Strawberries, natural companions to the roses, grow beneath their branches. *Alchemilla mollis* grows abundantly. *Alyssum saxatile* 'Sulphureum' and *Achillea × lewisii* 'King Edward' display similar shades of creamy-yellow flowers in the company of the softest of pink geraniums, *G. sanguineum lancastrense*. Dianthus in a variety of forms blooms abundantly and one bed is covered with an unbroken, glossy carpet of *Limnanthes douglasii*, from which rises the constant buzz of bees. The soft creamy yellows and the lime-green colours found in the alchemilla and limnanthes make the perfect companions to the slightly faded, shades of crimson, purple and pink of the roses and dianthus. There is silver provided by the leaves of the dianthus

to a glade which is bordered on one side by a walled rose garden.

The design of the rose garden is simple; it is the flourishing plants which provide the spectacle. Three sides of the garden are contained by high walls of mellow brick and the fourth, which borders the glade, is contained by a precisely clipped, hip-high hedge of box over which a row of 'Iceberg' froths with flower. The combination of the severe hedge and the mass of flower makes a dramatic invitation to enter the rose garden. The beds within are separated by straight brick paths and a centrally placed sundial is marked by clipped box buns. Apart from 'Iceberg' the roses in the collection are old-fashioned varieties. Here one finds the soft foliage and soft velvety violet petals of 'Reine des Violettes', the glossy leaves and globular pink buds and white petals of 'Boule de Neige', and the petals splashed pink and white of *R. × centifolia* 'Variegata', sometimes known as 'Village Maid'. 'Charles de Mills' shows its deep red-purple petals and 'Souvenir de la Malmaison' opens its beautifully proportioned, quartered, soft pink blooms throughout the summer months.

The golden autumn leaves of the grey poplar (*Populus canescens*) are reflected in the ripples of the small fountain set in the lake.

Rosa 'Iceberg' and *Alchemilla mollis* frame the view into the brick-paved rose garden where *Rosa* 'Wedding Day' climbs on the far wall above the stone seat.

logical and perfectly practical design which enhances the tranquillity water can bring to a garden. Here there are none of the strident colours, fussed-up designs or complicated plantings which so often surround swimming pools.

Colour, in the garden of Bolobek, is never used for its own sake but rather with discretion to extend a theme or emphasize an area. In its simple elegant design, reliance on the form and shape of plants, the texture of bark and leaf, the greens and whites, the scent of flowers and reflections in water, Bolobek shows clearly the hand of an artist. No one who has visited the garden would be surprised to learn that Lady Law-Smith is among Australia's finest water colourists specializing in plant portraits. The garden has enormous drama and strength of design but is not a garden in which the visitor rushes from one eye-catching blaze of colour to the next. Here the visitor wanders, without any feeling of pressure, examining the glories of nature and admiring the arrangements of man.

and a bank of *Stachys byzantina* which borders one wall. It is the controlled use of colour, the gentle contrasts of form, the simple design emphasized by simple, well-proportioned ornaments and the emphasis on scent which gives this rose garden its particular enchantment. Fruit trees are espaliered midway down opposite walls and clematis, grown on the outside, spills over the tops of the walls.

The swimming pool is placed close to the rose garden. Two sides are sheltered by great dark green walls of clipped cypress against which the sculptural forms, blue-grey foliage and spikes of creamy-white flowers of *Yucca gloriosa* are well displayed. When the interior of the swimming pool was painted the colour was carefully matched to the cypress hedging; the addition of chlorine to the water altered the precise shade to something closer to the bluey foliage of the yuccas. Today the three dominant shades of green – dark green hedge, blue-green water and blue-grey yuccas – have an elegant harmony and give the pool a peaceful tranquil atmosphere. The pool and its setting follow a simple,

Japanese cranes, made of bronze, stand before the flowers of *Yucca gloriosa* by the swimming pool.

Marnanie

MT MACEDON

Mr Kevin O'Neill

MARNANIE STANDS HIGH on Mt Macedon, a mountain whose ancient volcanic shape can be clearly seen from the surrounding plains. The area, with its cool wet climate, was developed in the last century as a place where city dwellers could escape from the heat of the plains. Marnanie began as a simple hill station in the 1890s, when a single-storey house was built beside a stream which pours its clear mountain water down the steeply sloping site. It belonged for many years to Sir Isaac Isaacs, Chief Justice and later Australia's first Australian Governor-General. It was in the 1930s, when Sir Isaac Isaacs was Governor-General, that a second storey was added and the buildings and surroundings given a more imposing appearance. However, when the present owner acquired the property sixteen years ago the garden had suffered some twenty-five years of neglect.

An immediate attraction at the time it was acquired was the driveway, which curves up the hill following the course of the singing mountain stream. Along its banks ran a dramatic ribbon of tree ferns (*Cyathea australis*). From the driveway, one still looks down onto the tops of the tree ferns and is able to enjoy the flat plains of green lace made by their widely spreading crowns. Old exotic trees added to the garden's appeal. They hung above the stream, were grouped round the house and lent their magnificent presence to a wilderness garden, which is known today as the dell. Sadly, the garden was hit by the Ash Wednesday fires of 1983 and the great trees of the dell were lost, although the house and many of the trees which surround it and line the stream's banks survived. Although the damage was

extensive and many trees have had to receive attention from tree surgeons, it is hoped that the garden has now stabilized and that future tree losses will not exceed the rate to be expected in an old planting. There are many well-grown, well-placed trees in the garden but two particularly magnificent specimens lend their real majesty to the site.

Below the house, close to the stream, stands a huge redwood (*Sequoia sempervirens*) and high on the hill where the upper garden merges with the natural vegetation stands an equally magnificent tree, the tree Australians call the mountain ash (*Eucalyptus regnans*). The mountain ash is the giant of the Victorian forests and the tallest of all

Left The small stream house, surrounded by tree ferns, once contained the electricity generator for the property.

A white-flowered horse chestnut and tree ferns frame the view of the house. Clipped bay trees grown as standards stand either side of the front door.

Australian trees. It is as if both the house and large garden (most of which lies on the spur of a hill) are cradled between these mammoth trees. In the mists which swirl through this mountain garden these great trees, and those of the gum-clad bushland which surround the garden, have an awe-inspiring presence.

A large common horse chestnut (*Aesculus hippocastanum*) spreads its wide leaves over the gravelled area before the front door, contrasting with the symmetrical dark branches of the monkey puzzle (*Araucaria araucana*) which stands close by. At a lower level, beside the stream, there is a little summerhouse or stream house. The building, dwarfed by the tree ferns which have regrown after extensive fire damage, once held the generator which supplied electricity to the property.

In the area below the drive, with the stream overhung by trees and edged with tree ferns, nature seems only half tamed. Plants grow in informal clumps and paths wind through the undergrowth. Great clumps of *Cardiocrinum giganteum* have been established and in mid-summer they raise their streaked creamy-white heavily-scented flowers to a height of 8 feet (2.5 m). White and green hydrangeas are planted near them to add their blooms to the scene and afford some protection from late frosts. Piles of logs, stacked in the Swiss manner and resembling circular huts, add their sculptural shapes to the woodland setting.

On the other side of the driveway the hill slopes upwards towards a crest of natural vegetation. This area, known as the Bluestone Garden, is intersected by bluestone (basalt) paths and steps and densely planted with flowering shrubs and trees. Designed primarily as a picking garden, today the extensive area has acquired a pleasant timeless quality. The bluestone paths and steps are weathered and the plants have grown into their allotted space and frequently overgrown it to flow over the edges of the paths creating an informal effect. The beds are filled with evergreen azaleas and rhododendrons chosen mainly from the small-leaved varieties. Many of the shrubs are planted in massed groups, rather than dotted about as single specimens, making the effect of their

blossom all the more impressive as the various groups come into bloom. The colours are mainly pastel and soft yellows, lavenders, whites and pinks predominate, offset with sheets of blue forget-me-nots, bluebells and bleeding heart (*Dicentra spectabilis*). Large stands of giant Solomon's seal (*Polygonatum commutatum*), apricot foxgloves and honey bush (*Melianthus major*) are used to edge the pathways. In the shelter of larger shrubs, clumps of small woodland plants such as erythroniums have been established. A group of *Rhododendron* 'Suave' is particularly effective scenting the air and adding its delicate waxy pinky-white blooms to the spectacle. Near it blooms a large clump of the daffodil 'Russ Holland', with flowers that open a uniform greenish sulphur-yellow and fade to white with a lime-green frill. The scent of Woodruff (*Galium odoratum*) hangs on the air. Occasionally the pastel theme is broken with a splash of scarlet provided by a group of tulips or a scarlet camellia. In the mist these flashes of colour bring the delicate colouring of the planting into focus.

A network of paths leads to the highest point in the Bluestone garden and from here the view out over the valley far below unfolds through the branches of *Prunus* 'Elvins'. Bred in Victoria in about 1940, this

terrace and it is edged with a strong border of the small-leaved lemon-coloured rhododendrons 'Unique' and 'Saffron Queen'. The drop from the terrace to the lawn below is masked by a curtain of Banksian roses, which bear double soft-cream flowers. The cascade of roses runs the entire length of the house and makes a dramatic backdrop to the curve of lawn which lies between the house and the lower garden. Here an impressive flight of steps leads through sloping beds filled with shrubs and carpeted with aquilegias. The paths which run across the slope are given height with simple wooden arbours over which roses are trained. A small pond curves round a supporting wall to which *Hydrangea anomala petiolaris* clings. A mask fountain plays water into the pond and adds its music to that of the stream below. Three great trees, a tulip tree (*Liriodendron tulipifera*), a New Zealand lacebark (*Hoheria populnea*) and an English oak (*Quercus robur*), link the lower garden to the upper garden which lies above the house along the upper section of the spur of hill.

Close to the house a section of the garden has been informally divided from the upper slopes by a curving row of silver pear trees (*Pyrus salicifolia*). Their willow-like silvery leaves form the background to a grand herbaceous border which lies in their curve.

Above High up over the valley at Mount Macedon, *Prunus* 'Elvins' frames the view in October.

Left The stream garden in April, with hydrangeas, a mixture of tree ferns, maples and cherry trees.

Right Banksias (*B. baxteri* and *B. coccinea*) and kangaroo paws (*Anigozanthos flavidus*) predominate in this arrangement of Australian native flowers.

ornamental plum bears white blossom tinged with rose very prolifically all down its branches. From this high point a path leads across the face of the hill to join a long flight of stone steps, whose descent down the steep slope is checked by a platform on which sits a simple fountain. Close to the steps the Chinese anise (*Illicium anisatum*) hangs its glossy leaves and many petalled flowers. The highest pathway is lined with white 'Iceberg' roses and baby's tears (*Erigeron karvinskianus*) and a row of pink dogwoods links the ornamental garden to the regrowth of the bushland beyond.

The remaining part of the extensive garden lies either side of the house on the spur of hill which is bordered on one side by the stream and on the other by the dell. A wide bricked terrace borders the house on the downhill slope. Azaleas, grown as standards, stand in large containers along the

A fountain set half-way up the steps of the Bluestone Garden is surrounded by native ferns, rhododendrons and azaleas, with *Prunus* 'Elvins' in full flower beyond.

Right The curved border, with a summerhouse designed by Paul Bangay, is set on the hill above the house. Plants with spiky, vertical forms, like verbascum, artemisia and foxgloves, emphasize the border's sculptural shape.

(The shallow curved lines used in this area follow the curve of the hill.) The central focus of the border is a stone summerhouse, the walls of which have been constructed from stone collected on the property, while the roof is clad with the wooden shingles used in the early pioneer days. Containers holding *Sisyrinchium striatum* stand on either side of the summerhouse. The border starts to show colour in early spring with waves of the white daisy-like flowers of *Anthemis cupaniana* and the blue spikes of *Ajuga pyramidalis*. These colours predominate in the border throughout the season and are mixed with creams and the softest of pinks. Silver-grey leaves are used extensively to light the border and pick up the foliage colours of the surrounding silver pear trees. *Cerastium tomentosum* and *Stachys byzantina* add their silvery hues at the edge of the border. Within the mass of flower, the magnificent felted, elephant-ear leaves of mulleins (*Verbascum bombyciferum*) contrast with the soft feathery foliage of the silvery *Artemisia arborescens*, which is clipped into shimmering balls of foliage. *Salvia sclarea turkestanica* displays its soft misty form with the white mallow (*Lavatera trimestris* 'Mont Blanc'). Delphiniums and monkshood (*Aconitum napellus*) add their strong spires of blue to the impressive display and a soft blue cultivar of *Scabiosa caucasica* produces a succession of flowers from its mound of leaves. To one side of the border stands the great oak; the ground beneath its branches flooded with the magical blue of the Himalayan poppy (*Meconopsis betonicifolia*). Behind the silver pears which edge the border lies a deep band of cultivated land which is devoted entirely to an extensive collection of lilies.

Further up the spur of hill, behind the herbaceous border, the garden changes quite dramatically. The border is long and deep and its scale suits the scale of the mountain spur, but the scene which is revealed behind its flowers has a majestic scale in keeping with the grandeur of mountain setting which is revealed behind the silver pear trees. Mown grass stretches upwards bordered by groves of silver birch and maple – trees which are well grown but which look like toys in comparison to the great mountain ashes which tower above mown grass and clothe the hillsides overlooking the garden. High on the hill in a glade of grass stands a huge urn mounted on a rendered brick platform. It is placed on an axis with the stone summerhouse which lies below at the centre of the herbaceous border. To one side of the urn there are two extensive plantings. The lower one contains a large array of deciduous azaleas in shades of cream, gold and flame. Separated from it by a wide band of level mown grass lies an equally extensive planting of well-grown rhododendrons. In the mists which frequently lie round the mountain the jewel colours of these shrubs and the autumn foliage of the deciduous trees glow in the gloom of the towering trees. To the other side of the urn lie a series of ponds, one of which is bordered with the unusual lily-like *Brunsvigia josephinae*.

This is a garden in which the controlled use of colour adds to the drama of the misty mountain scenery. Rich soil and adequate rain produce the remarkable abundance of flower but it is the sensitive handling of the site which gives Marnanie its special atmosphere. No one visiting this garden would be surprised to learn that Kevin O'Neill is recognized as Australia's leading floral designer.

Dreamthorpe

MT MACEDON

Penny & Philip Dunn

*T*HE GARDEN OF Dreamthorpe lies just below Mt Macedon in the heart of an area which was adopted during the early days of settlement as a cool spot where established Melbourne families could spend the summers. When summer at the sea became fashionable, many of the large estates and their gardens fell into disrepair. Today the proximity of Mt Macedon to Melbourne, adequate rainfall and good soil have brought renewed interest in the area and an influx of keen gardeners.

Dreamthorpe began as a daffodil farm in the 1870s and was owned by the major Melbourne florist of the day, Nat Ronalds. Massive oaks and massed daffodils, many of them now nameless cultivars, survive from this early era. Cypress windbreaks were established on the western and northern boundaries as protection from the bitter prevailing winds. In the 1920s Lady Hodges laid out what was, in essence, an Edwardian garden. There were neat circular flower beds and, in sharp contrast, rambling paths wandering through a dense wilderness, a lilac-bordered rose garden and the extensive cultivation which was normal in a large country garden. Lady Hodges was noted for her kindness to all and the neighbourhood children were allowed into the paddocks to pick the daffodils each spring. She had small tree houses built in the larger trees for birds and possums. It is her garden which, one way or another, provides many of the major elements in the garden of today.

When Mr and Mrs Dunn acquired the property in 1976, they embarked on a long programme of discovery, restoration and creation which shows no sign of coming to a halt. Many paths and flowerbeds had

vanished. The trees had reached great heights and their progeny were following their lofty example. Garden bridges had fallen in and rotted away and ponds had silted up. Some of the daffodil-filled paddocks had been sold and the plants uprooted but ten acres of overgrown garden remained. Only one of Lady Hodges' animal tree houses remained and this has been faithfully restored.

Right The leaves of a Japanese maple and the trunk of a liquidambar are the setting for a seat deep in the woodland.

In 1983 the Ash Wednesday bush fires swept across the mountain and the 120 feet (36.5 m) high cypress barrier, which protected the property from the west, was lost. The cypresses to the north survived and today these trees give an idea of the scale of the loss. Strangely, the house, which stands close to the western boundary where these trees once stood, was saved, as was much of the garden. It is thought that the huge flaming trees themselves provided a shield against the flying sparks and broke the fierce gusts of scorching wind. In the lower section of the garden, many of the Japanese maples, already under stress from the preceding months of drought, died immediately. Now, several years later, new casualties are becoming apparent as the deep damage to bark from burns to the trunks and the scorch from the radiant heat finally inflict their mortal wounds and ringbark the trees. A large hornbeam, which produced a full canopy of leaf for the first four years after the fire, has perished. It has been noted that

the greatest losses have been among ivy-clad trees, where the ivy held in the heat.

In removing the massive trees the fire saved the owners from making a difficult decision. The trees were taking much of the light, moisture and nutrients from the side of the garden sheltered by their gaunt frames and little would grow or grow well in their shadow. The main driveway remains a romantic dark passage through informal woodland studded with great trees, the majority of them Japanese maples. The side drive and lower part of the garden are now light and open and provide a pleasant contrast. This side driveway runs beside an open meadow containing the few surviving trees (all of which appear to be thriving in the additional light) and an open pond. The major scars have gone and gums, which were not present on the site before the fire, have appeared. A hawthorn hedge has been planted along the fence line and an avenue of tulip trees has been established. The fire has radically changed the atmosphere of one part of the garden but much remained and has been retained. Glimpses of the quiet roads which surround the property on three sides can now be seen through the trees; it is lighter and less mysterious. However, the essential atmosphere of a secluded country garden remains. It is still an interesting garden with many of the older elements now reaching their maturity.

The house looks on to a geometric formal garden. Straight clipped lavender hedges outline a path which leads down from the front door to a trellis clothed with the rose 'Albertine'. This long open trellis, simply constructed in rough wood, separates the formal garden (which in comparison to the rest of the garden is small) from the wild and informal gardens beyond. The grass on either side of the neat hedges is studded with old trees, largely pin oak, dogwood, cherry and golden ash, and the lavender hedges terminate neatly in mounds of box. Close to the house the raised beds are now filled with oak-leaved hydrangea, viburnums and the creamy-white French rose, 'Mme Georges Bruant'. A large michelia hedge stands nearby. This is the only area which retains any strong formal design (traces of old, probably Edwardian, circular beds have

Left A seat in the orchard is set amongst the yellow flowers of *Moraea huttonii*, a member of the iris family, now naturalized to grow in long grass.

One of the bluebell
walks in the
woodland.

been found but not restored) and most of the garden is informally planned with one naturalistic setting gently merging into the next. It is a garden for wandering around in a fairly aimless way ready to discover and enjoy whatever may unfold, not a garden to inspect, tick list in hand, in a military manner.

A creek runs through the property and much of the garden lies on its banks. Seven different bridges, most of them following a simple wooden cross-banded design, cross the creek. To the present owners' pleasure, after the new bridges had been installed early illustrations came to light and it was noted that the new bridges match almost exactly those in the first wilderness. A path (rediscovered by the present owners) leads down through the maple wood beside the creek. The ground here is densely carpeted with English bluebells, hellebores (*H. orientalis*) and winter heliotrope (*Petasites fragrans*). The three plants thrive under the trees, providing several months of winter and spring flower and superb leaf contrasts. The hellebores present great clumps of serrated dark leathery leaves throughout the year which swim in a sea of the lettuce-green waterlily-round leaves of the ground-hugging heliotrope. This greenery is punctuated in spring with the rich shiny green of the spikes of bluebell leaf. These three plants make up most of the ground cover but from time to time the theme is extended to include violets, wild English primroses, white wood anemones (*A. nemorosa*) and leucojums. As the dense undergrowth and rampant ivy are gradually brought under control and more light reaches the ground, new plants keep appearing. An old columbine cultivar flourishes in these woods, spreading its soft blue-green leaves over the woodland floor and producing its spring-time flowers in different exciting colours and colour combinations each year. Several different snowdrops, singles and doubles, have appeared in recent years and Mrs Dunn says that every year 'new' bulbous inhabitants are discovered. During the year of the drought and fire several unknown 'new' flowering bulbs appeared, never to be seen again. The path crosses and recrosses the creek, sometimes following the bank, at others veering off into the trees as it winds down the hill. At one point it opens out into a charming daffodil walk. Here each side of the serpentine path is thickly bordered with an old daffodil cultivar – the freely borne graceful flowers resemble light lemon-coloured stars. This part of the wilderness was once dark with trees and a row of large oaks still stands to one side of the walk but the fire took the trees on the other side and the path is now open to the light and the air circulation is much improved. The result is a change of atmosphere and bigger, more floriferous daffodils. The creek divides half way down the hill and feeds into a large open pond. It is overhung by large undamaged basket willows and the retaining banks are bordered with crocosmia and sword grass. White watsonias have grown into large clumps in this area.

A dark pathway bordered with high holly hedges which have been clipped into an overhead arch opens out to a large lawn. It is a sharp contrast after the dark main driveway, which is bordered by the heavily wooded wilderness and made more striking by its simple design. The lawn is almost entirely surrounded by high hedges of clipped pittosporum – the variety used is an old one with plain light lemon-gold leaves. Trees, mainly hollies (both the dark green

Rosa 'Wedding Day' softens the newly-built lines of a small raised pond.

The cross-banded bridge designed by Mr and Mrs Dunn is a focal point in the woodland.

Right A pond, set amongst large trees, has its margins planted with crocosmia and sword grass.

and variegated varieties), can be seen above the hedges. The great northern stand of cypresses make a dramatic backdrop. A few nicely shaped old trees stand in the lawn, most notably a golden oak which bears almost luminous lime-green spring foliage and a prunus, whose white spring blossom the owner describes as being 'like a wedding'. A peahen strolls about on the lawn. She just appeared out of nowhere one day and has remained to strut about in a setting that seems made for her.

The serene lawn gives no hint of the treasures beyond. An inconspicuous gap in the hedge is the entrance to an enclosed walk that runs round the back of the lawn, leading to an herbaceous garden, the lilac walk and the old orchard. One side of the path is edged with the lemon-gold pittosporum, the other by a line of *Garrya elliptica*. The herbaceous garden, which takes the form of a grassy glade, is dominated by a wisteria-clad arbour. The wisteria, growing from a massive trunk, almost hides from view the rustic seat within the arbour. The flowerbeds are thickly planted with white buddleias and the rose 'Général Galliéni' in the background, and annuals and perennials. The wealth of summer flowers includes delphiniums, peonies, sisyrinchiums, white verbenas, *Lychnis coronaria*, *Geranium endressii* 'Wargrave Pink', *Gladiolus* 'The Bride', *Convolvulus cneorum*, *Nepeta* × *faassenii*, *Digitalis lanata* and *Digitalis lutea*. *Gaura lindheimeri* and sidalceas bloom throughout the warmer months and plume poppies (*Macleaya*) reach a height of 6 feet (1.8 m). At ground level there are the interesting leaves of francoas and giant ajuga.

Beyond the herbaceous garden lies a lilac walk. Here too the plants are densely planted round a simple lawned space, a circle (which once contained Lady Hodges' geometric rose beds) surrounded by high walls of lilac (*Syringa vulgaris*). Rose arbours screen the paths which lead into and out of the lilac-bordered glade. Like the herbaceous garden, this is wonderfully secluded and you can enjoy the plants in peaceful isolation.

The orchard containing old apple cultivars remains much as it has been for many years. Rampant undergrowth was cleared to expose gnarled low trees and a field of bulbs beneath their boughs. Here belladonna lilies bloom in autumn, clumps of ixias and tritonias appear early in the summer months and in spring old daffodil cultivars flower profusely. All grow as they have for many years without human attention. The orchard reaches its dramatic peak in late spring, when the moraeas add their heads of yellow brilliance to an orchard dancing with apple blossom. A pathway through the flowering carpet is provided by one width of the mower.

The passage of time has left many marks on this garden. Some are tragic, but some of the oldest elements are only revealing their true beauty now after a hundred years in cultivation. For the most part the bulbs were dormant when the fire hit. They at least were preserved and, if anything, improved by the devastation. Many large trees and shrubs were untouched and unmarked. The scars have faded and the garden is blessed by a new generation of enthusiastic and creative gardeners. Dreamthorpe is, once again, a mysterious haven of dreams.

Cruden Farm

LANGWARRIN

Dame Elisabeth Murdoch

*D*AME ELISABETH MURDOCH came, as a young bride, to Cruden Farm sixty years ago and has been gardening there with enthusiasm and skill ever since. In 1929 the landscape designer Edna Walling was engaged to draw up plans and an architect employed to extend and improve the farmhouse. The gentle curve to the long driveway was extended by Walling to form a neat circle before the house. The rugged walls, built from stone collected on the property and enclosing two walled gardens, remain as Walling planned them. It is often remarked that this garden, which is one of the earliest Walling gardens to sur-

vive with the original documentation, dates from what is sometimes referred to as her formal English period. Certainly the driveway forms an exact circle in the formal manner before the front door but the arrangement of the trees on the original design has an informality which has nothing in common with the central placement of one specimen tree more usual in English driveways.

Today one of Australia's most famous avenues lines the gentle curves of the drive. The lemon-scented gums (*Eucalyptus citriodora*), planted by Dame Elisabeth herself, borrow nothing from English antecedents. The native Australian trees are planted closely together in a manner quite unlike any European avenue but using a style well suited to displaying the magical shaft-like trunks of these great trees. The bark of these gums is a pale powdery shade of grey-pink with an almost luminous glow to the silk-smooth dimpled surface. After the annual shedding of bark, the newly exposed surface is creamy white. Today the trees rise to some 150 feet (45 m) and the gummy-lemon scent is always in the air. High above the spectacular trunks the open canopy rustles in the smallest breath of air in a way no exotic tree can imitate. Light plays an important part in the enjoyment of the Australian scene and, where as in other parts of the world flower and leaf are used to add colour to a garden, here in Australia it is the play of light on leaf and bark which provides colour and changes the colour scheme in the course of a single day. Although these trees do carry large clusters of attractive cream flowers, which are later followed by interesting urn-shaped woody fruits, their chief

Left The play of light on leaf dapples the lawn in front of the imposing structure of the house.

Right The drive curves through an avenue of lemon-scented gums (*Eucalyptus citriodora*), their upper branches gilded in the setting sun.

branches have been systematically pruned over the years and now the strong tall trunks are revealed in their full glory supporting a high green canopy. In summer the canopy gives welcome shade without giving a claustrophobic sense of enclosure and the flicker of strong sunlight through the leaves makes an ever-changing pattern on the grass below. There are magnificent elms and two huge and unusual oaks, specimens of *Quercus × firthii* (thought to be a natural hybrid between *Q. phellos* and *Q. rubra*). To one side of the circle, a grove of trees contains both prickly paperbarks (*Melaleuca styphelioides*), which have thick spongy white layers of bark, and silver birches (*Betula pendula*). The barks and forms of these representatives of old and new continents make an interesting visual and tactile comparison, especially as both were scarred by the fires which severely damaged the

Left The lake was created in the last few years for its beauty and to provide a habitat for the waterfowl which, before the draining of nearby wetlands, were numerous in the area.

The lower walled garden, with steps designed by Edna Walling, includes the beautiful small swimming pool.

appeal derives from the play of light on the smooth bark and fine dull grey-green foliage. In the early morning and evening, when the long angled shafts of light gild the countryside, these trees have a bronze glow. At midday, when the harsh light drains the landscape of colour, their impressive forms look like sculptures in white, grey and black set against a sepia-tinted countryside. In moonlight, when the world fades to black, the pale bark has a life of its own and glows in the soft light. In wet weather these trees change again and their trunks gleam with a mauve-pink sheen and the dull green leaves glitter with the water. The long avenue, whose gentle curve seems to echo the lines found in the work of the artist Fred Williams, is bordered on one side by a hawthorn hedge. The other side has no hedge and through the post and rail fence the open paddocks can be seen as one approaches the house.

At the top of the avenue stands the house, its tall tapering verandah columns rising to the full two-storey height of the building and repeating the vertical lines of the lemon-scented gums. Between the avenue and the house lies the formal turning circle and in the central circle and bordering the sides of the drive several exotic deciduous trees rise to considerable heights. The lower

garden in 1944. Common box and *Coprosma repens* from New Zealand, with their brilliant green mirror-glossy leaves, are used to extend the feeling of a cool woodland glade. The contrast between the bright greens near the entrance and the dull greens of native trees in the avenue helps define the areas in an understated way. Today, little remains of Edna Walling's contributions, the garden being a reflection of Dame Elisabeth's considerable skill, energy and enthusiasm, but the avenue serves as a testimony to the vision of both these creative women.

To the left of the house a large rolling lawn embraces a sunken tennis court. The bank behind it is dressed with the contrasting foliage of various native trees. The fine weeping dull green leaves of casuarinas are displayed with the fresh green of grevilleas. Leptospermums grow with banksias, and *Agonis flexuosa* hangs its elegant boughs over the scene. From a position high on the bank it is possible to catch a glimpse of the sculptural avenue, while in another direction there are the fresh green tones of mown grass and exotic trees before the front entrance or, at a different angle, the odd patch of colour from the spring garden. These glimpses through the trees are typical of the garden today, for great care has been taken to ensure that its various parts relate to one another in a natural way.

The spring garden is overlooked by one side of the house and borders a lawn where a weeping elm takes up a central position. The lawn is edged with shrubs, trees and flowers. Azaleas in spring and hydrangeas in summer light up the shrubberies, and the deep pink of a well-placed crab apple (*Malus floribunda*) is picked up by an underplanting of crimson wallflowers. *Malus floribunda* and *M. ioensis* are used in several positions, helping to give an integrated appearance to the large garden. The garden comes into dramatic flower in spring when white broom (*Cytisus multiflorus*) and perennial white candytuft (*Iberis sempervirens*) highlight graceful kolkwitzias and clear blue ceanothus. The spring garden is linked to a grassy walk by a pair of *Prunus serrulata* 'Mount Fuji', which are underplanted with flourishing hosta cultivars. Above the walk, and bordering a corner of the house against

which *Clematis armandii* grows, lies a bed displaying hellebores in winter, peonies in late spring and, in summer, lilies and a foam of plume poppies (*Macleaya cordata*). To one side of the grassy walk lies a flowering border containing tall sculptural plantings of *Echium fastuosum* with drifts of yellow and brown daylilies planted in front of them. Every year large clumps of pastel zinnias, their seed collected annually, are planted out. The other side of the walk is devoted to silver-grey leaves and white flowers. *Plectranthus argentatus* is used extensively with *Senecio cineraria maritima* and *Teucrium fruticans* to provide a shimmer of silver-grey.

The garden gently leads the visitor past the house down a few stone steps where Dame Elisabeth keeps a selection of precious small flowering plants. These include gold-laced polyanthus; *Geranium phaeum*, with deep maroon flowers; *Geranium traversii*, from New Zealand; *Anemone blanda*, from Greece; the deciduous *Viola septentrionalis*, with its white petals rayed in clear china-blue; *Dicentra cucullaria* and snowdrops. Further down the mild slope grassy steps with a bluestone edging lead to the lake, which lies behind the house. The lake is a fairly new addition to the garden but old trees at the water's edge give it the air of something that has always been there. The paddock beyond the lake is dotted with gums (*Eucalyptus cephalocarpa*), whose gnarled trunks and greyish foliage do much to link the ornamental garden to the bush and paddocks beyond. Weeping willows stand on an island and border the banks. To one side of the lake stand two well-grown oaks and from time to time their progeny is added to the paddock round the lake. The indigenous gums too are added to quite frequently.

Separated from the rough grass round the lake by a simple fence clothed with *Lonicera nitida* lies the picking garden. It too is a comparatively new addition but looks well established. A simple wooden pergola stands in the centre, with the rose 'Titian' growing over it, and long gravel paths divide the simple geometric pattern of rectangular beds. These contain the citrus trees, herbs and vegetables required by the household but the overwhelming impression given is of

Acer negundo and copper beech are seen above a lawn encrusted with daisies.

The walled garden has a double border which includes a spectacular show of the yellow *Anthemis tinctoria* 'Mrs E. C. Buxton', the tall spikes of blue delphiniums, white and pink phlox, shasta daisies and dahlias.

abundant bloom. Here all the material needed for an enthusiastic flower-arranger is to be found. In spring there are polyanthus and primroses, and a soft yellow alstroemeria can be relied on to produce a few flowers whatever the season. Great clumps of aquilegias, foxgloves and tobacco plants join the rows of sweet peas in late spring. Lavender borders some of the beds and, in summer, there are pinks, lilies, dahlias and, above all, roses. One side of the extensive area is bordered with 'Iceberg' and separate beds are reserved for the various hues of rose petal; pink, red, soft pink and apricot. The British wild flower *Silene maritima* is allowed to grow here for its arching stems and balloon-like calyx. Steps, centred on a grey furrowed trunk of a *Eucalyptus cinerea cephalocarpa* specimen, which has grown out at a low angle to the ground, lead back to the upper level of the garden. From here one can walk back to the front of the house or diverge slightly through mown grass dotted

with large trees and visit the walled gardens.

The two linked walled gardens which Edna Walling planned for fruit trees and for a rose garden complete the circular walk and return the visitor to the greenery of the exotic trees which flank the entrance. Closely clipped ivy surrounds the iron gate which leads into the first garden. Over the gate stands a dancing brolga. The sculpture by Leslie Bowles was commissioned by Sir Keith Murdoch. Apples once lined the simple straight grass path leading to a small pond but they have long gone. The area proved too hot and, as Dame Elisabeth remarks, the fruit was stewed where it stood. Today the area is devoted to a dramatic and highly successful herbaceous planting. Dame Elisabeth says, 'It has taken me many years to achieve the effect I am after in my summer borders, which is an arrangement of colour, texture and form to delight the eye and nourish the spirit.' Through a long process of trial and error she has collected a range of plants which can tolerate the heat and will give months of bloom. A summer garden in Australia must remain in flower for a much longer period than the flowering borders of northern Europe and North America. At Cruden Farm the borders are thick with flower from November (early summer) through until mid-April. Each plant is carefully maintained and the dead heads are removed or the flowering stems cut down throughout the season. Dame Elisabeth knows exactly how to treat each of her plants to encourage fresh flower and keep the border at its peak for several months. As she says, 'The staying power of every plant is important. Even one failure can spoil the whole picture.' *Thalictrum speciosissimum* makes a splendid background curtain of fern-like foliage against the walls and holds its lime-green flowers for an extended period. *Thalictrum dipterocarpum*, known locally as lavender showers, flowers magnificently and displays its delicate foliage all through the summer. Perennial phlox (*Phlox paniculata*) in shades of soft pink, mauve and white will last through the summer with regular deadheading. Dahlias, too, which as Dame Elisabeth admits are not strictly speaking herbaceous, have the ability to last well through the summer and are used extensively. The small-flowered waterlily type, particularly 'Limeglow' and 'Gerrie Hoek', are favourites. *Delphinium* 'Blue Sensation' Dame Elisabeth finds most useful and more graceful than the commoner 'Pacific Giants'. *Anthemis tinctoria* 'E. C. Buxton' is regarded as invaluable for lighting the border with its lively lemon-yellow flowers and irrepressible habit. The borders at Cruden Farm do not faithfully follow the traditional British clumping of plants in groups of three, five and seven. This method is used but there are also brilliant bars of colour which run through the display. The soft speckled effect of a British border, which might well fade in the Australian light, is eschewed in favour of a more vigorous arrangement in which flower colour has the capacity to stand out in a strong light. Seen through the iron gate from the shadowy greenery of the trees near the main entrance to the house the glimpse of vivid colour is all that is needed to lure the visitor to look more closely. The walled rose garden envisaged by Edna Walling now contains a swimming pool; its quiet, green and well-trimmed formality contrasts sharply with the floral exuberance in the neighbouring walled enclosure.

The garden at Cruden Farm is the result of Dame Elisabeth's energy, vision and powers of observation. Few people have the opportunity to garden in one place all their adult lives and still fewer acquire the knowledge needed to establish an inspiring flower garden. The idea behind some of the more spectacular elements in the garden may be British but the skill to turn the vision into reality in Australia comes from knowledge which can only be acquired from practical experience. This is very much more than a British garden put together with great skill in a vastly different climate. It is a personal garden. Moreover it is a garden made by an Australian which, far from blocking out the natural scenery, seeks to enhance it and to establish a happy relationship between the exotic ornamental garden and the indigenous trees and shrubs which stand in the paddocks nearby. Of great significance was the choice of a native tree, in an era when the use of native plants in domestic gardens was unfashionable, to create what has become an avenue renowned for its beauty.

The white and silver border in the spring garden.

Garden of St Erth

BLACKWOOD

The Garnett Family

GOLD LED WHITE immigrants into the hills to the west of Melbourne in the last century and Simmons Reef was one of several strikes to attract a transient population. In the 1850s Matthew Rogers, a Cornish stone-mason who became a successful Australian gold-miner, built a simple stone house, which he named St Erth after his birthplace. The house, in time, was extended with a variety of wooden structures to service the needs of the Simmons Reef population and, at one stage, Matthew Rogers' property included a general store, a post office and a boot factory. Little remains of the early hillside settlement but the sloping garden which lies around his small stone house takes much of its form from the old roads and tracks of the isolated settlement.

Mr and Mrs T. R. Garnett bought St Erth in 1967, by which stage the bush, with the addition of imported brambles and self-sown pines, had reclaimed much of its former territory. The ground has since been cleared again but the forest which surrounds the garden (and now forms part of the Wombat State Forest) remains distinctively Australian and harbours a wide variety of native birds and animals, many of which frequent the garden. One section of the garden, in the area furthest from the stone house and at the highest point, is largely devoted to native plants. Here low-level gates have been installed in the fencing to allow wombats to pass freely between the forest and the garden. In the lower, cultivated area visitors are often given a quizzical inspection by the resident laughing kookaburras, which take a keen interest in all activities and appear to have acquired, like other birds in this garden, little fear of the human race. Blue wrens fix their beady attention on any freshly turned soil and are quite likely to use the gardener's foot or shoulder as a perch. There are no cats at St Erth.

Three closely grouped trees, an Irish strawberry tree (*Arbutus unedo*), a Portugal laurel (*Prunus lusitanica*) and an Italian cypress (*Cupressus sempervirens*), which were probably planted during the days of the gold rush, stand near the stone house. Today simple chairs have been placed in the shadowy grove made under the trees and, throughout the garden, other trees have now grown to match the stature of these original inhabitants. The garden today covers 10 acres (4 hectares) and has a well-established mature feeling. Unobtrusive new buildings, designed to merge with the surrounding bushland, have joined the old stone house, which, however, remains central to the garden's design. The garden itself

Left Three trees, dating from the first plantings of exotic flora, shade a sitting-out area.

Right Pinks and *Coreopsis* 'Sunray' take up the foreground in this November afternoon view of the house.

In the English garden a seat encircles a black mulberry tree (*Morus nigra*), beneath which flourishes lily-of-the-valley (*Convallaria majalis*).

owes much of its present form to Mr and Mrs T. R. Garnett and their son Stephen, all of whom are keen, energetic and well-informed gardeners. Today the garden of St Erth is a family concern and the modern houses are occupied by other members of the family. Mr T. R. Garnett is, in his active retirement, probably the best-known of the serious garden writers in contemporary Australia.

The property is approached by way of a dirt road which winds through the bush giving access only to St Erth and the State Reserve. A simple hedge, composed of flowering japonica (*Chaenomeles speciosa*), separates the house from the road and provides a solid wall of winter flower. There are no rolling lawns, elaborate statuary, artfully placed urns or grand seating arrangements at St Erth; it is essentially a country garden without affectations or mannerisms. Areas close to the house where foot traffic is heavy are paved in the local stone or gravel but mown grass is the favoured medium for the paths in this garden. Wide green ribbons, often broad enough for several people to walk together, lead through the cultivated areas, giving the garden a spacious atmosphere and providing a unifying element in a garden which displays a wide diversity of flower and foliage. In the wilder native garden the pathways resemble bush tracks and are layered with soft brown leaves. Throughout the whole garden it is the juxtaposition of paths, beds and trees

which define the long vistas and encourage the visitor to move from one area to the next.

Climbing plants and shrubs use the posts of the simple verandah on the old stone house as supports. *Abutilon megapotamicum* produces its small red and yellow lanterns throughout the year against the glow of the local golden stone. Summer adds the warm-pink flowers of the rose 'Baronne Prévost', the pink, trumpet-like flowers of *Podranea ricasoliana* and the yellow of *Clematis tangutica*. At ground level an edging of the bright rose-pink *Dianthus* 'Red Wings' adds its drama to the summery spectacle. A grass path lies between the dianthus edging to the verandah and a second flowering strip, which lies parallel to the house and adds its colourful display to the charming presentation of the old stone dwelling. Here, cotoneasters, both *C. dammeri* and *C. horizontalis* 'Variegata', provide their scarlet autumn-borne berries, dark leaves and strong shapes. During the summer months the bed is lit with mounds of flower provided by sun roses (*Helianthemum*); the garden is home to the Victorian State Collection of Cistaceae. When the borders and climbers are in full bloom the romantic little house is wreathed in flower (their shades well designed to enhance the colour in the glowing stone) and in winter the carefully chosen and well-trimmed plants provide a charming frame to the house and a link between it and its garden setting.

The stone house faces a broad grass path (once the main street of Simmons Reef), which leads from the road past the house and up the hill to the wild garden. Immediately opposite the house, on the far side of this wide grass path, lies what is known as the English garden. A black mulberry (*Morus nigra*), its trunk encircled with a simple wooden seat and the ground beneath its branches planted with a flourishing cover of lily-of-the-valley (*Convallaria majalis*), marks its boundary. On a rising slope beyond lie parallel herbaceous borders either side of a wide grassy path. One has an edging of the yellow *Achillea clypeolata* and, as the bed rises with the slope, the colourful heads of *Geum bulgaricum* and G. 'Tangerine', *Rudbeckia fulgida* var. *speciosa* and *R. californica*, *Phlomis italica*, bog sage (*Salvia uliginosa*), monkshood (*Aconitum napellus*), leopard's bane (*Doronicum* varieties), potentillas and *Sidalcea malvaeflora* become apparent. Throughout the length of the bed great clumps of Russell lupins are repeated, giving height, colour, leaf decoration, and the uniformity necessary to produce a natural harmony in such a wealth of colour and form. The other bed is delineated with a thick band of pinks and contains roses and irises. The wide pathway terminates at the foot of a deodar (*Cedrus deodara*), which lends its weeping greenery to all seasons of the year. To the far side of the borders daffodils have naturalized in the rough grass and the sloping area is set off with a curve of greenery. Throughout the ornamental garden care is taken with the relationship between the colourful exotic plants and the more muted shades of the surrounding bush. Blackwoods (*Acacia melanoxylon*) have been used extensively as trees which look at ease in both situations and their dark green leaves and unobtrusive but decorative cream-lemon balls of small flower make a strong backdrop to the ornamental garden and, at the same time, are in perfect harmony with the eucalypts of the bush. Looking down the hill into the ornamental garden from the native garden and bush, the blackwoods have the sculptural qualities needed to enhance the glimpses of bright colour which lie below.

On the other side of the main pathway, linked by wide shallow steps planted with pennyroyal (*Mentha pulegium*) and numerous different thymes, lies the orchard. The beds which lie between the path and the orchard contain a variety of well-grown interesting plants. The Chatham Island forget-me-not (*Myosotidium hortensia*), growing from a thick mulch of seaweed, thrives in this area. Here an unusual hellebore from Yugoslavia, *Helleborus dumetorum atropurpureus*, displays its large open flowers of deep maroon and *Angelica capipara* raises its fresh green ornamental leaves and whorls of whitish flower. Within the sloping orchard itself the gnarled lichen-encrusted fruiting trees, some more than sixty years old, are planted in neat lines. The trees give support to several clematis, including 'W. E. Gladstone', *C. venosa violacea* and 'Mme Julia Correvon'. The rows are given emphasis

with borders of box or lavender. In spring named daffodil cultivars, planted in groups, make dramatic bands of colour in these long narrow beds.

Above the orchard are a series of rockery beds, many devoted to plants from the same families or requiring similar conditions. One sunny bed, bordered with the purple-leaved ajuga, a deep purple-blue aubrieta and white arabis, contains a selection of true geraniums, including *G. versicolor*, *G. thunbergii*, *G. stapfianum roseum*, *G. albanum*, and *G. sanguineum* 'Album'. Another, topped with white pebbles to enhance the baking these bulbs require during the summer months, contains a number of unusual small-flowering bulbs, many of which are of South African origin. They include *Romulea bulbocodium leightiniana*, *Spiloxene capensis*, *Narcissus bulbocodium* 'Nylon', *Crocus angustifolius*, *C. etruscus*, *C. niveus* and *C. sativus*,

The wild garden has water lilies (*Nymphaea alba*) already flourishing well in the recently created dam.

stony course, and a stout simple wooden trellis. The wall is bordered with a dark form of *Iris unguicularis*, which enhances the blues of the rosemary 'Blue Lagoon' and aubrieta, which tumble from the wall above. The trellis carries *Pandorea jasminoides*, *Lathyrus sylvestris*, *Jasminum confusum* and the clematis 'Vyvyan Pennell'. The area within these confines (the small enclosed area in itself makes an interesting contrast to the more open spaces in this section of the garden) is thickly planted with a large number of edible or medicinal herbs. The thymes include an unusual orange-scented thyme, and the marjorams include a white form of *Origanum viride*.

Above these ornamental gardens at the top of the hill lies the site of the old Wesleyan church and the wild garden planted with a mixture of native and exotic plants. Beyond that the State forest rolls away through the hills. Here a dam-and-creek system has been developed quite recently to enable the cultivation of bog and water plants. The dam harbours water lilies and fish and a sunny sand bed contains tender native plants. One curved bank displays the silvery leaves of *Tanacetum haradjanii*, *Artemisia canescens*, *Anaphalis margaritacea*, and both *Glaucium flavum* and *G. corniculatum*. Another bed which curves round the water contains an extensive collection of callunas and ericas.

Pink *Camellia sasanqua*, grown from cuttings, are on the far side of the orchard, seen over long beds of white and yellow narcissus, edged with French lavender (*Lavandula dentata*).

Right In late September the house is just visible through the Australian native wattle (*Acacia prominens*), from the top of the garden.

Gladiolus alatus, *Nerine filifolia* and *Allium amabile*, *A. cernuum*, *A. murrayanum* and *A. neapolitanum*. Here too grows *Habranthus martinezii*, a species found in Argentina and Uruguay which was first described only seventeen years ago. The orchard and extensive plant collections contained in the rockery beds are separated from the vegetable garden and neatly enclosed herb garden by a hedge of red and white currant bushes underplanted with *Rhodohypoxis baurii* and crocus.

The vegetable garden occupies pride of place in the garden because 'well-grown vegetables are decorative'. Lupins and peas are grown here and used as green manure and the connecting paths are edged with globe artichokes. The herb garden is contained by low walls, designed so that plants can be established along the top of their

Below the peppermint trees, English prim-roses and bluebells thrive.

Far below the wild garden on the other side of the house and gate are two self-contained gardens. At the upper level, sep-arated from the road by a bank of massed cistus, which include *Cistus albidus* grown from seed collected in the Pyrenees and a specimen of *C. salvifolius* which has a purple tinge to its leaves, lies an important daffodil collection. Behind the bank of cistus a path marked with an irregular planting of sorbus and malus trees curves through the daffodil beds. Many of the daffodils growing in the light shade are of historic interest to Aus-tralians. Here one can find 'M.P. Williams', a daffodil bred by Alister Clark and named after the celebrated British daffodil breeder and judge who took a keen interest in Australian daffodils. (Mr Williams is recorded as having

noted that there were more pink daffodils in Alister's garden than in the whole of Britain. The first one, 'Pink Un', bred by Leonard Buckland, was exhibited in 1910.) The beds here contain many old cultivars and include some impressive clear pinks. Beyond the carefully nurtured and important collection, daffodils are naturalized in rough grass through which lies a wide strip of mown grass bordered by an avenue of urn-fruited gums (*Eucalyptus urnigera*). Blooming at the same time as the daffodils are thick stands of golden forsythia and kniphofia. Later in the year the extensive iris collection flowers at the same time as an impressive selection of foxtail lilies (*Eremurus*). Below the daffodil garden lies the garden of the butcher's shop. No trace of the shop remains above ground but gums and wattles thrive in the gritty rubble left on the site. A trial-and-error

Steps made from railway sleepers and grassed in-between sweep up from pinks and campanulas to the stately spikes of white watsonias on the right.

Above The long blossoms of the Portugal laurel (*Prunus lusitanica*) shade the beautiful thyme-covered steps.

The contrasting forms of red hot pokers and golden robinia fill the foreground.

method has been used to coppice gums with the aim of obtaining an interesting display of both mature and juvenile foliage. *Eucalyptus pulverulenta* shows its distinctive round blue-grey foliage, used all over the world in floral arrangements, against the magnificent early spring display of the Snowy River wattle (*Acacia boormannii*). Clumps of vivid grass-like foliage of the Tasmanian *Restio tetraphyllus* contrast with the blue foliage of *Eucalyptus cordata*. The Rottnest Island pine (*Callitris preissii*) adds strength, with its dense foliage and columnar shape, to the variety of foliage, form and flower this garden contains.

The garden of St Erth, taken as a whole, contains an astounding range of plants displayed in an attractive, unpretentious and logical manner. Simple seating, sometimes constructed from large tree trunks, is placed where the visitor might choose to pause and admire a particular prospect – not, as is so often the case in over-contrived gardens, as focal points in the garden's design. Here, with the exception of the low stone house, the plants provide the focal points and mown grass is used to lead the eye through from one part to another. The result is a peaceful garden but one full of excitement for those interested in plants and their culture.

Mawallok

Nr BEAUFORT

Mr & Mrs Peter Mitchell

*T*HE NAME MAWALLOK is said to derive from the sounds frogs make in spring, a sound which is fairly unusual in a dry climate. However Mawallok is blessed with natural water, which bubbles up from an unknown underground source in several places on the property and has been used to great effect in this garden. Victoria's Western District, in which Mawallok lies, is noted for its wool-growing capacity, wide wind-swept plains and low dry-stone walls constructed from the litter left by extinct volcanoes. The property was acquired in 1847 by Alexander Russell and remained in the Russell family until 1980, when it was bought by Mr and Mrs Peter Mitchell.

In 1909 the influential director of Melbourne Botanic Gardens, William Guilfoyle, was commissioned to design the garden and his plan is still in existence. He created an enclosed garden based on the English landscape tradition with Edwardian overtones. In the 1920s a large lake and island were constructed by General Sir John Monash (who commanded the Australian Army in the First World War). It was at this point that the previously secluded garden was opened up and the view over the lake to Mount Cole in the distance framed by the garden. In the 1930s the palms, typical of a Guilfoyle design, were removed from the lawn in front of the lake and various modifications made in the interests of easy maintenance. In spite of these changes, however, the garden remains true, in the main, to the Guilfoyle design.

The approach to the garden is through a tree-lined low-walled driveway and the entry arch is separated from a side lawn by a rockery and pond. Several tall *Eucalyptus viminalis* stand to one side of the garden and provide sustenance and an occasional home to the local koala population. Specimen trees grown on the side lawn include a well-grown, dawn redwood (*Metasequoia glyptostroboides*). This deciduous conifer, which was only discovered in China in 1945 and is rare in the wild, resembles somewhat a *Taxodium*. In autumn the leaves turn to an unusual shade of apricot. Many of the trees here and elsewhere in the garden carry wide metal collars around their trunks. The collar is slippery and prevents the destructive possums from climbing and destroying the trees.

Beside the pond, where water lilies bloom, stands the tall, elegant figure of a lead crane. The statue of a boy with an eel is used as a fountain. Behind the pond the massive Guil-

Dianthus 'Mrs Sinkins' and *Erigeron karvinskianus* provide soft tones against the angular shapes of the steps and the house.

foyle rockery is planted with evergreen shrubs and the surrounding beds are filled with flowering bulbs and plants. A lemon-yellow potentilla blooms with *Euphorbia characias wulfenii.* A sweep of reddish-pink valerian (*Centranthus ruber*) borders the pond in the company of irises and the cream-flowering *Tritonia lineata.* Some space is retained for annuals and a typical spring planting might contain white pansies and *Nemesia* 'Blue Gem'.

Behind the rockery is the imposing front door and parking area. Here the ground is covered with raked gravel and the area contained by wall-like clipped hedges. *Cupressus macrocarpa* has been used to create these impressive evergreen walls which are now about 12 feet (4 m) wide and 15 feet (5 m) high. From the front door the garden is hidden from view as the main vista lies on the opposite, north side, of the house.

A torrent of narrow steps leads from the wide rectangular grassed terrace which edges the north side of the house to a lawn which rolls through trees and shrubs towards the lake. A ha-ha, built in the 1930s, separates the close-mown grass from the rougher grass of the small golf course which borders the lake. Here black swans, musk duck, swamp hens and coots make their homes. In periods of drought the view from the emerald-green of the watered cultivated garden to the parched hills and paddocks of the Australian landscape provides as dramatic a contrast as any Australian garden can provide. It is a scene made all the more remarkable by the hundreds of water birds which appear on the lake as their wetlands dry out. The dark outlines of *Pinus radiata* and *Cupressus macrocarpa* 'Lambertiana',

Above left Red *Centranthus ruber,* phormium and tall white irises border a pond to one side of the house.

Yellow marguerite daisies and geums frame a glimpse of the lake from the west walk.

Below With cordylines in the vases at the top, *Erigeron karvinskianus* flows like a waterfall down the steps, past catmint (*Nepeta × faassenii*), to the full border below planted with *Euphorbia characias wulfenii*, *Artemisia arborescens*, the white *Dianthus* 'Mrs Sinkins', blue flag irises and pink campions. Beyond is the pergola, overflowing with climbing roses.

two trees which are widely used in the Western District as wind breaks, add to the drama of the view. The silvery leaves of well-grown *Populus alba* add to the varied foliage shapes and colours to be seen near the lake and the continual light movement of their soft leaves contrasts strongly with the more static appearance of the dark evergreens. The swamp paperbark (*Melaleuca ericifolia*) displays its bushy shape close to the water's edge and red gums (*Angophora costata*) stand in the paddocks nearby. Today two native plants, whose names were found on an old plan, *Eucalyptus alpina* and *Acacia elata*, which bears brilliant yellow flowers in winter and spring, are being added to the existing plantings. In spring the island is misted with a haze of pink bloom from *Tamarix parvifora*.

The view to the lake is framed by two great

The east walk, edged with *Helleborus orientalis* and iris, curves around the lawn towards a large planting of arum lilies.

banks of trees, many of them dating from the 1909 planting and today the full benefit of the care Guilfoyle took to contrast form, leaf shape and colour can be enjoyed. The purple-leaved cherry plum (*Prunus cerasifera* 'Nigra') provides its dark foliage. Three magnificent weeping lilly-pillies (*Waterhousea ventenatii*) rise to a height of 80 ft (24.5 m) and display torrents of narrow shiny leaves. A huge oak, which at some point in the past has been pollarded so that its branches hang down to ground level, dominates one side of the planting. Standing as a single specimen on the lawn is a beautifully shaped common horse chestnut (*Aesculus hippocastanum*).

In recent years much has been done to restore the garden to what was envisaged by Guilfoyle and the shrubs growing under the trees too are chosen for their ability to provide contrasting leaf and form. *Pittosporum crassifolium* 'Variegatum', a variety rarely seen in gardens today, and *Coprosma repens* 'Variegata' are used to light up the dark foliage of other plants. The gay patches of colour advocated by Guilfoyle have returned to edge important curves in the lawn. Today annuals are used informally, enabling the artist to change the colour scheme from time to time. Groups of flowering shrubs add their display and the addition of colour provided by the annuals and shrubs close to the ground channels the eye between the lofty walls of greenery towards the lake.

Two woodland walks run through the trees along either side of the long vista which lies between the house and the lake. Each are entered by way of the path which lies across the north face of the house just below the grassy terrace.

The west walk is approached through a wooden pergola over which ornamental grape vines are trained. The path, like its companion on the east side, has been restored in the last few years to the gently curving form of the original design. In the west walk plants which are at their best in spring are given emphasis. Great clumps of Solomon's seal (*Polygonatum × hybridum*), *Bergenia cordifolia*, *Arum italicum* and clivias are used under the trees. At one point the grass from the main lawn sweeps right in to border the path, creating a woodland glade. A grove of silver birch, a pin oak (*Quercus*

palustris) and a *Liquidambar styraciflua* stand in the glade and on the woodland side of the path purple honesty (*Lunaria annua*) flowers just as the purple prunus breaks into leaf. As the path winds down through the trees, to link with the main lawn close to the ha-ha at the bottom of the garden, a path leads off to expose a glimpse of the lake between a row of massive old pine trees. Here, quite recently, a lime walk has been established using *Tilia cordata*. The pleached trees have been neatly trained along wires close to the pathway so that the surrounding plants are seen through their branches. Below them the path is bordered with solid borders of *Iris unguicularis* and rain lilies (*Zephyranthes candida*). Turf lilies (*Liriope muscari*) are used extensively under the flowering shrubs, which include white lilac, the rose 'Sarah Van Fleet' and the highly effective *Prunus glandulosa*.

In the east walk plants which are most effective in autumn are given space. The walk is visually separated from the main lawn and has its own secluded, almost secret, atmosphere. Like the west walk, it links the path which runs across the garden just below the terrace to the bottom of the main lawn close to the ha-ha. The path winds through the shrubs and trees and at one point an old seat has been surrounded by lilac and a hebe with cerise flowers. Clipped bay trees stand at either end of the seat. Large patches of crocosmias and *Fuchsia procumbens* are used as ground cover. As the path approaches the lake it enters a simple but elegant self-contained garden. Here a section of lawn is bordered on two sides with huge cypress hedges and at the centre of the enclosed lawn stands a large blue cedar (*Cedrus atlantica glauca*). Two well-grown Chinese elms stand to one side and water can be seen through the flowers which grow around the gate leading into the paddock.

Between the wide path which runs across the north face linking the two walks and the grassed terrace in front of the house lies an extensive flight of narrow steps, broken in the middle by a rectangular landing of mown grass. Each step is edged with a neat frill of well-controlled *Erigeron karvinskianus*. It is as if the steps themselves form an integral part of the deep herbaceous borders which lie on either side and border three sides of the rectangular terrace above. The strong rectangular forms of the house and its immediate environs are emphasized in the plantings close to the house and are in gentle contrast to the naturalistic atmosphere of the wider garden surrounding the house and terrace. The terrace itself is edged with plantings of the rose 'Sea Foam' and *Nepeta × faassenii*, which add their soft flowery forms to the border lying beneath the terrace. *Convolvulus sabatius* tumbles over the stone wall and lends its blue flowers to the border throughout the summer months. The beds are edged with a solid wide band of the white *Dianthus* 'Mrs Sinkins', emphasizing the strongly rectangular elements in the design. All along the border at regular intervals stand great buns of *Artemisia arborescens*, which are about 6 feet (1.8 m) wide and 5 feet (1.5 m) high. Regular clipping gives these buns of silver foliage a wonderfully feathery effect and when the border dies down in winter the foliage of the artemisia and the dianthus remain to give the border the strong form needed to balance the imposing house. In summer the border is filled with flowers, mainly chosen from a pink, white and blue palette. *Convolvulus cneorum, Digitalis hey-*

woodii, and the white form of *Lychnis coronaria* lend their silvery foliage to the border and bloom for several months. Pink silenes and verbenas provide large patches of colour all through the summer months. Lupins and monkshood (*Aconitum napellus*) add height to the planting. A blue-flowering clematis winds up the stonework above the border and a fuchsia with rose-pink leaves is planted among the stones to decorate both the terrace above and the border beneath.

The garden of Mawallok today has been restored to the glory planned for it in 1909. It is a garden lucky to have the talents of Jocelyn Mitchell. As Chairman of the Australian Gardening History Society she has a particular interest and knowledge of the problems which face the owners of large historic country gardens. Happily Mawallok is in the hands of people who combine artistic talent with energy and approach the past, present and future of the garden with sensitivity and knowledge.

In springtime, bleached willow branches by the lake frame the view across the lake to Mawallok.

Left The main vista, looking from the front terrace over the lawns and lake to the distant hills.

123

A Country Garden
TARADALE

Mr & Mrs Graham Geddes

*I*N THE ROLLING hills to the west of Melbourne, lies a property bordered by the Coliban River which was first developed in the middle of the last century. In the early years availability of water must have been a major attraction of the site. However, the soil is an uncompromising clay, which bakes into an impenetrable block in the heat of summer and lacks any of the qualities needed for good drainage during the wet winters. In spite of these difficulties, exacerbated by hot gale-force summer winds and bitterly cold winter winds, the growth rate in this climate is rapid. With the right treatment a garden can be created in a few years – and lost in a single season of neglect.

The farmhouse and buildings date from 1860 but, when Mr and Mrs Geddes moved in, the buildings, after years of neglect, were

Along one of several colourful paths *Geum* 'Mrs Bradshaw' leads the eye on to rugosa roses, yellow anthemis and tall lupins.

close to the end of their useful life. Little remained of previous gardens and the yards and home paddocks were littered with old farm machinery and derelict cars. A few old pines, some with massive girths, shade what was once the working area of the farm and a grove of elms, probably springing from the suckers of an earlier tree, stand to one side of the house. The trees form the bones and background to the modern garden and when some of the home paddocks were included in the ornamental garden a few magnificent ghost-like gums were incorpo-

before the house alpine strawberries grow from a base of fine gravel. In summer the courtyard looks as artless as the effects of nature itself; in winter the plants are thinned and the fine gravel raked with neat precision and the craft of the gardener becomes obvious.

What is now known as the Old Garden lies on the side of the house farthest from the working area of the farm and looks out over the trees which mark the river bed to the rolling hills with their rocky outcrops and groups of eucalypts. The house, with its simple traditional verandah, is hung with the rose 'Albertine' and summer-flowering jasmines. Before it lies lawn encompassed by a densely planted half-moon border of shrubs and flowers. Directly opposite the main doorway a path leads through the informal planting to a gate from which a narrow paved path leads out, at a tangent, over the paddocks and down to the river. Like many of the paths in this garden, it is paved and kept clear of the low vegetation which in this climate quickly covers any vacant space; this is to avoid the risk of stepping on the venomous tiger snakes that are found in the area. An old hawthorn tree, typical of many established near early homesteads, stands on the lawn. The wide bed contains a backbone of shrubs: shrub roses grow through strong but simple iron supports; winter flower and scent are provided by the shrub honeysuckle (*Lonicera fragrantissima*); and a pair of forsythia bushes standing to either side of the central pathway display their bare flower-encrusted branches in early spring and their decorative yellow foliage in autumn. A loquat tree (*Eriobotrya japonica*) adds stature and leathery white felt-backed leaves to the winter scene.

In spring the beds display yellow daffodils and the pathway is bordered with thick clumps of deep blue grape hyacinth. The odd lucerne plant (*Alfalfa*), growing from seed blown in from the paddocks, is permitted to add its clear blue lupin flowers to the beds. In this garden plants are given space if their colour and form pleases the owners, not because of some classification which decrees which plant should be treated as a weed, crop or ornamental variety. In summer,

Left The summerhouse, frosted with *Solanum jasminoides* 'Album', is set at the end of a border containing poppies, delphiniums and shasta daisies.

rated within the garden. Today the eucalypt-bordered dirt road leads into a neat tidy grassed area where the old buildings have been restored and painted a uniform quiet green and the bare earth beneath the pines is now covered with a glossy green carpet of blue-flowering periwinkle (*Vinca major*). To one side stands the old farmhouse where, in sharp contrast to the towering pines, two silver birches pruned to a waist-high umbrella shape, spread their branches on either side of the steps which lead down to the front door. In the informal courtyard

White roses flourish in heavy shade beneath a sheltering wooden arch.

when the roses bloom the ground beneath their branches is hidden in the mass of flower and foliage. Spires of delphinium, hollyhock and *Allium giganteum* rise from a flowery bed of *Vinca minor*, Californian poppies and rock roses. The scent of Persian lilac (*Syringa × persica*) mingles with the fragrance of roses. Behind the broad flowery plantation stand apple trees elegantly encased in individual iron mushroom-shaped cages. The iron framework holds a wide unobtrusive umbrella of wire-netting over the branches, affording protection from the marauding flocks of sulphur-crested cockatoos which frequent the area. Behind the Old Garden the fence line has been planted with a hedge of tree lucerne (*Chamaecytisus proliferus*), a plant introduced from the Canary Islands in the early days of settlement for use as cattle fodder, and now widely naturalized throughout Victoria. It bears elegant long sprays of white pea-shaped scented flowers, which are enjoyed by the bees in winter and early spring.

To one side of the house stands the grove of old elms and from their shade one can view the area known today as the New Garden. An extensive flower garden has been created where the home paddocks were once situated, and a long high wall separates this part of the garden from the well-treed paddocks. The gentle slope on the land is such that the view out over the countryside is visible from the upper garden but the garden itself gains protection from the winds which sweep through the hills. During the summer months when the growth is at its maximum the high wall is hidden and the extensive view to the summer-bleached hills is given an edge of bright, exotic flowers. The New Garden consists of a series of simple rectangular flowerbeds dissected by straight gravel paths. Height is given by an old iron summerhouse, rose-clad arbours which reach over the paths and by some existing gums, which are now situated within the garden. The beds themselves present an abundance of flower. Annuals such as cosmos, cleome, corncockle, Queen Anne's lace (*Daucus carota*), evening primrose, mallow, nasturtium, Shirley poppy, love-in-a-mist and larkspur are allowed to seed themselves

throughout the garden. *Helleborus lividus corsicus* has naturalized beneath an elm, and, under the gums, where it is often hard to establish any ground cover, mesembryanthemums and *Sedum spectabile* carpet the ground. The geum 'Mrs Bradshaw' forms great clumps and hangs over the pathways, its bright colour picked up by the vivid shades of self-sown Californian poppies. In this climate, even in mid-winter, the geum can be relied on to display a few flowers. Wallflowers bloom from earliest spring and give prolonged displays of colour. Here they are treated as perennials and reach the size of small shrubs. *Lychnis coronaria* 'Alba' carpets the ground below the spikes of blue *Verbena rigida*. The glowing colours of Sweet williams are set off with the grey foliage and white flowers of aquilegia hybrids. Sidalceas, lupins, verbascums, bergamot, bog sage (*Salvia uliginosa*) and a large variety of campanulas all add their colours and forms to summer's glory.

To one side of the flowerbeds the fence line is edged with a solid hedge of gleaming silvery *Artemisia arborescens*, against which is planted a thick band of pink watsonia. The well-held pink sprays of flower are displayed against the silvery foliage and when the flowers die down the spikes of sharp-green foliage make an interesting contrast against the soft, lacy forms of the artemisia. Lamb's ears (*Stachys byzantina*), *Phlomis fruticosa*, violets and *Vinca minor* and *major* are used to provide leaf decoration during the winter months. Gallipoli heath, an Australian common name given to *Physostegia virginiana*, forms strong clumps of flower throughout the borders. The flowers were once used to commemorate the Australians who fell during the First World War on the Turkish coastline at Gallipoli in much the same way as the wild red poppies are used in memory of those who died on the battlefields of Flanders. These beds with their exuberant use of colour, healthy well-maintained plants and informal fairly crowded plantings, represent what many contemporary Australians would consider to be cottage gardening at its best. Preference is given to old-fashioned plant varieties and the flamboyant glory of summer is achieved through careful attention to the condition of the soil and the

Well-established elm trees (*Ulmus*) provide shade for the Geddes family's outside eating area.

choice of plants which, provided they have adequate water, thrive in this climate.

Beyond the flourishing flowers of the New Garden and parallel to the high wall lie neat rows of vines, trained along waist-high wires. The wall itself is used as support for espaliered fruit trees. The geometric shapes made by the trees and vines are reflected in the simple rectangular layout of the flowerbeds and paths. In winter the New Garden has a pleasing simplicity appropriate to a country garden. In summer there is a dramatic contrast between the straight lines of the fruiting plants and the irregular confusion of form and colour of the flowerbeds.

The latest additions to the garden are a large wall-enclosed formal rose garden and Olivia's Garden. The design of the impressive rose garden is simple and the space large enough to display a huge central iron rose arbour. Olivia's garden is designed for the Geddes' small daughter. It contains a large child's playhouse and sunken stone paths

(ideal for small vehicular traffic) and the raised beds are thickly planted with roses, scented shrubs and perennials. Down by the river the grass is mown. Here, the narrow path leads through a grove of cherry-plums (*Prunus cerasifera*), trees which have seeded themselves from an old orchard plantation, and new fruiting specimens are being added to old survivors.

This garden speaks of the enjoyment its owners get from planning, planting, expanding and caring for a long-neglected country garden. It is a garden which, in the height of the flowering period, teams with what appears to be an extensive but random arrangement of bright flowers but in winter and in the dry heat of late summer the strength of the controlling design is evident. It is the thought given to the site and the attention given to the scale of the land which makes these brilliant groupings sit happily in the often dusty soft shades of an Australian landscape.

Dalvui

NOORAT

Mr Raymond Williams

DALVUI LIES ON the rolling volcanic plains of Victoria's Western District. Mt Noorat, an extinct volcano, overlooks the garden and accounts for the rich soil on which the garden feeds. The land was taken up in 1839 but the present garden dates from 1898 when its owner, Mr Niel Walter Black, commissioned the landscape designer William Guilfoyle to advise on the layout and planting of the garden. No plans have survived but his letters referring to the garden are still in existence and, with a few documented minor alterations, the original 5 acres (2.5 hectares) of garden, are thought to conform to the structure imposed in 1898. One surviving letter indicates that Guilfoyle paid considerable attention to the garden. In it he discusses the 'harmony of the various tints of greenery as viewed from a distance' and the necessity for 'a good background ... for showing up variety of colour, whether the background be near or distant'. An imposing house was planned and by the time it was completed the garden was well established. However, in 1909 Mr Black died (in the wreck of the *Waratah*) and never saw the completion of his house or the maturity of his garden. After his death the property was divided and passed to the Palmer family, which held possession until 1974. Mr Raymond Williams has lived at Dalvui, restoring and developing what had become an overgrown garden, for the past five years. He has also added 2 acres (1 hectare) to the ornamental garden.

The main drive, which on the original plan was to have swept round the outside of the garden and up to the house, was never used, but its avenue of trees still stands and provides a dramatic backdrop to much of the

Left   Jacaranda mimosifolia vies for attention next to the house.

Below   A cordyline stands beneath one of the Indian-style arches on the verandah.

garden. Today the silver poplars (*Populus alba*) are of impressive grandeur and their silvery summer leaves, yellow autumn leaves and dark winter skeletons contribute much to the atmosphere of the garden. Equally interesting is the driveway in use today, which approaches from a different angle. It too is bordered with poplars (*Populus alba* 'Pyramidalis') and curves gently across the paddocks. Fine wire is attached to posts hidden from view behind each tree, and, as one enters the park-like paddocks, the trees which line the edge of the garden can be enjoyed without the usual visually obtrusive constructions needed for controlling stock.

As the driveway approaches the garden a small planting of ornamental trees heralds what is within the gates. Two varieties of *Cedrus atlantica*, *C.a.* 'Aurea' and *C.a.* 'Glauca', stand with fine Monterey pines (*Pinus radiata*) casting their shade on the garden's plain white gates, which are set in white cross-banded wooden fencing. Within the gates the wide driveway curves through a particularly fine avenue of ninety-year old silver birches (*Betula pendula*) growing in

Previous page   The main drive winds out from the house under old silver birches.

mown grass well back from the drive's edge. Shrubs, such as philadelphus, choisyas and viburnums, border the generous swathe of grass. The silver variegation on the leaves of a blue lacecap hydrangea lights the shadows helped by a band of white-flowering *Corydalis ochroleuca*. Nearby stands a dark and massive clump of New Zealand flax (*Phormium*), which, like the palm (*Phoenix canariensis*) standing at one side of the garden, probably dates from Guilfoyle's early plan. As the driveway approaches the house other well-grown trees, a *Tilia cordata*, a great elm and a Norway maple (*Acer platanoides*) shade the area. More recent additions to their ranks have included the exquisite tricolor beech (*Fagus sylvatica* 'Tricolor') and *Robinia pseudoacacia* 'Frisia'. The harmony of the various tints of greenery extolled by Guilfoyle are still there and to this day the garden exemplifies many of his thoughts on foliage and his love of trees. Interesting tree groupings are typical of the garden, which is surrounded by drifts of carefully contrasted foliage and, typical of many early Australian

gardens, little of the countryside beyond the confines of the garden and its surrounding avenue of silver poplars can be seen from within the garden. The aim in many of the grander Australian gardens dating from the late Victorian and Edwardian era was to recreate a corner of England and eliminate the foreign landscape.

As the house comes into view the garden opens out, plant groupings are lower and the house is displayed surrounded by the open greenery of rolling lawns. In summer a bed of hydrangeas holds the attention and in winter the eye is caught by and directed into the garden by a series of beds, arranged like the slices of a cake, which today contain a collection of ericas. The carriage loop before the main door is contained by a wall of greenery composed of Chinese elm (*Ulmus parvifolia*), *Jacaranda mimosifolia* and grey myrtle (*Backhousia myrtifolia*). Apple trees are espaliered round the window frames and pears and peaches are trained against the wall of a service yard. A bed containing lemon-yellow and soft mauve iris is edged

A fan of heather beds by the drive has a small fountain as a focal point.

Agapanthus and arum lilies flank the path which leads towards the newly-created bridge over the pond.

with *Stachys byzantina* 'Limelight' and *Helichrysum orientale* 'Lime Glow'. The contrast between the spiky blue-grey leaves of the iris and the soft golden glow of the two silvery-leaved plants is strikingly effective. The violet petals of a cultivar of *Tulbaghia violacea* which carries its flowers through the summer months completes the charming study in colour, texture and form.

Apart from the carriage loop and a small service area (which today contains a pergola covered with Banksian roses), the setting for

wind through the more distant parts of the garden.

The lawns which surround the house are interrupted on one side by massive rockeries, which Guilfoyle used to mask a natural outcrop of rock. The huge rocks are arranged in a somewhat gothic rather than a naturalistic style. The plantings match the scale of the rocks and large clumps of watsonia, bulbinella, *Wachendorfia thyrsiflora* and *Campanula rapunculoides* bloom from the rocks in the company of plants which have strong,

Below left An island is planted with a paulownia tree and agapanthus.

On an autumn afternoon, the blue-purple flowers of *Plectranthus ecklonii* light up the borders.

the house consists of sweeping lawns. The garden was clearly designed with the house as its focal point and all the major windows look out over the wide lawns to the mixed groupings of trees, shrubs and flowers. The arrangement is informal and the mixed plantings surrounding the lawns reveal informal vistas through the trees and expose different views of the garden as the visitor moves through it. Views of the house are kept clear although two magnificent specimens of *Tilia cordata* stand on the south front. A number of paths, varying in character,

A wide pair of herbaceous borders unfolds beyond the pond in November.

sculptural shapes. One impressive rockery is topped by an equally impressive, well-grown coral tree (*Erythrina crista-galli*). Beyond the rockeries lies a pretty mown path which leads through the shrubs and trees that border the garden. The planting includes clivias and *Melianthus major*, with strong sculptural forms, and beneath these there are delicate colour associations. The combinations of pink veronica planted with *Geranium endressii* 'Wargrave Pink' and the luscious yellow *Trollius europaeus* 'Superbus' with *Phlomis fruticosa* are particularly effective.

A second path leads away from the major expanse of lawn through a pair of ancient Lombardy poplars (*Populus nigra* 'Italica'). These guard some rugged stone steps and take one to the far side of a chain of ponds, studded with small islands, which lie at the bottom of one long sweep of lawn. A chinoiserie bridge links one island to the lawn. From this position one can look back up the green expanse to the house or across the garden at the decorative planting. Splashes of white or blue are used throughout the year to link the selection of orna-

mental plants and to lead the eye through the garden. The blues are provided by the native Australian hibiscus, the flowers on the jacaranda and paulownia trees and in spring there are sheets of forget-me-nots, bluebells and omphalodes. In summer an attractive agapanthus cultivar dating from the early garden blooms from the shrubberies and, in the early autumn, the spikes of the blue-flowered *Plectranthus ecklonii* take up the theme. White is provided with bands of the ever-blooming *Corydalis ochroleuca*, *Romneya coulteri* (which is grown to great effect in this garden), viburnums, *Catalpa bignonioides* and the bracts of *Davidia involucrata*.

bery which backs one section of lawn. An arbour, hung with *Rosa banksiae* 'Alba Plena' leads back through a flowery border.

The extensive new garden lies to the west of the house. The area is contained within a planting of trees and shrubs which include a Chinese elm (*Ulmus parvifolia* 'Frosty'), the glossy leafed *Viburnum odoratissimum*, *Ribes aureum* and an exquisitely scented osmanthus. The gigantic sculptural shapes of *Doryanthes* 'Guilfoyliana' and *Doryanthes excelsa* with leaves 8 feet (2.4 m) in size and tree-like flower stems which rise to a height of 20 feet (6 m) give the area great character. Huge beds in the centre of the area contain bold drifts of perennials.

Right Hedging of clipped *Lonicera nitida* gives this area its strong form. The avenue of silver poplars can be seen in the background.

Behind the pond a new garden unfolds. A ha-ha marks the boundary of this part of the garden and beyond it can be seen the parklike surroundings. A seat is placed between beds edged with low hedges of clipped *Lonicera nitida* and the path takes a course between a wide pair of herbaceous borders. The borders are filled with a mass of hostas, astilbes, candelabra primulas (*P. helodoxa*), *Campanula glomerata* and *C. latifolia*. Returning to the lawns which surround the house the path, its line marked by stands of blue agapanthus, leads through the large shrub-

The large garden of Dalvui is lucky to have been rescued. Too often gardens of this type and size prove impossible to maintain. Dalvui has been restored by its owner who not only attends to all the maintenance himself but has extended the area under cultivation. This is an occasion when, happily, a garden of historic importance has fallen into enthusiastic hands.

A Garden of Australian Native Plants

MONTROSE

Gwen & Rodger Elliot

*T*HIS GARDEN OF native plants lies on a block of about 5 acres (2 hectares) of which about two-thirds is still indigenous bushland. In 1980, before the Elliots bought the land, a real estate agent had 'improved' the land by bulldozing nearly all the under-storey plants. Only the mature eucalypts and a small bush area remained and a number of large *Pinus radiata*. The pines were removed and as their progeny appeared they were removed too. Happily, a dry season followed the agent's planting of clover and rye grass and so very little of it germinated.

It has been the Elliots' intention, 'as far as possible, to foster the development of the native vegetation and total ecology of the area.' After devastation by the bulldozer the land was allowed to regenerate with little assistance from the hand of man. Exotic wind-borne and bird-borne weeds such as pittosporum, ivy, raspberries, brambles and Spanish heath have been systematically removed as they appeared over the years. Indigenous plants were allowed to regenerate and only the hairpin banksia, *Banksia spinulosa cunninghamii*, which is indigenous to the local hills, was actually planted. The long, narrow leaves are dark green and borne on woody sculptural plants. The upright bottlebrushes of yellow to amber flowers with black styles can reach a length of 10 inches (25 cm) and width of 3 inches (8 cm) and make interesting sentries at the entry to the bush-bordered gravel driveway. The flowers are carried throughout the winter months, providing ample nectar for many native birds, and are followed by impressive woody fruits.

Little else has been done to foster the natural vegetation but today, less than ten years since the bulldozer did its work, the simple driveway curves uphill through what looks like natural bushland. The large trees include the narrow-leaved peppermint (*Eucalyptus radiata*), messmate stringy bark (*E. obliqua*), red stringy bark (*E. macrorhyncha*) and swamp gum (*E. ovata*). The blackwoods (*Acacia melanoxylon*), which bear trusses of pale yellow flowers in early spring, have suckered and formed pleasant copses. The common heath, the floral emblem of the State of Victoria, splashes the scene with its white or pink flowers in winter. In early spring the bushland comes to life with flashes of bright yellow from the small shrubby *Acacia myrtifolia*. The thatch saw sedge (*Gahnia radula*) is very dense in some areas. Its sharp-edged foliage makes it unpopular with gardeners and bushwalkers but it is kept because it makes an important habitat for the sword-grass brown butterfly and because the blue wrens favour it as a nesting site. A major aim of the garden is 'to provide and maintain a habitat for the wildlife of the region' and Rodger and Gwen Elliot enjoy sharing their garden with over fifty species of native birds, echidnas, ringtail and brush-tail possums, numerous lizards and skinks, the occasional copperhead snake, the harmless white-lipped snakes and an enormous number of butterflies and insects.

The house, a typically Australian long low structure, whose recycled hand-made bricks and woodwork have been carefully chosen to merge with the soft colouring often found in the foliage of native plants, stands on a south-facing slope, just below the crest of a small hill. Around it lies the

Left Pink *Boronia serrulata* and blue *Conospermum caeruleum* flower against the bark of *Eucalyptus leucoxylon* spp. *megalocarpa* and *Jacksonia scoparia*.

A white-flowered variant of *Tetratheca thymifolia* sets off two forms of *Telopea speciosissima*. To one side the yellow flowers of *Banksia spinulosa* var. *spinulosa* can also be seen.

ornamental garden in which grow some thousand plant species and cultivars collected from all over Australia. In one corner there is a small collection of Californian plants as over the years botanists and horticulturists from California have made regular visits and the inevitable plant swap which occurs when gardeners meet has taken place. The nearby Dandenong Ranges dominate the view from the garden which follows a simple, logical pattern and is designed with the aim of blending and merging the ornamental garden with the indigenous plants of the bushland which surrounds it. There are no artificial barriers between the bush and the garden.

A pale pink form of the balm mint bush (*Prostanthera melissifolia*) froths its delicate-looking blooms over the outbuildings and a soft gravel path (in a shade which picks up the earth tones from the bush) leads from the driveway towards the front door. The eye is attracted immediately to the flashes of deep clear blue which decorate the parking area. Australian flora, sometimes described as drab by those who can only see colour if it is set off with brilliant green, is rich in the jewel blues found elsewhere in cornflowers, gentians and iris. Here *Dampiera linearis* covers the ground with swathes of glowing blue. Several forms have been collected and established in the garden and it is of interest to note that while one vigorous plant flowers freely from late July (mid-winter) until December, others bloom for more limited periods.

A bed to one side of the path is given strength and height with a golden form of *Banksia spinulosa*, which was selected from plants growing in Toowoomba in Queensland. Several other forms are found within the ornamental garden. *Eucalyptus leucoxylon megalocarpa* hangs its fine, open branches over the bed and path and decorates the scene with its pale pink to raspberry-pink tufts of flower and long-stalked pointed caps set against leaves which display the same shade of greyish green on both sides. The tree moves as the nectar-eating birds clamber about and the movement makes the sheen on its smooth bark, its arching branches and tufted blooms all the more eye catching. (It used to be thought that *E. leucoxylon* only produced dark-brown bark in areas where gold was present in the soil.) During winter and spring the ground beneath one fine group is carpeted with the brilliant blue of dampiera through which pink and white forms of the native heath appear and the bed is given textural and architectural form at ground level with mounds of the native grass *Poa morrissii*. In late spring and summer the dominant yellow of *Helichrysum apiculatum* takes precedence as a ground cover.

There is a wealth of flower and contrasting foliage near the main door. Over the pergola which leads to the door a white form of native lilac (*Hardenbergia comptoniana*) hangs its multitude of tiny pea-like flowers from late winter until mid-spring. The dense form of the golden bush pea (*Pultenaea gunnii*) is contrasted with the airy light forms of mint bushes (*Prostanthera*) and boronias. In spring the bed is lit with soft mauves, the palest of pinks, carmine-pinks and white in conjunction with the stronger yellow of the bush pea, and the air is scented with the lingering perfume of various boronias. The ground beneath the shrubs is covered with a dense green mat made by the foliage of *Viola hederacea* 'Baby Blue', whose generously produced sky-blue flowers stand well above the foliage. At the far end the dark green foliage and spikes of yellow flower on the pine-leaved geebung (*Persoonia pinifolia*) give emphasis to the planting. The yellow flowers are followed by clusters of green to purplish fleshy fruits called geebungs, which were once eaten by Aborigines.

The space beside the front door is usually decorated with container-grown native plants which are brought up from the propagating area as they come into flower. Pink, white and purple forms of the pink rock orchid (*Dendrobium kingianum*) join star-like clusters of *Phebalium* spp. and wax flowers (*Eriostemon* spp.). Shade-tolerant dwarf native ferns are used to set off the more colourful plants. To the other side of the path *Thomasia grandiflora* is massed with mauve flower – its curious petal arrangement reminds one of the skirt of a ruffled silk ballgown. Close by *Guichenotia macrantha* (a flower which is beginning to find its way

An *Eriostemon* hybrid blooms with *Boronia muelleri* 'Sunset Serenade' in a bushland setting.

onto the international flower market) displays its pinky-white buds and flowers through the winter months.

Bordering this side of the house is a single informal bed of flowering plants and trees. The gravel path surrounds the bed but there are no neat edges or straight lines, the plants themselves softening the edges and defining the gently curving pathway. Flannel flowers (*Actinotus helianthi*) have self-sown through the bed and add their curiously fabric-like texture to a variety of textures – some of which are rarely found in the flora of other continents. Perhaps the most extraordinary of these textures is found in the rare blue tinsel lily (*Calectasia cyanea intermedia*) which produces abundant violet-blue stars of flower with golden anthers. The polished petals are so smooth that they look as if they have been made from a man-made substance and the metallic colouring is so rarely found in nature's paintbox that one suspects the dye pot. A large clump grows and flowers well in this bed. The spider-net grevillea (*Grevillea thelemanniana preissii*) has an attractive mounded form and gnarled branches; it displays its bright red gold-tipped flowers against greyish leaves from May until December. *Dampiera teres* can be relied on to produce blue-mauve flowers thoughout the year. One of the prettiest and most dramatic sights in this bed is the West Australian dwarf shrub *Commersonia pulchella*. A profusion of pink buds open to reveal star-like white flowers with crimson centres and crimson staining on the petal reverse. The small leaves are a soft grey-green and the new growth has a pleasant tint of dusky red. The bush produces flush upon flush of flower between September and March and a few flowers can usually be found during the rest of the year.

At the far end of the bed, placed so that their dramatic qualities can be appreciated as one walks towards the front door, stand a group of waratahs (*Telopea speciosissima*). There are selected forms taken from the well-known red variety and the 'Wirrimbirra White' form, which is rarely seen outside botanic gardens. Although in general it seldom sets seed, in this garden it blooms well and the flowering of the first

seedlings is awaited with anticipation. Various forms of *Grevillea lavandulacea* are used in this bed and an as yet unnamed relative of the common everlasting *Helichrysum apiculatum* produces its clusters of tiny golden-yellow flowers for nine months of the year. The bed is backed by the bush plants and the colours of the foliage within the ornamental garden and the foliage in the bush itself give the whole area a harmonious peaceful atmosphere. Some of the plants have strong forms and there is a wealth of flower but there are no strident colours or colour comparisons which might interfere with the natural surroundings. The bush borders one side of the path and on both sides the fascinating grass-leaved trigger plant (*Stylidium graminifolium*) blooms. The long column or trigger is held below the petals and when an insect lands on the petals the column, which contains both a pollen receptacle and a pollen distributor, shoots forward and deposits its burden on the insect.

The path leads past the geebung and round the side of the house to the garden behind the house. The drama of the brilliant yellow of *Helichrysum bracteatum* 'Dargan Hill Monarch' is there to lead the eye and feet towards this second section of garden. Here open space is used to great effect to display the plants but here too the bush lends its gentle colours as a backdrop to the decorative elements of the plant collection.

Edging the house and sweeping under the verandah on the northern side lies a wide border of raked, fine gravel broken by the dense small bright-green leaves of the matted bush pea (*Pultenaea pedunculata*). The commoner golden form is there in company with the much rarer shell-pink form 'Pyalong Pink'. The tiny, fan-shaped flowers of *Scaevola* 'Mauve Clusters' rise from a dense mat of small bright green leaves. The use of bright green in the area close to the house, in a garden where softer grey greens and sage greens predominate, coupled with the simplicity of the broad band of fine gravel, softens the man-made lines of the house and gives the area its distinct character and relaxed design. At one end of the wide, gravel terrace a small compartment is contained within a low wall. Here blue-tongued

Conospermum caeruleum and *Hibbertia inconspicua* grow together in a container.

Right Notice the textural contrasts to be found in Australian native flora. In the foreground is *Dampiera linearis* 'Early Blue'. The frothing pale-pink *Boronia muelleri* 'Sunset Serenade' is well displayed against the narrow greyish stems of the leafless *Jacksonia scoparia*.

lizards, excellent for controlling the snails and caterpillars in the garden, bask in the sun. Shallow steps, their edges clad with thick bleached wood and the treads gravelled but planted with ground-hugging plants, lead up to an open lawn which runs the length of the house. The lowest step is given emphasis with a great clump of tassel-cord rush (*Restio tetraphyllus*). Looking away from the house from the top of the steps the lawn is contained within a sweep of natural bush made all the more dramatic by the blackwood groves. In one corner these trees have been given emphasis by the rough clearing of the undergrowth and the trimming of the lower branches on the tree trunks. The result is an informal vista in which a group of tree trunks make the focal point rather than some man-made sculptural or utilitarian object. The bank between the gravel terrace and the upper lawn is covered by a wide planting of individual specimens. The corner devoted to Californian plants includes a selection of *Mimulus* species, but most of the area is devoted to the extensive collection of Australian native plants. A gungurru (*Eucalyptus caesia magna*, also known as *E. c.* 'Silver Princess') hangs its large clusters of brilliant silvery-pink blooms over the area. A great clump of *Scaevola auriculata* gives the bed both form and colour and the clump provides an unending supply of fan-shaped mauve flowers with golden centres. The mauve is picked up by one of the gardens most dramatic specimens. In one corner stands a selected form of the native blue hibiscus (*Alyogyne huegelii*). The huge blooms have petals which are folded to give a multi-petalled appearance and, like many hibiscus, looks as if someone had given the flowerhead a small twist before allowing the flower to unfurl its petals. The colour of this sensational plant changes, as do many Australian plants, with the light and with the maturity of the flowerhead. At one moment the petals seem to be a deep silky blue-purple, at the next they may appear sky blue or even change to a shade of navy blue. Near the hibiscus and beneath a small copse of blackwoods the ground is covered with the prostrate growth of *Brachysema praemorsum*, which bears elongated red pea-shaped flowers, which are eagerly visited by nectar-feeding birds.

The garden is rarely watered and the hose turned on only after prolonged dry weather, perhaps once a year. Slow-release fertilizer is usually incorporated at planting time but subsequent feeding is uncommon. Weeding and pruning receive regular attention but spraying is almost never necessary as the birds and insects clean up most garden pests. This garden is a truly Australian garden and the creation of two people, who are both respected horticultural and botanical writers and whose extensive knowledge of the Australian flora is constantly being extended and revised. It is a place of great botanical interest and discovery, containing many plants, collected from throughout Australia, whose habits are unknown in cultivation. Finally, it is a garden which has its own colours, scents, shapes and sounds.

The Bush Gardens
ELTHAM

*S*INCE THE LAST century the hills of Eltham, 14 miles (22 km) from the heart of Melbourne, have been the home of artists and craftsmen. The first group of artists working in this area earned a reputation for producing what is now recognized as some of the first distinctively Australian work. More recently the gardeners of Eltham have inspired a general interest in Australian flora and today many gardens are devoted entirely to Australian flora or contain a 'bush walk'. Such plantings play a vital part in the preservation of native birds.

JOHN STREET

Cécile & Peter Glass

When the artist and landscape consultant Peter Glass bought land at Eltham just before the Second World War he bought open space. Like most hills in the neighbourhood, the land had been cleared of all native vegetation and a commercial orchard had been established. The only other tree was a large Peruvian peppercorn (*Schinus molle*), a species of decorative tree which was much planted in early settlements to provide quick shade.

The peppercorn tree still weeps beside what looks today like a steeply climbing bush track, dwarfed by massive gums. This 'track' is, in fact, a curbless hard surface, its colour matched exactly to its dirt borders. A closer look reveals several houses squatting low in the vegetation, a few cars tucked between tree trunks and rocks. This is an urban development but there are no boundary fences.

Peter Glass planted the first sugar gums

(*Eucalyptus cladocalyx*) in 1939. The trees were acquired from the only source available in those days, the Forestry Commission. Today he feels he would have preferred to have used a plant native to the area. The sugar gum originates from South Australia and was widely planted throughout Victoria as a windbreak. As it was he chose from

Right The soft, dimpled bark of *Eucalyptus citriodora*, by the front door, is given emphasis by the contrasting circular wooden grill and concentric rings of bricks.

Above The view from the terrace is reminiscent of the bush.

Below *Bauera rubioides* flourishes beside some steps.

what was available and the results are spectacular. The massive straight trunks rise to the sky like cathedral columns, supporting a leafy roof some 130 feet (40 m) above. The air below is sharp with the clean smell of eucalyptus. Birds dash about in the busy noisy fashion of native Australian birds and the air is always filled with their squawks and ringing bell-like tones.

After the initial planting little was done until 1948, when Peter Glass came to live in Eltham. Later he was joined by others who shared his love of the bush and by a French wife, Cécile, whose small plant nursery, the first of its kind, was entirely devoted to native plants. (When family groups came to visit, invariably the parents chose one of the smaller shrubs. Cécile Glass always gave the children a tree to plant and she is, perhaps, responsible for the custom today of presenting each new Australian citizen with a native tree.)

By the front door, in a circle of paving (the inner circle composed of slatted wood copied from a design used in French parks) stands the shaft of a huge lemon-scented gum (*E. citriodora*). Its soft cream-white fluffy flowers and urn-shaped, warty and woody fruits are held high above, almost out of sight in a crown of sparse open foliage.

Below rises the straight column of trunk. After peeling, the bark is a luminous lime-white, which changes to an equally luminous shade somewhere between a pale powder-grey and a lavender-pink as the smooth bark hardens. The bark at all times looks soft, almost spongy, and has an appealing, smooth-as-flesh tactile quality. (Those who knock at this front door are frequently found stroking or hugging the tree.)

Much of the traditional gardener's demand for colour is satisfied by the bright plumage of the native birds that flock in to feed. The traditional gardener looks for colour on the ground or at eye level; here, throughout the year, it is to be found high above in the tree tops. Bright flashes of colour arrest the eye and sometimes form outstanding colour matches and contrasts. In this garden the top of an iron bark (*Eucalyptus sideroxylon*), with its gum-grey foliage and great trusses of crimson-pink flower, is a favourite spot with the crimson rosella, a bird large enough to be seen easily from the ground.

The house is enveloped in bush which has a sculpture-like appearance when viewed from the windows. At ground level, a massive doryanthes (*D. excelsa*) from the east coast of New South Wales with huge spear-like leaves has been established as a focal point by a small pond. For the most part, however, these sculptures are composed of barks, whose hues and shapes change with the seasons. Many of the smooth-barked native trees shed their bark as exotic trees shed their leaves. New shades appear constantly (some of them bright enough to satisfy those whose craving for colour can only be satisfied by the most vivid of hues) and fantastic shapes and patterns are revealed as the bark peels or flakes away from the tree trunk.

In a courtyard below a window a *Melaleuca nesophila* has grown in an unusual way with its long low boughs spread horizontally. Leafless and grey, they have a rough papery texture that makes a play of light and shadow on the ground below. The branches provide the focus in this courtyard, a reversal of the more traditional pattern, in which man-made objects provide the focal point and plants the background.

JOHN STREET
Gordon Ford

Across the road Gordon Ford, the well-known landscape architect, has established what is now a renowned bush garden. Massive flat-topped rocks dominate the path leading into the block and the area surrounding the house. Although now encrusted with moss and lichen, these were brought to the site, a crane being needed to lift them into position. Native shrubs, especially grevilleas and species of *Correa*, are used extensively throughout this garden, their fine forms and delicate flowers contrasting sharply with the solid forms of the rock.

Near the house a torrent of water pours over the rocks into a still pool. There is movement and tranquillity. The horizontal surfaces of the rocks surrounding the pool are thrown into sharp focus by the linear leaves of the native iris (*Orthrosanthus multiflorus*). In spring the area is lit with their leafy racemes of soft mauve-blue flowers. The front entry of the house is approached across a chain of huge stepping stones which traverse the base of the waterfall. This is no exercise in prettiness; these rocks have a strength of design which dominates the low dwelling to such an extent that one hardly notices its presence.

During his early years in Eltham Mr Ford used some exotic plants to achieve a natural effect and there are still a few survivors. A huge willow hangs over the pond and some shrubs flower near the house, among them the abutilons 'Sydney Belle' and 'Emperor'. In this climate they bloom through the year.

The eye is not drawn to the house but to a small leafy path which bypasses it and leads round the still pond. The unmade path is soft with a bed of dried gum leaves and whispers slightly when used. It leads from the man-made elements into trees, inviting one to explore. Soon the pathway is forgotten; even in this small area it is easy to understand how early settlers got bushed (lost).

The language used to describe traditional gardens is quite inappropriate applied to this setting. Australia, after all, is different from the northern hemisphere: the perspective is different, the angle of light is different; the smell is different; the sounds are different; and the flora and fauna are also different. Many who are unaccustomed to the Australian landscape find the bush strange, frightening and lonely. Some even find it ugly. Here, dwarfed by the pole-like trunks, one can feel the bush in all its splendour. Prettiness and cosiness take second place to space and light, scale and proportion, mass and void. One feels small and alone, in awe of the grandeur of nature, and yet the space is a mere acre and a half (0.6 hectares).

Traditional gardens are often divided into 'garden rooms'. Here too the garden divides into rooms but the arrangement is vertical, not horizontal. The first room is at ground level and equates with a traditional garden. There are ground-cover plants, species of *Brachycome*, tufts of native grass and the deep decorative leaf litter. The 'shrubs' of the bush bloom head-high in this room. Winter is splashed with bright yellow wattle (*Acacia baileyana*), known in the northern hemisphere as mimosa. In summer the fine grey-green to silver-blue foliage of wattle casts its soft shadow here. Light is the important element in this lower room. It is dim under the trees, the light being filtered through a tracery of leaves high above which casts constantly changing patterns.

The garden is on different levels and this path, with the fern *Nephrolepsis cordifolia* in the foreground, leads up stone steps from the house to the top of the garden.

Water, stone and foliage are used close to the house to create a bush-like setting.

The pool is bridged by a series of stepping stones which cross the base of the waterfall and lead to the front of the house.

For a moment the elegant flowers of species wattles, grevilleas and correas are caught in the light and then they are lost in shade. The second room, standing directly above the ground-floor room, begins at the level of the human head and soars above the visitor. Great cylindrical columns of straight smooth bark rise to the leaf canopy far above. The peeling and flaking barks which decorate the changing seasons are lit by the angled shafts of flickering light. The relationship between the awe-inspiring columns of wood and the spaces which separate them gives this room its form and shape – no man-made masonry is needed here to give the garden form. High above hangs the third room, a canopy of leaf silhouetted against the changing shades of sky. The tracery of leaf moves constantly with the wind, finding new shapes and designs as it exposes a fretwork of blue. To this elegant background the birds add their motion and vivid hues.

At one point the canopy opens and light streams to the ground giving greater emphasis to the shafts of trunk. The muted shades of new bark have a silken sheen. These great silky pencils seem to drop from the sky rather than rise upwards. The point where they reach the earth is left showing the bare intersection of geometric lines; vertical lines, right angles and circles interact without interference to enthral the onlooker with their elegance. There is no frill of stones or bed of ground-cover plants here, just the triumph of nature's simplicity. Although these gardens have colour, texture is much more important.

Today the hill in Eltham is peopled by those who share the philosophy of Cécile and Peter Glass and Gordon Ford. The area provides a lung for the city nearby and a refuge and feeding place for native birds. One characteristic of this area should be mentioned. Sounds here take on a special quality, making them quite different to the sounds of other gardens. It is not just the calls of the birds but the way in which, rebounding from the leafy tracery above to the leafy carpet below, all sounds have a curious all-Australian mellow ring.

The Castlemaine Gardens

CASTLEMAINE

GOLD WAS FOUND at Forrest Creek (which flows just below Badger's Keep) in 1851 bringing an influx of people to the Castlemaine district in central Victoria. The climate is typical of inland areas, with hot summers and cold frosty winters. The local sandstone lies in reefs through the area, providing an attractive and easily obtained building material and a challenge to those designing and nurturing gardens. The area is noted for its early-Australian architecture, its cultural life and its beautiful gardens.

BADGER'S KEEP

Margaret & Clive Winmill

The sandstone miner's cottage at Badger's Keep sits low on a hillside. Its garden, created by Margaret and Clive Winmill, runs along the side of a creek valley and merges with the hills above. The valley itself is barren and weed infested, the result of un-sympathetic bulldozing of the old mining site by local authorities. The garden now shelters behind a planting of native trees and shrubs. These have the three-fold effect of screening the garden from the devastation below, linking the view from the garden to the hills beyond, and sheltering the garden from the west wind which sweeps up the creek valley.

Little remains of previous gardens but the current owners' interest in old fruiting trees was more than satisfied by the quince and damson trees which had spread through the site. Only well-placed, well-grown speci-mens have been retained. A massive pear

tree, described as 'old' in the 1920s, still survives. Today the modern orchard contains some three hundred different apple culti-vars (all old varieties, descended from those imported in colonial times) and to the old bones of previous gardens more trees have been added, many of them fruiting varieties.

A small flight of steps leads to the cottage. A rather insignificant spot just below these steps (a spot only noticeable because a few paths intersect there and because it leads directly up to the cottage) forms a pivotal spot in the garden. A strong diagonal axis runs through the garden from this point to a

An informal cottage-garden planting dominated by blue aquilegias.

Above The ground is encrusted with flowers in front of the cottage.

Below A path, shaded with the foliage of *Acer negundo*, is edged with flowers.

pine standing to the south on the hillside. A simple one-room sandstone cottage, a recent addition, now stands beneath this pine. Much of the garden is contained in a natural bowl in the hillside which falls between these two points. Along this axis in the lowest part of the shallow bowl, there is a wheel-shaped arrangement of flowerbeds. Above there is a pond and a neat orchard, its rows of trees sited to follow the diagonal line across the hill.

At another angle from this pivotal spot a mown glade opens out shaded by a black mulberry, one of the original plantings. This small area has a bright Mediterranean atmosphere. Pockets of perennials in shades of red, orange and yellow pick up the warm shades of a dry-stone wall. A fat low rosemary hedge, through which one reaches the front gate, borders one side and an olive tree has been added to the planting. Elsewhere in the garden colours are largely confined to paler pastel shades.

Just below this glade a grass path is bordered with flowers. In summer there are lavenders and roses such as 'Frau Dagmar Hastrup', 'Ispahan' and *Rosa × alba* 'Maxima'. The lavenders are outstanding and with the pink bergamot (*Monarda didyma*) give a long display. An unusual tall nodding dianthus adds to the charm.

This garden contains many unusual

plants; some have been collected over the years from other old gardens, others have been grown from imported seed. The wide selection of roses, many of them chosen from the groups often referred to as 'old or shrub roses', are grown throughout the garden. They festoon old sheds and climb through the trees. One of the gardens most dramatic sights (and this garden in full bloom is dramatic) is 'Dorothy Perkins' growing through an almond tree. Irises are used extensively and the garden includes a selection of species and hybrids of the bearded iris.

From the pivotal point just below the house one path leads uphill and to one side of the house. Here the sunken pathway is bordered with herbs and the area shaded by an apricot tree (*Prunus mume* 'The Geisha') and a box elder (*Acer negundo*). The raised

A walk along this path begins with Californian poppies and passes catmint, flag irises, roses, geums, scabious and the creamy blossoms of the common elder *Sambucus nigra*.

borders are planted with a selection of herbs, many of which are rarely seen in Australian private gardens. Among the thymes is *Thymus pannonicus*, the oreganums include the Cretan dittany (*Origanum dictamnus*) and the historic mandrake plant (*Mandragora officinarum*) flourishes here.

The gums screen the view below and the garden merges above into the tree-crested hill. Yuccas are dotted through the trees on the lower part of the hill. The steep curving slope above the garden is contained by rough dry stone walls. In summer these walls foam with orange Californian poppies, the silken sheen of their petals contrasting with the sandy roughness of the rock. These plants are perennial in this climate and the fine blue-grey foliage remains in winter to pick up the blue-grey shades of the gums above and below the garden.

This garden is never without flower. In summer it is spectacular. The beds glow with soft flowing colour set off by the greens of grass, tree and shrub. In winter the borders make a fascinating early-morning silvery display. In spite of the heavy frosts few of the perennials winter underground and their varied leaves are stiffened with glistening frost. The plants, grouped with as much thought for their silvery winter leaf contrasts as they are for colour harmony in summer, cover the ground with a patchwork of silver lace. The silver-grey theme is taken up by the white felted stalks and grey leaves of shrubby germander (*Teucrium fruticans*) and the lavish use of lavender.

In summer, when the garden is in full flower, a first glance reveals little by way of formal design. Paths seem to wander about in an inviting and exciting but somewhat random manner. It may not be a formal garden but it is a strongly designed garden and its well-known collections of exotic plants sit happily in the local landscape because the design, following a traditional axial pattern, is firm. Designing a garden which runs across the face of a hill is never easy but the usual solution of levelling and walling severe rectangular 'rooms' has not been employed here. The garden follows the natural form of the land and with its strong vistas enhances rather than denies its Australian setting.

CAMPBELL STREET

Barbara Maund

THE BLOCK IS typical of many to be found on the outskirts of a country town. A low cottage, the front door standing between two identical windows shaded by a verandah, faces a wide quiet road and hides the back garden from view. The setting is quiet but one must walk round the side of the house, entering the garden through a pergola, before the garden's serenity can be fully appreciated.

A large gnarled peppercorn tree (*Schinus molle*) stands to one side of the small site, its height and grandeur too large for the perspective. It serves the useful purpose of forcing the eye down onto the land and to the detail below. Moreover, its foliage provides summer shade, brightens the wintery scene and its soft pink berries enhance the colour themes in this delicately toned garden.

The land slopes gently away from the house, rippling downward like shallow water running over rock. The square lines of the house itself have been softened with the addition of an octagonal tent-like structure. The natural levels have hardly been changed. The gentle lie of the land is emphasized by the design rather than dissected by straight lines and sharp drops. The soft curves increase the feeling of gentle movement and add to the sense of space. Like the scales on a fish, the paths and beds interlink elegantly and lead the eye across the surface to explore one detail after another. In spite of the fact that most of the garden is closely divided by curving lines the design has none of what Vita Sackville-West described as 'weak wavering curves and wriggles'. Here, her demand for 'simplicity, symmetry and surprise' would be satisfied, even if the strong straight lines she often advocated have been replaced by the curve of the new moon.

To break the surface (as water breaks over a rock) some beds are edged on their lower side with low hedging. *Lavandula stoechas*, *Rosmarinus officinalis* or lad's love (*Artemisia abrotanum*) have been put to good purpose. One curve is marked with a row of knee-high ivy-covered mushroom shapes. Others take their form from colour not height, and are

The pink *Dianthus deltoides* appears to flow into and out of this typically Australian shallow pond.

White watsonias, pinks, campanulas, thrift and variegated iris illustrate the characteristic colours of this garden.

edged with scales of pale house leeks (*Sempervivum* and *Jovibarba*). Like eddies in a stream, bowls of pale ivies light the ground in the shade of a focal tree. Each bed is given attention with either a carefully balanced evergreen grouping or a tree. In winter the rhythm of these careful plantings is revealed. In summer one looks through trees and shrubs as one circle leads to another.

At the lower end of the garden, on a diagonal line from the pergola through which one enters, a pool of pale raked gravel is surrounded by the silver-white leaves of *Artemesia arborescens*, *Chrysanthemum ptarmicifolium*, *Senecio bicolor cineraria* 'White Diamond', and *Dianthus* 'Mrs Sinkins'. It is like looking down onto water by moonlight – real water is contained in a circular pond to one side of the site. Throughout the garden leaf is important and winter is decorated by many pale leaves. The pride of Madeira (*Echium fastuosum*) makes mounds of huge pointed silver silk leaves contrasting with a small cylindrical blue conifer and the lettuce-green spikes of *Euphorbia rigida*. The almost luminous green is picked up by the flowers of *Helleborus × sternii*.

In spring blossom from the trees and spiraeas lace the air while the ground is studded with flowering bulbs. The lilac-pink Cretan tulip (*Tulipa saxatilis*) is a particular favourite and yellow kniphofias add the strength of their upright spires to the design. In summer the whole garden dances with bloom. Cosmos, *Gaura lindheimeri*, *Salvia uliginosa*, bronze fennel, and *Verbena bonariensis* are used to add their light movement to any breath of breeze that blows in the fierce heat. There are also the more rigid uprights of mauve verbascums, pale physostegias and lilies. Throughout the garden mauves, lavenders, burgundies and lemon yellows are given preference. Barbara Maund favours plants which seed themselves so that she or nature can 'change the colour pictures' with ease.

The first ambition of most gardeners when faced with the solid high fences which

surround three sides of an Australian suburban plot is to mask the heavy line with shrubs and creepers. In this garden there is no feeling of being surrounded by heavy fencing and yet one can take the unusual step of following a narrow pathway (which is unnoticeable from the rest of the garden) right round the perimeter behind the plantings. This 'walk' affords views into the garden which are denied in most confined gardens, adds depth to each vista, and creates a sense of mystery and excitement which is rare in a small garden.

In this garden every inch of space is used and used in such a way that it can be seen from every angle. This is a garden of quiet ordered beauty and fulfils Barbara Maund's intention to create 'comeliness at all seasons' and 'a place of grace before anything else'.

GAINSBOROUGH STREET

Felicity & Vic Say

*T*HE GARDEN has a sensible structure dictated by the sloping land, the house, the presence of a little-used railway line just outside the boundary, the needs of a young family, and the owners' enthusiasm for native birds and 'painting with plants'. The house and garden stand at the far end of an open street where, in summer, the heat, dust and glare are fairly oppressive. The front path enters the garden at its highest point and leads through a cool dark tunnel of fragrant buddleia. The tunnel opens onto a strongly planted slope, where the sun is filtered by trees and the grass is refreshingly green. The path leads across the slope and

In a garden of bright colours, *Iris sibirica* features strongly against Californian poppies, while the white foxgloves stand in the deep shadow on the bend of the brick path.

down to the front door. Purple-leafed prunus and smoke bush hang over the path from the upper bank. Below these trees, so that the aromatic scent of its foliage scents the air when touched, *Lavandula × allardii* is used as an edging shrub. The imaginative leaf contrast is typical of this garden and, when the trees above are bare in winter, the foliage of the lavender remains to frost the scene. The lower side of the pathway picks up the silvery theme (a theme which is visible in winter and summer alike) with an edging of lamb's ears (*Stachys byzantina*). This too is typical of the garden, where no area is totally without foliage in winter. In summer the low-growing *Acaena buchananii* and *Nierembergia repens* add their decorative petals to the mauve flower spikes of the lamb's ears. The path's edging merges softly and without any sense of visual abruptness with the sloping flowerbed which lies immediately below. An old white hawthorn guards the front door.

Below the front pathway the garden can be seen swirling its colours through a lawn which rolls down the hill, through trees, past the west side of the house to the lower level of the garden. Giant stone steps link the lawn to the driveway below. The informal driveway, strongly reminiscent of a bush track, is thickly planted with native shrubs and trees and follows the line of the lower boundary along the back of the house. Among the gums are *Eucalyptus leucoxylon* ssp. *megalo-carpa. E. polybractea* and *E. pauciflora* var. *nana* and the under-storey includes banksias, correas, eremophilas, and grevilleas. Species, hybrids and cultivars have been used. The area now elegantly fulfils its purpose – to provide a refuge and bush-tucker for native birds. The driveway also gives access to vehicles and screens the house and garden from the view of the railway embankment. It also adds depth to the perspective by merging the garden foliage with that of the trees beyond.

The lines in this garden are soft and curve with the contours of the land. The old house, part of which was once a Wesleyan chapel, is painted in the muted shades of green one finds in native plants. In this garden it is the plants which attract the most attention not the house, which sits unobtrusively and peacefully in its garden. In autumn the

dusky green of the house makes a magnificent backdrop to the dramatic deep pink and crimson foliage of an ornamental vine which clothes one entry. Where changing levels have created harsh lines between the foundations of the house and the garden, evergreen native shrubs have been used to soften the line and marry the house to the gentle curve of the land. On occasion these native plants are mixed to great effect with exotic plants. The pine-scented green lavender (*Lavandula viridis*) and the daphne hybrid (*D. × burkwoodii*) look superb planted informally in a group containing the creamy-green bells of *Correa reflexa* and bordered by the fresh green foliage of *Myoporum parvifolium*. The foliage of this group is punctuated with spikes of kangaroo paw (*Anigozanthos*). In another area red annual poppies (*Papaver rhoeas*) self-sow in a bed of winter-flowering native shrubs, greatly adding to the area's decorative value in early summer.

In this climate, some exotic perennial border plants will produce the odd flower, geums and wallflowers among them, in mid-winter and in this season the garden makes the most of these little touches of colour. Wallflowers are grouped in one corner with the unusual lavender-blue flowers of the native olearia (*O. phlogopappa*). Hellebores are used extensively under the trees and on one sunny bank. *Helleborus foetidus* has established well and a striking group of plants now light the wintery slope with their upright spikes of luminous lettuce-green flower, companions to a winter-flowering lemon and white daffodil. Both pink and white forms of *Daphne odora* present the garden with strong mounds of winter flower and fill the garden with their clear scent. A mid-blue shade of *Ipheion uniflorum* stars the ground in the company of an unusually dark variety of the Algerian iris (*I. unguicularis*). The winter picture cannot rival the burst of early summer bloom but specks of colour outline the gentle curve of the herbaceous beds while the lower garden is embroidered with winter-flowering grevilleas and correas.

The burst of summer bloom in this garden is spectacular. Mixes of blues and pinks predominate. In early summer mounds of pink-flowering true geraniums (*G. sanguineum*) bloom next to blue gromwell (*Buglossoides*

Rosa 'Buff Beauty' and perennials produce a mass of flower.

theme, its pink petals surrounding a warm golden centre.

No garden is static and this garden used to be flamed with patches of bright scarlet. Some will remain (the master stroke of mixing the annual poppy with native plants will stay) but as the owners' interest in shrub roses grows the use of scarlet is being limited in the areas where the subtle shades of *Rosa macrantha*, 'Stanwell Perpetual' and 'Quatre Saisons' bloom. Here they are banished and the old-fashioned Shirley poppy, its colours strictly confined to those with soft pink petals and golden stamens, is encouraged.

In early spring this garden is blue and yellow: yellow daffodils bloom with blue ipheion, Spanish bluebells and grape hyacinth. Then, as summer approaches, comes a flash of triumphant colour set off by cream as the deep purple irises, scarlet geums and cream Californian poppies reach their peak. As summer settles in the colours pan out into soft mauves, pinks and blues – misty colours to take over as the shade from the trees spreads across the hot garden. Although the needs of the family and native birds are of primary importance here, the year-long blends and contrasts of colour and shade are a major consideration.

purpureocaeruleum). Spikes of the soft mauve-pink *Penstemon* 'Evelyn' and *Penstemon heterophyllus* mix with mounds of catmint (*Nepeta faassenii*) and the well-held heads of blue brodiaeas (*B. laxa* 'Queen Fabiola'). In late summer, when the blue delphiniums fade, pink hollyhocks come into flower picking up the pinks of the sweet bergamot (*Monarda didyma*). These mauve-blue and pink-blue pictures are lit with flashes of creamy golds. The columbines (*Aquilegia* hybrids) have been confined to shades of rust, mustard and yellow; the lavish clumps of sparaxis confined to a shade of cream laced with pink; and the Californian poppies limited to a gleaming shade of cream. *Helianthemum* 'Pink Gem' takes up the

TASMANIA

Malahide

FINGAL

The Hon. Rose Talbot

MALAHIDE TAKES ITS NAME from Malahide Castle in Ireland, the seat of the Talbot family, which lies ten miles (16 km) to the north of Dublin. It was from here that a younger son, William Talbot, set out for Tasmania in 1820. He was granted land in the Fingal valley where the South Esk and Break o'Day rivers converge and soon established large flocks of sheep and cattle. By 1835 he was advertising for stonemasons and it is almost certain that the generous stone buildings which stand on the property today date from this period. The buildings he erected were unusual in their layout. Although the idea of integrating the house with the farm buildings was widely advocated in English pattern books of the era, the concept was rarely adopted in Australia. The house itself was built to a simple design, one-room deep, with a second storey largely contained within the roof space. A massive stone wool store, attached to the house, was erected at right angles to it. A further large L-shaped stone building, known today as the coach house, formed with the wool store three sides to a central courtyard.

Malahide was planned as an efficient farmstead, modelled on a grouping of buildings common in the countryside of Ireland, rather than on the grandiose country houses built by the emigrating English gentry of the time. What distinguishes Malahide from its European antecedents is the scale of the buildings, which have a dignity only size can impart. There is, too, a wide stone-flagged verandah with a concave roof running along the front face of the house. The stone buildings have seen many vicissitudes, but they remain, and now form the nucleus of the garden. For the gardener the stone walls have special significance. The golden mellowed stone provides a perfect background to

Left A great collection of old-fashioned roses flourishes in the long border by the coach house walls, including R. 'Black Boy', R. 'Constance Spry', R. 'Ballerina' and R. 'Mme Alfred Carrière'.

Right The stone house and buildings seen from the garden.

the roses for which the garden is noted and the walls hold the sun's warmth and give shelter in an area in which sharp frost can occur at any time of the year.

The Talbot family made a considerable contribution to the government of colonial Tasmania and stretched their influence across Bass Strait to Victoria with the victory of Blink Bonny in the 1884 Caulfield Cup. However, when the property passed, in 1940, to Milo, the seventh Baron Talbot de Malahide, the family had been absent for nearly sixty years, during which time the property was managed by agents. By then the buildings were neglected and all that remained of past gardens were a few trees and plants grown in a bed contained by car tyres. Lord Talbot restored the building and began the long process of remaking the garden. Keenly interested in botany and horticulture, Lord Talbot was a Fellow of the Linnaean Society and in 1963 sponsored the publication of *The Endemic Flora of Tasmania*, a work which remained unfinished when he

A potentilla flourishes between two rugosa roses, the reddish-purple . *R.* 'Roseraie de l'Haÿ' and *R.* 'Frau Dagmar Hastrup', backed by blue and white irises, ceanothus, lupins and buddleia. On the other side of the picket fence grows a young red horse chestnut *Aesculus × carnea* 'Briotii'.

died in 1973. It was later completed under the guidance of his sister, the Hon. Rose Talbot. Miss Talbot now lives at Malahide and the garden, created from a plan drawn up by Dr Brian Morley, of Adelaide's Botanic Gardens, reflects her taste and interest.

The valley in which the garden lies plays a major part in the garden's atmosphere. The light here has the clear bright quality familiar to Australians. The sky seems to be bigger and the horizon wider than elsewhere. The house, facing east, looks towards a gap in the hills which border the valley and dominate the view from the garden. These hills present a fascinating backdrop, sometimes appearing so close that the native eucalypts and pine plantations on their slopes can be seen in detail, at other times

Gleditsia triacanthos glows in a corner by the coach house, backed by lilac and willow, and contrasting with the catmint (Nepeta × faassenii) and the yellow arching branches of Genista lydia.

tralia, where the clumps formed by their suckering habit give welcome shade. They require little attention but are usually found in overcrowded groups of badly grown stunted specimens. Here, at Malahide, they have reached a considerable height and stand as single, noble specimens surrounded by mown grass. Their dark furrowed bark, elegant fern-like leaves and long drooping clusters of white pea-like scented flowers do much to set the atmosphere in this garden. Perhaps the most striking of the trees to border the central expanse of lawn are a second pair of *Pinus roxburghii.* These ancient trees, whose trunks look as if they are composed of great scales of beaten copper, frame the view down the valley. The naked trunks rising to a height of 120 feet (37 m) are now topped by somewhat sparse dark foliage. Their presence dominates the scene, dwarfing the house and adding, with their great height, the character only old trees can impart. In the early morning the long parallel shadows of their trunks dissect the central expanse of lawn and point to the house. In the evening when the sun is behind the house the shadows lie across the lower lawn, directing the eye towards the gap in the hills. After severe frost, when the great trees are hung with long icicles and the ground beneath them is white with frost the garden offers one of its most dramatic sights.

To the left of the house as one enters the garden lies a grove of old elms. Australia remains unaffected by Dutch elm disease and magnificent specimens remain in many old gardens. The area is enclosed on two sides, as is the whole garden, by old hawthorn hedges (*Crataegus monogyna*). These hedges are common in Tasmania and their gently rolling forms, reflecting the landscape, now look as much a part of the natural scenery as do the eucalypts and acacias. Under the elms grow daffodils and to one side a bed contains mahonias, *Helleborus foetidus*, lily-of-the-valley (*Convallaria majalis*) and a variety of hosta cultivars. On the south (shady side) of the house, which borders the elm grove, *Schizophragma hydrangeoides* has been established on the stone walls.

To the far side of the house lies the coach house and two sides of its stone walls are edged with deep flower borders. The walls

distant, when all that can be seen is their outline and an unbroken sheet of colour which changes constantly – from mauve to blue or grey or black. Then, quite unexpectedly, they will turn to a ghostly white or vanish behind a screen of rain or mist.

New avenues of *Eucalyptus viminalis* and oak now lead across the paddocks to Malahide where the garden gates are guarded by two old longleaf pines (*Pinus roxburghii*). The drive forms a gentle loop round mown grass before the front door. Several magnificent specimens of *Robinia pseudoacacia* stand on the open lawns with roses trained around their trunks. One supports the peach-coloured 'Meg' and another supports the vigorous white rambler, 'Wedding Day'. Robinia trees are often found in rural Ausare hung with roses and great masses of the evergreen *Clematis armandii* 'Apple Blossom', which in spring is covered in soft blossom. The Californian tree poppy (*Romneya coulteri*) and cultivars of *Paeonia suffruticosa* grow in great mounds and blend their varied leaf shapes, colours and textures with their glorious summer-borne flowers. *Anchusa italica* and delphinium cultivars add their shades of blue and the Chatham Island forget-me-not (*Myosotidium hortensia*) raises its profuse white-edged blue flowers from its great glossy veined leaves. The plants used at the back of this border are of generous proportions and they are grown in large clumps that look splendid against the high wall. The beds are misted with mounds of catmint (*Nepeta × faassenii*) alternated with the clean-cut form of silvery lamb's ears (*Stachys byzantina*). In winter when the perennials die down and many of the roses display only bare branches a small mauve-purple primrose peeps from the beds and reflects the colours found in the clumps of pansies which bloom well through the winter months. Early spring sees Solomon's seal (*Polygonatum × hybridum*) and aquilegias decorating the beds and some also grow from crevices in the stone walls. But it is the roses which give the main display. In keeping with the scale of the buildings, the roses here are allowed to grow into large bushes. This appears to suit their temperament, for they bloom freely. The specimens are large enough to give the viewer the happy experience of looking up into their petals. Here the sumptuous pure white 'Mme Hardy' blooms with the floriferous 'Marguerite Hilling' and the semi-double deep-crimson 'Mrs Anthony Waterer'. On one wall 'Lady Hillingdon', which has flowers of apricot colour, makes an unusual colour companion with *Magnolia grandiflora*. The dark foliage and plum-coloured wood of the rose and the shiny thick dark green leaves of the magnolia, red-brown and felted on the undersides, are shown to advantage against the glowing stone.

Between the outer side of the coach house and two low stone buildings, one a gothic cottage and the other a disused simple low farm building, lies a lawn separated from the garden at the front of the house by a row of *Viburnum plicatum*. Bordering the two small buildings, a lavender hedge encloses another flower border. Roses, which once again are the main plants, are here kept low in harmony with the modest height of the two small buildings. 'Danse des Sylphes' parades her rich red petals and 'The Fairy' and 'Green Ice' carpet the ground in the company of a soft pink *Alstroemeria* Ligtu Hybrid. Old viola cultivars and Canterbury bells (*Campanula medium*) are used between the roses and the bed is given height between the two buildings with plantings of kolkwitzia and rugosa roses. Behind the two small stone buildings there is a gravel terrace, which separates the garden from the surrounding paddock and river, where roses are also trained against the walls. Here 'Albertine' and *Rosa filipes* smother the stonework and flower abundantly.

A pleasant rectangular garden has been created in front of the stone outbuilding with its lavender-edged flower border. Here stand neat rows of *Betula jacquemontii*, their papery white barks peeling to reveal brilliant white trunks and their elegant long winter-borne catkins decorating what might otherwise be a bleak scene. One side of the rectangle is bordered by a picket fence smothered in *Clematis montana* and honeysuckle. And in the corner which allows access to the courtyard behind the coach house stands a superb *Gleditsia triacanthos* against a backdrop of lilac. This small partly enclosed garden, which lies to one side and behind the larger garden, has its own character. The contrast in scale of the two areas adds to the interest of the garden as a whole.

A further area, small by comparison with the garden at the front, lies behind the house and brings the abundant roses and flowers into view from the windows. Here 'Altissimo', which, it is sometimes claimed, will not grow on a wall, flourishes against its stone support. A curved bed circles the area and white buddleia, irises, lupins, nerines and dianthus mingle with roses such as 'Complicata', 'Cornelia', 'Maiden's Blush' and 'Roseraie de l'Haÿ'. All combine, through sight and scent, to invite and lure those within the house to come out into the garden.

In front of the house, where the land slopes down to the rivers, a long lawn leads

the eye beyond the great trees of the garden to the land beyond and to the circle of hills. One side of this lawn has been planted with flowering and fruiting trees. Here there are greengage plums, 'Cox's Orange Pippin' and 'Granny Smith' apples, medlars, crab apples and 'Satsuma' plums. All are planted in rows set at an angle to the stretch of mown grass and trees are pruned to low open shapes. When looked down on from the higher level near the front door they present, in late spring, a chequerboard pattern of pink, white and cerise blossom, which combines with the sharp green new growth of the hawthorn hedges and the willows that line the river beds to make a particularly lovely effect.

Malahide today is a garden of perfect scale in harmony with its surroundings; a place of space, light, trees and roses. It is the sort of garden early settlers from the northern hemisphere might have dreamed of making. They would probably have taken great pleasure in the way familiar plants have flourished in the antipodes but there would be no mistaking this for an Irish or English garden. The hedges planted for shelter and to protect the garden from farm animals do not block out the Australian landscape with its wide horizon bounded by eucalypt-clad hills.

Neat rows of silver birches (*Betula jacquemontii*) are framed by *Gleditsia triacanthos* and the flowers of *Cistus × cyprius*.

157

High Peak
NR HOBART

Mr & Mrs C. H. Grant

*T*HE HON. C.H. GRANT M.L.C. (a member of the Tasmanian Legislative Council and representative at the Australian Constitutional Convention of 1898) built his imposing house in 1892. The site was covered in stupendous trees (a sure indication of good soil) and enjoyed one of the most dramatic views nature can provide.

A cider gum (*Eucalyptus gunnii*) is said to have stood to 360 feet (110 m) and an early photograph attests to the veracity of the legend of a Tasmanian blue gum (*Eucalyptus globulus*) with a girth of 70 feet (21.5 m). These two magnificent trees have now gone, but other great gums clothe the mountain sides nearby (in the company of stringy bark, mountain gum and other Tasmanian hardwoods). A few large eucalypts still stand within the confines of the garden but today the trees are, in the main, the result of Mr C. H. Grant's plantings in the 1890s. His trees and shrubs, many now of exceptional size, were imported from Britain for the Great Exhibition of 1896. After the Exhibition these already well-grown trees were purchased for the garden.

The house and its garden sit slightly below the mountain peaks, gaining protection from the prevailing westerlies but suffering short sharp bursts of frost and snow which last well into the summer months. This is one of the few gardens in Australia known to have endured a white Christmas. But in a climate of extremes such as that enjoyed in most parts of Australia anything can happen and in the 1967 bush fires the wild garden on the lower slopes, where native plants were encouraged, was lost. The annual rainfall is about 50 inches (1270 mm), about twice that received in the nearby city of Hobart.

Perhaps the most dramatic aspect of High Peak is the view. The house and garden sit at a level of 1400 feet (427 m) above sea level and look down, over and through the trees, to a sweep of land and sea far below. The islands and promontories which surround the estuary of the river Derwent are, on clear days, laid out as if one were looking down on a contour map. It is like the view from an aeroplane, but in this case the view is static and framed or pierced by great trees and edged with flowering shrubs.

The Hon. C. H. Grant M.L.C., died in 1901 and never saw his garden, his pride and joy, in its mature form. His son, Senator C. W. Grant, with the aid of Mr James Scott, who was head gardener at High Peak for forty years, preserved his vision. Since 1943 Mr and Mrs C. H. Grant have maintained the garden, making the necessary changes as the garden matures, but preserving the intrinsically formal character of the early design. Some trees have had to be removed as they outgrew their allotted space but many remain and the extensive hedging has been preserved and well maintained. Throughout the garden there are still thick hedges of barberry, box, pittosporum and cotoneaster, which not only give protection from the wind but are decorative in themselves and have the visual force needed in this strong scenery.

The approach to this house is by a gently winding driveway bordered by hedges. Near the house a giant redwood (*Sequoiadendron giganteum*) stands on a sloping lawn. This noteworthy tree is now over 150 feet (46 m) tall and has a girth which would stretch the arms of eight men if they were to try to link hands. However, it still has the pleasing pyramidal form (carrying branches near to the ground level and tapering upwards) of a younger specimen. The driveway runs across the front of the house to a level grassy glade. This modern addition to the garden, installed to provide extra parking space on the steep slope, contains a mixture of tall gums and young rhododendron cultivars. Protection from the slope is provided by a stout row of tree ferns. The front door is bordered by a glowing ruby-pink rhododendron which now reaches the top of the second storey windows. High Peak is noted

for its extensive rhododendron collection and rhododendron flowers are to be found in this garden from May through to Christmas. The well-known varieties such as 'Pink Pearl', 'White Pearl' and 'Alice' have grown to a great size but the names of many other early cultivars have been lost.

The driveway in front of the house is bordered with a low wall masked by a thick

Below The clipped battlements of the pittosporum hedge in the drive off-sets a froth of rhododendrons, backed by a giant redwood.

Above The original fountain in the box-enclosed pool is backed by a mass of rhododendrons, including *R.* 'August van Geert', on the house, *R.* 'Alice', *R.* 'Pink Pearl' and *R.* 'Sappho', with *R.* 'White Pearl' in the foreground.

Previous page An early November view from the house to the Derwent estuary, with *Rhododendron* 'August van Geert' in the foreground, and *R.* 'Pink Pearl' with *R.* 'Alice' growing together on the left. The white *R.* 'Sappho' is in flower by the path.

hedge of pale green pittosporum neatly clipped to resemble battlements. Opposite the front door the hedging is pierced and the exposed wall curves outward to provide a viewing platform. On either side of the platform, steps lead down into the garden. The view to the sea is seen through the tops of flowering shrubs such as camellias, forsythias, *Garrya elliptica*, hydrangeas and a multitude of rhododendrons. There is always the trim of rich greens and it is rare for there to be nothing in flower. There are a few large trees, most notably two massive monkey puzzles (*Araucaria araucana*) which, like most of the larger trees, have probably passed their centenary.

The size of the shrubs is only appreciated when you are down in the garden, the pathways leading from the steps being so overhung with shrubs that they are invisible from above. It is like entering a dark tunnel where dense foliage forms the ceiling and only the great tree-like trunks are visible. The tunnels are short and the paths soon connect with the light wide open pathway bordered with clipped box which traverses the steep hillside. This garden is full of these contrasts between light and dark, sunlight and shadow. In line with the front door and viewing platform, but at a much lower level, is a circular pond. From the upper level only the fall of water from the fountain can be seen. The pond is outlined in clipped box and the parallel rows of stone coping which surround it are inset with small flowering plants. Blue kingfisher daisy (*Felicia bergeriana*), iris and hyacinth all bloom beside the water. The pond is backed by the solid greenery of the shrubs which are interlaced with foxgloves, carpeted with multicoloured primroses, both doubles and singles and jewelled with gentians.

The broad open gravel path leads across the hillside to a tennis court edged with agapanthus, roses and rowan trees. A summerhouse stands to one side of the court and to the other a half circle of grass bordered with evergreen trees opens out – a pleasant level space from which to watch tennis. Set at the back of the glade the remains of a massive tree trunk still stands. Today the remains are covered with ivy but the tree trunk was once large enough and stout enough for chairs to be placed within its wood and the 'structure' used as a summer-house. King George V and Queen Mary on their visit in 1901 sat in this tree house during an afternoon reception.

Beyond the tennis court there is a fairly level stretch of land which used to be the old orchard. Today fruit, mainly raspberries and strawberries, are grown and a few fruiting trees remain, but much of the space is used as a picking garden. The area is protected by a bank of tall trees and low ivy-clad walls (which were built from rock gathered when the land was cleared). A straight mown path leads down the hill and terminates in a weeping silver birch, through which the view to the sea unfolds. One side of the path is bordered with a stout box hedge and backed with evergreen trees; chinese elm, lilly-pilly, escallonia, yellow-berried holly and cryptomeria are used here and elsewhere in the garden. Deciduous plants such as forsythia, flowering plum and japonica are placed within these strong bands of greenery. It is a pattern employed in various parts of the garden which not only gives tender plants the protection they need but has strong visual form throughout the year. When the deciduous plants are in bloom or displaying their autumn colours they are all the more dramatic for their solid surround of greenery. The other side of the path is like a field of flowers. Daffodils (the collection has been added to regularly since the first specimens were imported from England in the 1890s) are maintained in rows and lifted every four or five years. There are rows of an old red gladiolus cultivar cherished for its ability to bloom at Christmas. Carnations, dahlias, calla lilies, grape hyacinth, lupins, pink and white peonies, roses, a hedge of red pineapple sage, and strong bushes of *Fuchsia* 'Bridal Shower' all flourish in this informal area, which is never without colour.

Impressive as the picking garden and the daffodil and rhododendron collections are, the major interest at High Peak is its history. It is rare to find a well-maintained garden which retains the spirit of the 1890s and, rarer still, one which has not seen periods of neglect, been damaged by fire, or reduced to a mere shadow of the original intention through fashionable vandalism.

Churchill
CAMPANIA

Mrs Phyllis Barnett

CHURCHILL LIES in the Coal Valley of southern Tasmania. The unobtrusive wooden house, which is hardly noticeable against the natural vegetation, looks out over the wide flat valley floor to the hills in the distance. The house and garden, on a bank above the river, are contained in a simple rectangle of land which has been fenced off from a paddock. Below the bank lie the flat marshes cut by the coiling river. A few clumps of trees punctuate the level plains. For most of the year the colouring in the valley is sage-green, dull green and a sandy olive-green. The river has a brown tinge to its water, and trees provide darker tones of the same muted shades. There is grandeur in the scale of the valley and the subtle colouring, Australian colouring, which those accustomed to the verdant hues of a northern European landscape find hard to appreciate, gives the area an air of mystery.

Herons and cormorants fish in the river, ducks rear their young just below the house, native hens are plentiful in the marshes and, when the river floods, sea hawks hover above the valley while the black swans grandly glide in to claim their share of the abundant food supply. However, if the river water and marsh attract a wide variety of water birds, Mrs Barnett describes the area as being 'like a second Sahara, where every drop of rain is as precious as time itself'.

The garden is not large and takes its form from the marsh below, echoing the shapes of the coiling river, the flat plains with their low mounding grassy vegetation and the occasional darker, higher forms of trees. No mown grass is used in the garden. Plants are established in gravel and allowed to spread

A winding path, edged with pinks and felicia, has been designed to flow into the meandering river beyond.

Previous page The tea tree (*Leptospermum scoparium*), on the right, is planted on the edge of the garden by the straight thyme path.

out over the hard surface. Where necessary paths are paved in stone but in the open areas of the garden paths are simply areas with no vegetation and one can walk in a less constricted manner than is usual in most small gardens. It is as if one were wandering on the marsh itself.

At the entrance there is a path to the front door and one going downhill, along one side of the house, towards the marsh. The path itself is a brilliant ribbon of golden thyme threading its way through mats of flowering plants. On the other side of the fence the river threads its way through the marsh. Seen from the top of the slope the path and river look like natural extensions of each other. To one side of the path lies a curving cushion of prostrate rosemary (*Rosmarinus officinalis* 'Prostratus') which carries a speckle of blue flower on its dark foliage throughout the year. In late autumn, when the mass of blue flower is so dense that none of its dark foliage

can be seen, it resembles a curve of water. The blue of the rosemary picks up the blue in the sky; the sky, in turn, is reflected in the water of the river below and the composition of plant, water and air achieve a remarkable harmony.

Between the side of the house and the path are mounds of the pink *Verbena × hybrida* 'Parry's Pink', *Verbena tenera* 'Maonettii' and pink pelargoniums. All the low-growing plants here are encouraged, in early life, to form neat mounds of foliage. Later, as the plants fill out, the winds which blow across the marshes control the soft shapes and forms of the ornamental plants as they do the drifts of marsh grasses. The sharp gold of the thyme path is picked up here and elsewhere in the garden with golden forms of neat dwarf conifers; *Thuja plicata* 'Collyer's Gold' and *Taxus baccata* 'Aurea' and varieties 'Aurea Nana' and 'Semperaurea' of *Thuja orientalis* are used throughout the garden.

The same sharp yellow tones are found in the generous mounds of *Euphorbia myrsinites* and stonecrop (*Sedum acre*) and contrasted with the neat mounds of a particularly dark purple variety of *Lavandula stoechas*.

The path leads round the house and across the narrow stretch of land which separates the house from the marsh lying below the bank. At either end of the house stand single tapering deep-green conifers, which provide a simple frame to the house. The verandah which borders the house is planted with a hedge of the *Ceanothus* 'Autumnal Blue', and, again, a soft rounded form reflecting the forms found on the marsh below is used in preference to the geometrical shapes often found in clipped hedging. The hedge softens the man-made lines of the building and helps it to merge with the mellow landscape. The path is edged with mounding groups of *Helianthemum* 'Wisley Pink', their sharp yellow centres matching precisely the yellow ribbons of thyme. *Convolvulus sabatius* pours over rocks, matching its blue disks of flower to the rosemary and the ceanothus. Shades of sky blue and pink set off by silver leaves and touches of sharp yellow, provided either by petal or leaf, predominate in the garden's colour scheme.

The path leads across the house to a lawn shaded by a silver birch, where the dark-green form of *Thymus serpyllum* is used in place of the more usual mown grass. When the thyme is not in bloom it looks like a dark pool of water, but in summer, when the plants flower profusely, it resembles undulating mauve and pink velvet. Mrs Barnett notes that her lawn is much easier to manage than grass. There is no mowing, no weeding and very little watering. Lemon-scented pelargoniums (*Pelargonium crispum*) are planted beside the thyme lawn and *Leptospermum scoparium* 'Walkeri' presents a pretty picture bordered with *Penstemon* 'Pink Endurance'. The path then leads up past the side of the house to the open garden behind it, where the extensive view of the marshlands is hidden by the building.

As the garden opens out, trees are more widely used and one may wander through the plants in a less directed manner. A group of three *Betula jacquemontii*, the whitest of all birches, forms a small grove balanced by a single spreading crab apple. The ground is covered with low mounding flowering plants and broken by the taller forms of the dwarf conifers. Different armerias or thrifts are widely used and the garden contains an extensive collection of dianthus, many of which are at the height of their flowering glory when the crab apple is hung with blossom. All the old favourites are found here, 'Little Jock', 'La Bourboule' and 'Mrs Sinkins' blooming with numerous cultivars of *D. alpinus* and *D. gratianopolitanus*. The silvery effect given by the leaves of the dianthus is further enhanced by *Cerastium tomentosum*, which forms comfortable-looking cushions of silvery-grey foliage patterned with white star-like flowers. Milky pink-tinged houseleeks trickle between rocks and *Arabis ferdinandi-coburgii* 'Variegata' forms thick mats of green leaves splashed with white and carries a frost of white springtime flower. A yellow-flowering gazania adds its yellow-variegated leaf to the tapestry of leaf and flower. Baby's tears (*Erigeron karvinskianus*) rise in dense mounds and present their daisy-like heads of flower for nine months of the year. A gazania cultivar carrying dusky-pink flowers spreads over the ground and in one corner *Ver-*

Right The ornamental garden merges harmoniously with the landscape beyond.

The blue *Convolvulus mauritanicus* and pink thrift (*Armeria maritima*) provide an effective edging to a path of golden thyme.

bena × *hybrida* 'Amethyst' blooms with the white daisy-like flowers of *Osteospermum ecklonis*. The blue reverse of the osteospermum's petals and a central blue disk pick up the colouring in the blue flowers of *Plumbago auriculata* which blooms for several summer months in this climate.

There are stronger colours near the house and here the grey-leaved *Gazania pinnata* carries its deep bronze-red flowers close to the yellow and red of *Abutilon megapotamicum*, which is almost never without a few drooping lantern-like flowers. By the front door a golden variegated ivy climbs the wall and the ground is encrusted with the tiny rosettes of *Sedum spathulifolium* 'Cape

Blanco', whose acid-yellow flowers pick up the yellow in the ivy and whose pink-tinged leaves reflect the pinks of the many dianthus and armerias found throughout the garden.

The garden at Churchill is not large or complicated and does not seek to impose its forms on the landscape. It is a garden perfectly adjusted to its severe climate and the owner's desire for a harmonious relationship with nature. The garden echoes the shapes and forms of the marsh which dominates the scenery; what has been added is colour. It is as if, in this peaceful secluded spot, the marsh had suddenly been spangled with colours – pinks, carmines, blues, bright white, acid yellows and silvery tones.

Red Hill Farm

DELORAINE

Mrs Edward Ranicar

MRS RANICAR and her husband were looking for somewhere to farm, garden and fish on retirement from tea planting in India. With the world to choose from, Tasmania came closest to meeting their needs. The land round Red Hill rolls gently, the shallow pastured valleys are dotted with fine trees, the hilltops retain their native vegetation and, in the far distance, the peaks of blue mountains break the sky line. The earth is rich and red and an annual rainfall of about 40 inches (1016 mm) ensures a steady growth rate. There is always a chance of frost, even in mid-summer, and mid-winter temperatures sink to 7–9 degrees below zero.

When Mr and Mrs Ranicar moved to Red Hill Farm in 1951 the pleasant Georgian house by the side of a road stood forlorn and gardenless. It and the nearby store date from 1840, when Red Hill Farm began life as a farm, public house and store. People from the outlying stations came here to collect their provisions, rest their horses and have a drink before setting out once more for their remote settlements. On a hill behind the two classical stone buildings stands a large weathered wooden barn of the same date.

Today it is hard to believe that even the largest of the trees were planted no earlier than 1951 and that the large oaks sprang, at that date, from a pocketful of acorns. A billowing hawthorn hedge and high row of poplars separates the property from the nearby road. In front of the house the cobblestones where the wagons once parked have been unearthed and restored for use as the front path. Beside the house stands a golden ash (*Fraxinus excelsior* 'Aurea') in a sea of hellebores and *Cyclamen hederifolium*

(both plants adding their charm to many parts of the garden). Cotoneaster is trained against the house and *Camellia sasanqua* 'Red Willow', which takes its name from its weeping willow-like appearance and the reddish shade of the new growth, hangs its glossy leaves by the front door. A magnificent specimen of *Hydrangea petiolaris*, which is a challenge in many Australian gardens, clings to this shady wall.

Right Roses 'Marguerite Hilling' and 'Buff Beauty' flourish in the mixed border which curves up the garden.

Beside the short driveway, which runs between the simple classical buildings of the house and store, stands a Mexican hawthorn (*Crataegus pubescens*), a tree of irregular shape which adds its dark leaves and glowing yellow fruit to the winter garden. In summer its white flowers attract bees. Another hawthorn stands in the same area, this time the smaller *Crataegus orientalis*, which is deciduous but comes into leaf early and displays the downy silvery reverse to its small jagged leaves for many months. A cut-leaf birch and a medium-sized evergreen, bought as a 'dwarf conifer' but which turned out to be the Californian redwood (*Sequoia sempervirens*), stand nearby. Happily the redwood remains 'medium sized' at present.

To one side of the drive lies the path to the back door. As at most farms, this is the most important door of the house and the path is bordered with well-grown glossy-leaved camellias and surrounded by a garden in which white and silver predominate. A rectangular lawn, surrounded by beds containing small trees, shrubs, perennials and bulbs, lies along this level stretch of land behind the house. At a higher level is a thriving vegetable garden before the hill slopes up to pasture and trees. On the lawn stands an old triple-grafted apple which produces abundant Cox's Orange Pippins, Sturmers and a few Jonathan's every year. It decorates the garden with its spring blossom, its autumn foliage and its gnarled lichen-draped boughs in winter. In one corner there is a strong planting of *Itea ilicifolia*, grown as much for its dark holly-like evergreen leaves as for its long drooping catkins and froth of greenish-cream summer flowers. Another bed is given a strong backing with the classical dome-shape of a weeping silver pear (*Pyrus salicifolia* 'Pendula') and a particularly silvery silver birch stands behind a corner bed. In summer a scented white rose adds its spectacular presence to the scene. It was acquired some years ago from a mixed vase at a party and has yet to be identified. At its feet a prostrate starry white rose (with a similar pedigree) carpets the ground through the summer months. In winter, when the roses have been cut back, the ground is studded with crocuses in lavender and white shades (with a silvery reverse to their leaves). These

soft shades are complemented with an early blooming lemon-yellow polyanthus and lavender primroses, which combine with *Helleborus niger* to give this garden a delicate and unusually flowery winter appearance. Clipped variegated box and silvery grasses are used to add their form and shades throughout the year. In summer the beds burst with flower. A white campanula blooms through the summer months adding to the drama provided by the grey-silver leaves and majestic white flowers on the great clumps of *Romneya coulteri*.

The major part of the flower garden lies below and to one side of the house. Beneath one window is a seat from which one can look down the lawn and enjoy the flowers and shrubs. The conservatory beside it has a Chilean evergreen, *Berberidopsis corallina*, trained against its walls. This plant has a lime-green leaf and small red flowers. The essential characteristic of this garden is the way it has been carefully contained to make it quite secluded. A few trees can be seen above the strong flowering evergreens which border the garden, providing shelter for the smaller plants and forming a visual barrier. A big hawthorn hedge forms one boundary, the edge furthest from the house and at the lowest level is bordered with thick holly and the other sides are strongly bordered with large camellias, the well-behaved *Escallonia* 'Gwendoline Anley', *Eucryphia cordifolia* and other evergreen shrubs. Within these solid but decorative boundaries a magical flower garden unfolds. Lawn streams down the centre curving round the beds and from time to time isolating an island bed. The man-made lines are soft and reflect the gentle slope of the land. The strong forms and drama of glowing colour are provided by the plants themselves. This garden is full of interesting leaf shapes and contrasts but its most outstanding feature are the flowers and, even in mid-winter, the garden is never without a trim of petal.

The winter garden is rich with the flowers of camellias. *Camellia* 'Cornish Snow' has now reached a dramatic size and its branches are encrusted with buds from May (early winter) to September (spring). The odd harsh frost nips the buds from time to time but there are always more ready to take their

Left Towards the lower end of the garden azaleas and rhododendrons surround a small pool. *169*

and one small pathway densely bordered with their nodding heads is now called the Hellebore Walk. There are the better forms of *H. orientalis*, *H. foetidus* (the form with the interesting maroon-rimming to the petals) and *H. × sternii*, grown from seed given to Mrs Ranicar by Professor Stern. *Erythronium tuolumnense* gilds the ground and the group includes a rare white form which Mrs Ranicar describes as looking like a miniature lily. Above the hellebores hang the dark leaves of a magnificent *Mahonia lomariifolia*, whose panicles of bright yellow flowers decorate the garden for months. Beside it stands a rarely grown Himalayan magnolia, *M. campbellii*, which, according to its habit, took nineteen years to bloom. Now, when it blooms it attracts an audience from far and wide.

Late spring brings the emergence of the hosta leaves. (A local botanist describes the collection here as 'the best grown, best collection he knows'.) There are the bluish leaves of the *Hosta sieboldiana* cultivars, the

Left A pin oak and a dwarf Japanese maple back this lily pool where the poached egg plant *Limnanthes douglasii* overflows a classical vase, surrounded by a miniature campanula, *Senecio maritima* 'Silver Dust' and the wiry stems of *Ixea viridiflora*.

Below The happy association of the circular shapes of *Clematis* 'Nelly Moser' and the foxglove spikes of *Digitalis purpurea* is off-set by the yellow combination of leopard's bane and poppy in the hedgerow.

place and continue the torrent of flower. *Camellia* 'Donation' and *C*. 'Salutation' give months of winter and spring flower. Mrs Ranicar favours the softer forms and shapes of the Williamsii hybrids and finds they do well in her climate.

The ground in winter and early spring is carpeted with flowering bulbs and various leaf forms. Nothing looks bare or bleak here in spite of the cold conditions. Great patches of the marbled ivy-shaped leaves of cyclamen are broken with thick tufts of crocus. First come the frail lavender petals of *C. tomasinianus*, then a wave of yellow crocuses takes over, to be followed by the larger blue cultivars such as 'Pickwick'. Thick clumps of snowdrops, the species and cultivars of *Galanthus nivalis* predominating, follow the crocuses. Then comes the glory of the snow (*Chionodoxa luciliae*). Grown from a single packet of seed supplied by the Royal Horticultural Society in London thirty years ago, these enchanting dancing china-blue flowers now spread through the garden, charming all who see them and reminding Mrs Ranicar of the china-blue Indian boxes of her childhood.

A wide variety of hellebores bloom here

pale glossy-green leaves of *H. plantaginea*, which produces pure-white trumpet-shaped scented flowers in autumn, and the heart-shaped richly veined leaves of *H. ventricosa*. Many of these plants now reach a re-markable size but were started from seed some years ago.

As summer approaches the roses burst into their full glory supported by a wealth of flowering perennials. Among the roses 'Buff Beauty' is a great favourite and David Austin roses have proved ideal in this climate. 'Proud Titania' and 'Chaucer' flourish and produce masses of huge flowers. But if one rose only were to be awarded a prize, the owner would probably single out 'Titian', whose coppery-rose single blooms are pro-duced for months against a background of dark camellia leaves – a spectacular combin-ation. Clematis, too, are great favourites and grow informally through the flower garden. Cultivars of *C. macropetala* are used exten-sively. In one bed a striking twenty-five-year-old tree peony now reaches a height of 6 feet (1.8 m) and decorates the garden with its dramatic dark yellow petals, which are so shiny they look as if they have been polished. The plant was grown from a single seed supplied by the Royal Horticultural Society's Wisley Garden twenty-five years ago and is probably one of the first of its kind to be grown in Australia.

Beneath this eye-level flowering bounty is an equally lavish flowery ground. Foxgloves bloom in spring and clumps of penstemon bloom all through the warmer months. Dianthus, *Alchemilla mollis* and *Geranium sanguineum* froth the ground pierced by the spikes of a double form of *Papaver atlanticum*. The red Kaffir lilies, *Schizostylis coccinea*, together with a pink cultivar, produce their lily-like heads during one brief lull in the flowering season. Mrs Ranicar generally avoids orange in the garden but a few lilies in this shade have crept in and have done so well that she does not have the heart to remove them. One rule, however, is strictly adhered to and no perennial is given space in this garden if it has to be staked.

To one side of the lawn is a small pond planted with waterlilies and surrounded by dwarf trees, which include a miniature deodar, a dwarf Japanese maple and dwarf

pomegranate. Here, too, the ground is studded with flower throughout the year. Winter bulbs give way to primulas in spring and are followed by small campanulas in summer.

This treasury of flowers is surrounded (but hidden from view) on two sides by a paddock, which has been turned into a small arboretum. There are plantings of single specimens of *Cedrus deodara*, *Ginkgo biloba*, red hawthorn, Brewer's weeping spruce, paulownia, walnut and oak. The ground is richly carpeted with daffodils and bluebells and slopes down at the lowest level to a lake. The lake itself has weeping willows overhanging the water. The banks are edged with arum lilies and to one side there is a great clump of pampas grass (*Cortaderia selloana*). After the wealth of flower, form and colour within the garden close to the house, this simple green tree-studded sward reflected in water gently reintroduces the eye to the majesty of the surrounding scenery.

The garden of Red Hill Farm is, in essence, an informal country garden. What makes it outstanding are the plants, their successful nurture, and the artist's eye which has arranged the flowery effects. What has been achieved here owes little to rigid formal design and yet the garden has a strong logical plan. It is a design where the paths follow the obvious route and the plants make the pictures and form the barriers. There are what are often called garden rooms, but there is nothing obvious or over-contrived about the way they are defined. Man-made decorative contrivances are kept to a minimum in what is essentially a highly decorative garden.

Nothing here is prettied-up or self-consciously charming but the abundance of flower is astounding. The garden has a relaxed natural air to it and sits at ease with the peaceful countryside beyond its boundaries. Above all this garden is a plantsman's dream. Here, partly for climatic reasons but in large measure as a result of the skills of Mrs Ranicar, plants which many in Australia find both difficult to grow and difficult to obtain, grow to formidable size and flower abundantly.

Previous page
Winecups (*Babiana rubro-cyanea*) flower at the front of this springtime scene. The pin oak (*Quercus palustris*) and the tall Lombardy poplars fill the sky behind.

Left At the beginning of November arum lilies (*Zantedeschia aethiopica*) grow naturally under the willows surrounding the dam.

173

SOUTH AUSTRALIA

Willyama

ADELAIDE

*T*HE EXTENSIVE STONE HOUSE, in an Adelaide suburb close to the city centre was built in 1876 and today retains two and a half acres (1 hectare) of garden. In 1888 it was bought by a German, Charles Rasp, who had arrived in Australia as a young man in 1869. Early jobs as a drover and boundary rider and the discovery of silver at Silverton and Daydream led him to a serious interest in prospecting. In 1883 he announced what he described as 'a mountain of tin' at the place which came to be known as Broken Hill. His 'mountain of tin' turned out to be what is probably the richest silver and lead ore source in the world. He renamed his city property Willyama which was, at that time, the official government name for the Broken Hill area. He added extensive stables, a ballroom and gallery to the property.

Charles Rasp died in 1907 and his widow, also a German, was trapped in Germany during the First World War. On her return after the war anti-German sentiment was so strong that it needed a special Act of Parliament before she could regain her Broken Hill shares and Willyama. On her death in 1936 the property was bought by Mr and Mrs Hew O'Halloran Giles. They removed the deep verandahs trimmed in the cast iron of the earlier era and replaced them with a Georgian style concrete balustrade. Mr and Mrs O'Halloran Giles lived at Willyama until recently when, on their deaths, it was sold once more. The property remains in private ownership and, discounting its first brief period and the recent new ownership, the property has had only the two major owners, each spanning about fifty years. The gardener who retired recently had looked after Willyama for thirty-two years. The garden has had an unusually consistent life with only the vagaries of climate to contend with for over a hundred years.

Mr and Mrs Rasp are known to have favoured eucalypts and palms. Two of their now massive palms still shield the garden at the rear of the property but only one eucalypt remains and it is infected with borer. However, the size of many of the magnificent trees indicates that they probably date from the first garden and were planted before the Rasp purchase in 1888. A bunya pine (*Araucaria bidwillii*) that stands in the middle of the driveway has grown to a height of 66 feet (20 m) and every three years drops weighty pineapple-shaped cones, each capable of inflicting serious injury to cars or people. On the other side of the garden a Canary Islands pine of magnificent stature necessitated, some years ago, the unroofing of the conservatory, the glass of which was continually broken by the falling cones. Atlas cedars up to 66 feet (20 m) high which dot the garden and a huge *Ginkgo biloba* probably date from the period of the first owner too, giving them at the least a full century of life.

Old iron gates hung from stone pillars lead into the property. A wide path veers from the drive to cross the front of the house, connect with the steps leading up to the front door, and give access to a formal side garden to the east of the house. Beside the path and driveway are great tubs of pelargoniums which add clumps of ruby-red flower to the scene beneath the trees for long periods. It is unnecessary in this climate to provide winter shelter for pelargoniums. They can and in this garden have, reached the size of small shrubs. The strip of garden separating the front of the house from the road is dominated by three huge poplars (which only hold their leaves from October to March) underplanted with bamboo and shrubs. The house has a wide border of silvery leaves and the ground beneath the trees is thickly carpeted with ground-cover plants including the blue/white variety of *Osteospermum ecklonis*. This is particularly successful and blooms throughout the year. A myrtle has just been added to this shrubbery by the new owners. It is 'a family plant' and its direct ancestor was brought by the family of the present owner on one of the first ships to arrive in South Australia, the *Africaine*.

Here and elsewhere in the garden the ground under the trees is lit with thick plantings of blood-leaf (*Iresine herbstii*). The plantings are so thick that the dark ground under the tall evergreen trees glows with the mounded banks of ruby-red leaves and almost iridescent ruby stalks throughout the year. This ruby-rose shade has been used extensively through the formal garden and makes a glowing companion to the dark greens of the trees.

The Canary Islands pine stands at one end with the foundations of the conservatory making a sunken garden beneath it. This sunken garden is now planted with irises. A large clump of strelitzia flourishes beneath the tree, the sword-like smoky-blue foliage making a focal point throughout the year and during the warmer months there is a long succession of bird-like flowers. At the other end of this garden, surrounded by lawn, stands a large Atlas cedar. A path running between the two great trees is bordered with broad rose beds. The blood-leaf is used once more to great effect and a

large tree-like hibiscus stands at one end. The beds contain a mix of multicoloured roses: 'Iceberg' and 'Peter Frankenfeld' are particularly successful, with 'Peter Frankenfeld' picking up the strong pink of the pelargoniums and blood-leaf. Next to the house a large *Magnolia grandiflora* hangs its bloom and branches. Some of the roses have been there many years and the canes spring from massive crowns of wood. In spite of the overhanging trees and age of the rose bushes, these beds are spectacular in all seasons except winter. However, as the trees impinge more and more on the light at ground level, consideration is being given to moving some bushes to a more open spot and to the establishment of the roses often referred to as 'old shrub roses'.

A nectarine hangs over the urns which guard the entry to a courtyard garden.

Previous page While pink pelargoniums in tubs and hydrangeas line the approach to the house, *Jacaranda mimosifolia* sets its mauve-blue blossom against the blue of the sky.

When the ballroom and gallery were added to the west and rear of the house it left a central courtyard, which is entered from the garden by way of a pretty but well-concealed iron gate. Two sides of the courtyard are bordered by wide verandahs and the third side by the gallery which, being composed largely of glass, gives the totally enclosed courtyard a great feeling of space and light, which contrasts with the open shady garden. The courtyard contains a central planting of columnar cypresses which surround an old urn and are underplanted with arum lilies. In one corner an ancient rosy-pink bougainvillea has been grown as a standard. Its solid trunks and a large well-clipped head of foliage makes it look more like a small tree than a sprawling creeper. Pink camellias thrive in the shelter here and an ornamental vine which clothes the walls casts a ruby glow on all in autumn.

The wide driveway leads past the west of the main house and broadens out between the house, which is bordered on this side by a series of small courtyard gardens, and a large building, which contains a cottage and what were once the stables. The space here remains as wide as ever and it would still be possible for the horse-drawn carriages, dropping guests to a ball, to turn round the bunya pine with ease. A formal pathway leads from the carriage loop to the gallery and ballroom. A female specimen of *Ginkgo biloba*, large and old, shades the path with light foliage, which in autumn turns bright yellow. The tree still bears fruit and seedlings are often found beneath it. The broad path is densely planted with hydrangeas and fuchsias. Small courtyard gardens either side of the entrance courtyard run into one another, providing a decorative scented and flowery border to the house, gallery and ballroom. The series of courtyards seems inexplicable until it is understood that one

The Victorian fountain, surrounded by roses, irises and columns of junipers, forms the focal point of the rose garden.

A summerhouse stands in the wilderness garden where the leaves and flowers of *Acanthus mollis* are used to great effect.

was once a shade house. During the occupancy of Mrs Rasp, one of today's 'courtyards' was enclosed with trellis and shaded by vines from the strong sunlight. Today all that remains are the swirls of brick flooring which decorate and define one of the series of small courtyards. Low vegetation is thickly massed round the swirls of brick with an emphasis on scented and silvery plants. In the centre of another courtyard stands an elaborate high urn with silvery leaves tumbling over the rim. On one side of this are urn-topped pillars and on the other a pair of ball-cut bay trees.

The trees in the western side of the garden are old and large but, for the most part, are varieties with lighter foliage than those in the eastern formal garden. Here the ginkgo, peppercorn tree (*Schinus molle*) and jacarandas move their light foliage in the summer breezes. The spectacular hyacinth-blue of the jacaranda's summer-borne flowers are popular with all birds. As well as the introduced birds found in most Australian cities, several native species still find a home in this city garden. There are honey-eaters, galahs and even a pair of boobook owls. A golden chalice vine (*Solandra grandiflora*) clothes the sunny stone walls of the stable building. The large plant bears flowers throughout the year which tone perfectly with the warm dull yellows of the stone.

To the western side of the driveway the remains of a bulb garden surround an old wooden summerhouse. Today the romantic little summerhouse is seen above a sea of glossy deep green leaves. *Acanthus mollis*, arum lilies and crocosmia have taken over and created what the Victorians would have immediately recognized as a romantic wilderness, the perfect companion to the summerhouse. In spite of the rampant growth, unknown flowers occasionally show through and when this happens efforts are then made to preserve and identify them. An informally decorative vegetable patch borders the wilderness. Its paths are lined with bulbs and the fence line is planted with tumbling roses. This charming informal mix of flowers and vegetables has the pleasant unstructured air which belonged to country gardens before the contrived potager was reinvented. Here anything that is needed by the household for either eating or picking is planted together in a random but pleasing fashion.

Beyond the wilderness and kitchen garden and behind the stable building lies a grass tennis court. The border separating it from the neighbouring garden has been recently planted with fruit trees and its wire netting borders used for fruiting vines. Chinese gooseberry (*Actinidia chinensis*) and passion fruit (*Passiflora edulis*) have been established and are flourishing. Soon they will provide a green wall of leaf. Unfortunately the garden, like many other well-treed city gardens, is home to numerous possums and it is doubtful that the human inhabitants will enjoy much of the fruit.

Today this old and historic garden is facing the problems of many old gardens. The hundred-year-old trees have reached sizes which might have taken twice as long in other parts of the world. Settlement in Australia has not been long enough to give us any reliable view of the life expectancy of these fast-growing trees. Giving them the considerable quantities of water they need is a real problem in what is essentially a dry climate. An automatic watering system has been installed but water is an expensive commodity and the thirst of these trees is unquenchable. Happily the garden is in sensible and sensitive hands and a new family is there to enjoy its magic.

Mt George

STIRLING

Betty & Bob Lewis

A SECLUDED VALLEY in the Adelaide Hills was taken up in 1851 by Abraham Ashhurst. He established fruit trees and berry bushes in the rich alluvial soil and relied on the water from the creek, Cox's Creek, which runs through the valley. The winters here are cold and wet with up to 40 inches (1016 mm) of rain falling during the colder months. In summer there is little rain, the creek is reduced to a trickle and bushfires are a constant threat. In the 1983 Ash Wednesday bush fires the valley was surrounded by fire on three sides and the gums in the bush nearby could be heard exploding as the fire approached.

Happily the property at Mt George escaped. The valley sides are still clothed with theatrical gums. Great candle bark gums, both *Eucalyptus viminalis* and its close relation *E. rubida*, hang over the creek and the house. The upper hillsides are well covered with stringy bark scrub (*E. obliqua*) and the under-storey laced with native cherry and blackwoods. Hans Heysen, the great South Australian painter of native trees, worked in this area and what is now called the Heysen Trail leads through the hills bordering the property at Mt George. In the back paddock behind the house a theatrical stand of white-trunked *Eucalyptus rubida* salutes the skyline. This stand of gums is now noted in the National Trust's Register of Significant Trees. The creek splashes through the valley in winter and in summer usually manages to maintain some flow; only in severe drought does it shrink to a string of pools. The hills are broken with craggy outcrops of rock which are encrusted with the rich green velvet of moss in winter. In the summers the dry hills fade to the soft sandy shades which suit the muted sage greens and misty blues of the gums and undergrowth.

The Ashhurst family remained in possession, cultivating their fruit farm, until it was bought in 1938 by Miss Margaret Murray, who established the bones of the present garden. Close to the house a walnut tree, now over one hundred years old, is all that remains of the early fruit farm. It is said that Miss Murray had to fell some of the stringy barks to help pay for the property and in their place she established the first exotic

Right *Eucalyptus viminalis* rises behind the house in this view down the garden from the upper terrace.

When they came home permanently in 1983 the garden at Mt George consisted of an overgrown arboretum stretching up one hillside and some solid attractive stonework. The valley and hillsides were hidden from both the house and the driveway by a selection of densely planted trees (many now seriously misshapen from the overcrowded conditions) and the creek bed was infested with weeping willows which were causing serious erosion of the creek itself. A few lines of poplars close to the skyline marked the boundaries of the property and these remain. In the tree and shrub thinning which followed, great care was taken to expose the valley and creek, to enhance and reveal the

Left Steps through the old stone wall, covered with *Erigeron karvinskianus*, lead from the terrace to the upper lawn.

Below Fraxinus excelsior 'Aurea' is one of many trees providing excellent autumn colour at Mt George.

ornamental trees on the site, a grove of silver birches. There followed a lifetime of tree planting (perhaps, with hindsight, over-planting would be a better description of her arboreal enthusiasm). She employed stone-masons to extend the cottage (which acquired a kitchen and bathroom for the first time) and laid out the garden. This work was carried out just after the Second World War, but her tree planting is known to have pre-dated her building. One side of the valley was informally dissected into three tiers. One level carries the driveway up to the house and on the remaining two she laid broad sweeps of superbly crafted stone paving, which curve round the hill sides flanked by retaining stone walls and linked with wide shallow steps. Simple retaining terraces were built in front of the house.

All building at Mt George is done in a local stone using an informal but sturdy pattern. The man-made creations have strong simple lines and merge easily with the bush surrounding them. The grassed terraces in front of the house have no elaborate balustrading; they drop, without any form of barricade, to the valley below. Only the corners are delineated with low hedges of rosemary, just big and high enough to hint at the sharp drop but not impeding or distracting from the view down the valley or into the rocky hillsides.

Bob and Betty Lewis bought the property in 1967 but it was some years before they were able to live at Mt George and devote their considerable talents to the garden.

The house looks down to the river which is bordered by willows and rhododendrons.

Previous page
Foxgloves (*Digitalis purpurea*), delphiniums, pinks (dianthus), *Centranthus ruber*, *Rosa* 'Veilchenblau' and lamb's tongues (*Stachys lanata*) lead to a rough-hewn stone seat on the lower path.

182

natural bush on the property, and to retain the careful and pleasant way in which the ornamental exotic plantings and the man-made elements merge with the bush. The recent addition of a carport and workshop has been carried out with such care, leaving one side open, that the view to the bush-clad hillside from the garden and entry area is hardly interrupted.

A few rhododendrons, survivors of Miss Murray's planting, grow along the creek banks, where they draw attention to the gleam of water, the curve of the banks or an outcrop of rock. The majority of the willows were removed and now wild duck can be seen from the terraces chugging merrily about in the open pools and the sacred kingfisher pays an annual visit. During the

period of the owners' absence, sheep had been allowed into the property to control the undergrowth and minimize the risk of fire. It was discovered that rhododendrons are great survivors; sheep leave them alone and, in spite of wilting badly on hot days, they live through high temperatures, hot winds and dry spells.

As you approach the house the drive curves gently along the hillside and to one side the valley opens out into a meadow. The low stone house sits serenely half way up the hill with a view down into the peaceful valley. The huge gums on the hill behind the house make it look small, almost insignificant in the strong natural scenery. A spacious area behind the house has been levelled for cars and stone steps lead from this area up to a wide lawn. The stone paths lead from this wide grassy area up the hillside through shrubs and trees until the cultivated area gently merges with the native scrub. Beside the house stands the ancient walnut in the company of catalpa, magnolia, maple, *Nyssa sylvatica*, parrotia and persimmon.

A rose bed has been added to the slopes and the path here is edged with 'Green Ice' which flows over a wall, frilling it with flower for long periods in the warmer months. 'Apricot Nectar', 'Ice Ginger' and 'Veilchenblau' set the colour theme in the rose bed. Shades which enhance the green leaves above but do not compete for attention are chosen for the rose plantings. The sloping beds and ground between the retaining walls and paths are liberally planted with irises and *Leucojum vernum*. Nerines pop up in autumn and the ground is embellished with great clumps of hellebores in winter. Tulips have naturalized with *Trachelium caeruleum*, belladonna lilies, *Verbena rigida* and the blue lily (*Aristea ecklonii*). Flowers spring up all over the garden throughout the year. Thryptomenes and jonquils scent the air and the ground in spring is thickly carpeted with daffodils and bluebells. One stone retaining wall is covered with a cascade of gentian-blue *Lithospermum diffusum* and another is draped with *Clematis montana*. Camellias, syringas, Mollis azaleas and japonicas (*Chaenomeles*) flourish with forsythias and rhododendrons beneath the trees. *Cyrilla racemiflora* and *Cedronella triphylla*, both rare in Australian gardens, thrive under the trees. In recent years grevilleas and correas have been added to the collection. The stone well's cover is held in place by cast-iron replicas of the animals on the Australian coat of arms, the emu and the kangaroo.

The trees, however, are undoubtedly the chief strength and interest of this garden. Miss Murray, it would appear, tried any unusual tree she could lay her hands on, ancient or modern. A stand of Douglas fir, some cypress and blue spruce provide winter greenery and summer contrast but the majority of the trees are deciduous. Perhaps of the greatest interest are the specimens of claret ash (*Fraxinus oxycarpa* 'Raywood'). The dark-leaved seedling sport was found in about 1910 in a nursery nearby by Mr T. C.

Wollaston, who took it home to his garden at Raywood. This property, later known as Arbury Park, lies on Cox's Creek about half a mile below Mt George. Cuttings were taken and a local nurseryman, from whom Miss Murray is known to have acquired many of her trees, added it to his range. The grandsire of all claret ashes everywhere has now perished and there is a possibility that these still healthy trees may be the oldest of their kind. They stand behind a group of golden ash providing, when seen from below, a deep wine-coloured crown to the burst of yellow foliage below them. Apart from the drama provided by the ashes the hill displays dogwoods, including an evergreen dogwood, tulip trees, a red horse chestnut, *Quercus dentata* and the fabulous foliage of *Cercidiphyllum japonicum* and lindens.

Miss Murray is known to have collaborated with local nurserymen in importing and propagating rare trees and the driveway is bordered by a short avenue of the English oak (*Quercus robur*). Further up the bank there is a witch hazel (*Hamamelis virginiana*). An acer with a peculiarly crinkly, bunched foliage has yet to be positively identified and there are several cornus varieties including one with unusually red stems. Several rowans, prunus, flowering apples, *Parrotia persica*, *Nyssa sylvatica* from the north-east of America and a *Ginkgo biloba* complete the picture. Many of the trees in this arboretum are rarely seen in Australia or elsewhere.

Today the arboretum is being judiciously and sensibly managed. Miss Murray's trees have been thinned but without the total devastation sometimes resorted to on an overgrown site in a climate which produces rapid growth. Bob and Betty Lewis are adding new trees and flowers to their hillside, planting with a sensitive eye to the future and the natural beauty of the valley. In Australia, where many beautiful valleys remain untouched by development, it is easy to feel that one valley is much like another and that, if one has to be sacrificed to make a freeway or to build a factory, there are always others. Fortunately the owners of this historic, special and enchanting valley, which combines a tree collection so well with the natural setting, are doing all that can be done to preserve it for the future.

Forest Lodge
STIRLING

Mr & Mrs John Hervey Bagot

*T*HE ADELAIDE HILLS, in which Forest Lodge is located, enjoy a cooler summer climate than the plains below and a winter rainfall adequate to the requirements of the plants favoured by the avid collectors of the Victorian age. In 1890 John Bagot commissioned an imposing house to be built of the pleasant local stone in a simplified baronial style on a site covering 27 acres (11 hectares), with a garden 10 acres (4 hectares) in extent, laid out in the Gardenesque style. Modifications, however, were made to the styles of both house and garden to reflect local conditions and the good sense and taste of the owners. While the house and garden were under construction, Mr and Mrs Bagot travelled to Canada, England and Japan, acquiring specimens for the garden and visiting any person or place which could extend their botanical knowledge and collection. Unlike many contemporaries, whose gardening intentions sometimes seem to amount to a denial of Australia, John Bagot was interested in all plants. Early records indicate that he made unsuccessful attempts to establish waratahs in the heavy soil, but he was more successful with *Cordyline australis*, which was used as an accent plant.

There was nothing mean or small in the design of the original house and garden. An illustration made in 1892 shows the house, with its impressive three-storey tower, looking somewhat stark on its hill surrounded by a network of paths and small, but carefully placed, scraps of evergreen vegetation. Today the paths remain, faithful to the early illustration, but the house no longer dominates the scene. The scraps of vegetation now rise as high as 100 feet (30 m) and the house is surrounded by curtains of greenery.

The property passed in 1910 to Mr and Mrs John Bagot's only child, Walter, an eminent South Australian architect. He shared his parents' enthusiasm for the garden, maintaining the integrity of the original plan and preserving, as much as possible, the early plantings. Observing the climatic similarities between his garden and parts of Italy he also developed a great interest in Italian design. Throughout his half-century occupancy he made regular visits to Italy, studying garden architecture and collecting statuary and plants. In 1963 Forest Lodge passed to his son John Hervey Bagot, who, with his wife Helen, maintains it today.

Left The lawn in front of the house provides a formal area at Forest Lodge.

Right Combining the inspiration of two cultures, this view from the Japanese bridge, through palms and rhododendrons, looks down the Italian Vista, lined with tall cypresses.

The original stone fountain stands by the bridge amid dense shrubs and trees.

The garden is approached through imposing gates set in dense trees, the majority of which are evergreen. The driveway curves gently upwards through large dark trees and dense shrubs, emerging in a shaft of light in front of the house. From here it leads across the entrance to a half circle of clipped hedge, which forms an elegant backdrop to a central iron fountain depicting a boy and swan. The turning circle, placed to one side of the house (rather than in front of the main entrance as was more usual in the Victorian period), gives this area a great feeling of space and purpose.

The area facing the main entrance and driveway is left open to a wide, gently sloping semi-circle of lawn, behind which is a backdrop of stupendous trees. The majority of these are evergreens, part of Mr John Bagot's collection of conifers, but on one side a magnificent weeping elm makes a contrast, its great cascade of leaves and branches sweeping right down to the ground. The grassed space is on a generous scale so that neither house nor trees look overpowering, despite their size. In the centre of this peaceful greenery three copper beeches are grouped closely round a massive uncarved rock; the rock gives the impression of being locked in by the strong trunks. (The unusu-

ally close planting of the trees and their grouping in the lawn's centre, illustrates the original and successful touches Mr Walter Bagot often brought to his designs and plantings.) Edging the lawn are solid ranks of agapanthus, with great blue heads that match the blue of the sky. In winter their impressive clumps of foliage are not lost in this grand setting.

Below the lawn, the network of paths created by Mr John Bagot still leads gently down through rhododendron walks and azalea beds to the fountain, grotto and Japanese bridge where the first garden ended. It is difficult to believe that these are the same paths (in some cases restored) as those shown in illustrations dating from 1897. Although they are easily negotiated, the paths are now so hemmed in by towering shrubs and trees that the neat concentric patterns of the Victorian shrubbery are lost. It takes some time to realize that there are three identical circular beds, each containing variegated holly trees. Much of the famous Japanese plant collection has diminished over the years but enough remains of the early plantings to gain a strong impression of the intentions of the first design. Today one 'discovers', just as one was intended to discover, the fountain, grotto and bridge after a journey through a dense botanical treasury.

When Walter Bagot inherited the garden he felt that it lacked form in comparison to the Italian gardens he ·so admired. In 1917 he cleared a long narrow strip of land below the Japanese bridge and created an avenue of Italian cypresses, grown from seed he had collected in Italy. The Italian-inspired vista and the Japanese garden merge happily together, giving no sense of the cultural conflict one might expect from such a bold step. The powerful presence of the trees as they are today is reinforced by the stands of Californian redwoods and Douglas firs which rise behind them. At the far end he constructed a monument inlaid with marble relief sculptures and inscribed with tablets commemorating his forebears. The huge edifice, which looks tiny seen from the bridge and framed by trees that are now 60 feet (18 m) high, is topped by a terracotta replica of a

Medici vase, planted with *Crassula argentea*, which flows over the rim and down the sides. Behind the monument a semi-circle of *Cupressus lusitanica* was established. Grand marble steps were installed to allow entry to the wooded walk, which is now covered with soft turf studded with daffodils. Once more Mr Walter Bagot's ability to stamp his individuality on what is an impressive but standard format is apparent.

Until recently a large, single candle-bark gum (*Eucalyptus rubida*) stood off centre in the semi-circle of dark trees behind the monument. The tree was retained from the existing indigenous vegetation and for many years held its fragmented clumps of foliage high over the monument, its whitish bark matching the waxy texture of the marble beneath. The tree made a brilliant addition to a classical formula and it made a lasting impression on all who saw it, standing as an example of past glories.

The beds bordering the verandah have recently been planted with a variety of hydrangeas.

By the time Mr Walter Bagot took over the garden, many of the small geometric flower-beds in the other major expanse of lawn, to the south-east of the house, had become unmanageable. The roots of the trees were absorbing too much of the available moisture to allow flowers to flourish. The trees were retained and the lawn, which is used for croquet, is now bordered on three sides by dense greenery: solid blocks of yew, *Cupressus torulosa*, *Cedrus atlantica* and *Chamaecyparis* species. Straight gravel paths, a low wall, and shallow octagonal stone steps still give the area its geometric shape but the strongest impression is made by the surrounding foliage. There also, stout hedges of euonymus and two specimens of *Chamaecyparis obtusa* which stand to either side of the

Rhododendrons frame this view along the gully to the Japanese bridge.

lawn strike a formal note. Formerly much of the collection of Italian statues and containers was used to highlight the geometry of this area. Pairs of statues guarded pathways and gave emphasis to stone steps, while stone containers were planted with zonal pelargoniums and daisies. Today there are still fewer flowers; a small number of roses and hydrangeas bloom beneath the windows and much of the Italian collection has had to be put in storage, as theft and vandalism have become a constant problem. Nevertheless, the smooth croquet lawn provides a disciplined formal green space in perfect proportion to the house which it borders.

What was once a second croquet lawn, lying at a distance from the house, is now a rose garden. The geometric beds are bordered with quartz stone and surrounded by solid plantings of azaleas, camellias, heathers, magnolias and maples. The huge conifers that form the boundary of this area overshadow the site but in spite of the competition the roses bloom well. Among smaller plants that survive and bloom under the dense tree canopy are babianas, freesias, ixias, lily-of-the-valley, crocosmias and sparaxis. Many other small plants that were once grown here have gone and the proxim-

ity of the large trees makes it impossible to establish new plants. The difficult growing conditions presented by these conifers has to be set against their highly dramatic contribution to the garden.

Forest Lodge well deserves its name; the house stands on a heavily wooded hill and the garden merges into extensive woods. Furthermore, the drama of the garden as a whole relies on contrasts of foliage and shape provided by the heavy green trees that were much favoured in England in the last century. These trees now reach great heights and on a dull day can create an atmosphere of faded gothic gloom. However, on bright days the clear Australian light beams down like powerful stage lighting, throwing the lines and colours of the trees into sharp focus. When the gloom disperses, the blues and greens glow like a peacock's tail in a colour spectrum that is rarely seen under the grey skies which so frequently hang over English gardens of the same period. This garden is more than a relic of past glory deriving from standard schools of gardening. It has perfect scale, botanic collections, striking colour and unusual variations on well-known themes. It is an impressive garden, although, unlike many Victorian gardens, it was never designed purely to impress.

Right The seat on this long walk was sited at the time of the garden's creation.

Panmure

STIRLING

Dr & Mrs Christopher Laurie

*T*HE HILLS TO THE EAST of Adelaide, where the climate is cooler and wetter than that of the surrounding plains, have become home to many South Australian garden enthusiasts. The Panmure property is situated on the spur of a hill and its garden lies in the converging valleys and on the spur's slopes. The garden dates from the depression of the 1870s, when stone-masons working on the railway (which was ultimately to lead to the development of the area) were laid off. These men were employed to construct the first garden on the property, and their stone constructions play a major role in the form of the modern garden. Panmure has seen periods of development and neglect. When the present owners bought the property in 1970, the

'Four Seasons' putti recline in this long curve of ivy under a row of cedars (*Cedrus deodara*).

190

area was overgrown with brambles and self-sown trees. Aspens, birches, maples, and radiata pines were flourishing and some cypresses, part of the original plantings, had reached a massive and disproportionate size.

The entrance is from the upper side of the spur and the drive curves gently downward towards the house bordered by evergreen shrubs. Close to the house the driveway divides, one branch leading to the garages and the propagation area, the other curling into a parking area near the front door. The modern house and swimming pool stand on level ground on the crest of the spur. This is the first house to stand on the site reserved by the early architect for the main dwelling. Previous owners had enlarged a coach house and used it as the main residence. This extended coach house no longer forms a part of the property and cannot be seen from the house or garden of Panmure as they are today. Two splendid stone staircases lead from the higher ground to the gardens below. The garden has been reclaimed after the years of neglect, the superb stonework exposed and an irrigation system installed. The design is largely unaltered apart from minor adjustments made necessary by the use of modern machinery.

A narrow strip of lawn and an ivy-covered low wall separate the house from the fairly steep drop into the valley below. Impressive reclining 'Four Seasons' putti rise from a bed of ivy, and a row of majestic deodars (*Cedrus deodara*) shade the neat lawn and house. The strong row of trees, neat grass and statuary give the entry a geometric formality. From this high vantage point one looks through the trunks of the deodars to the far side of the valley, which is thickly covered with native vegetation composed mainly of stringy bark (*Eucalyptus obliqua*). From this position there is hardly a trace of other human habitation to be seen and little of the garden is visible; only the top of the stone steps can be seen below. When the garden is at last revealed, there is a view down to weeping willows on the valley floor indicating the presence of water in the lowest part.

The hillside garden is entered by the imposing stone steps, which are all the better for a hundred years of weather. At three levels, paths wind round the slopes, linked

Right This terracotta statue is found, half-hidden, on one of the many walks at Panmure.

periodically by simple flights of stone steps and opening out into broader terraces where the slope permits. The garden still contains several of the follies the Victorians enjoyed and the present owners have added pieces of statuary.

The many paths cutting through this garden invite exploration. Some are neatly gravelled, some green with mown grass, while others are little more than bush tracks. The sloping beds between the paths are filled with collections of rhododendrons, azaleas, camellias and conifers. Some beds are reserved for a particular group, others contain well-balanced mixed plantings. The beds on steep terrain are planted with trees rising from a thick ground cover of ivy. Care is taken to prevent the ivy from strangling trees but the owner enjoys the tracery of ivy against bark. On gentler slopes the planting is of smaller shrubs, which grow from a mulch of deep leaf litter. In winter the garden presents a patchwork of greens and browns enlivened with the odd flower. As the season progresses the greens and browns change to patches of bright colour and the design is broken by the irregular lines of leaf as the trees develop their summer canopy. The retaining stonework provides the seams to this patchwork. In some places it is left

naked, in others clothed with *Ficus pumila* or draped with ivy. Here and there a wall is made more conspicuous with a rim of bright green foliage, such as that of snowflakes (*Leucojum vernum*).

A number of trees at Panmure date from the early garden. These include several large English oaks, the deodars, tulip trees, magnolias, beeches and lindens. Other, many self-sown during the period of neglect, have been removed. Most of the trees now growing have been planted by Dr Laurie who has a particular enthusiasm for deciduous species and varieties. Those established in the past twenty years include a grove of the Chinese rowan (*Sorbus hupehensis*) which carries claret autumn foliage and panicles of pale rose-pink berries. In winter its bark has the orange-yellow glow often associated with Chinese porcelain. Another Chinese tree, *Stachyurus praecox*, has established well. It holds its coloured leaves well into the winter months, and in spring carries rather stiff drooping racemes of lemon-yellow

flowers. The Tibetan *Michelia doltsopa*, which has wonderfully fragrant magnolia-like flowers, is planted among groups of beech (*Fagus sylvatica*) in a variety of forms. The beeches provide a European touch in a garden rich in Asian trees and shrubs.

The huge English oak shelters a thriving group of camellias whose evergreen leaves and pink and white flowers do much to enhance the winter garden. In another area *Luculia gratissima*, both the species and an improved form, add their pink winter-borne flowers to the scene and lapageria (a relic of an earlier garden) winds its way through the trees displaying its pink bells. Winter is cold here, but it is not bleak and there are always a few flowers. As the trees gain the sharp-green lace of spring-leaf, the scene below is lit with a great bank of Kurume azaleas.

More recently another slope has been planted with a collection of conifers. The owner prefers to plant these close together and remove the excess when necessary. The young conifers already display a good cover

Left Seen from under the vine-covered verandah, the swimming pool is decorated at one end by a skilful association of *Acer palmatum* 'Dissectum Atro-purpureum' and the spreading juniper *Juniperus × media* 'Pfitzeriana'.

Ash tree leaves in April cover the old stone steps which link the paths circling the hill.

of sculptural shapes and contrasting greens. The grouping of similar plants which bloom or carry spectacular new growth in the same area gives the garden great drama as the seasons bring waves of colour or interesting detail to one part of the garden after another. In spite of much restoration and replanting (some quite recent but some of it nearly twenty years old), no part of this garden looks raw or new. Part of this impression is undoubtedly achieved through the fast growth rate, but a large measure of this success is due to the owner's skill, enthusiasm, and considerable plant knowledge. Dr Laurie has found all his rare trees within Australia, sometimes buying unknown unlabelled trees and sorting out their correct botanical names later. The collection includes *Nyssa sinensis*, *Magnolia campbellii*, *Davidia involucrata*, several specimens of *Acer palmatum* 'Senkaki' (which displays glowing red stems in winter), fifty to sixty persimmon trees and lots of *Laburnum* × *watereri* 'Vossii'.

The Tasmanian *Nothofagus gunnii*, one of the few deciduous native trees, and a number of leatherwoods (*Eucryphia*) are also included in the collection.

The area along the base of the valley now forms a series of interlinked gardens which harbour an extensive rhododendron collection (the tropical varieties are planted elsewhere in a sloping bed to give them the warmer conditions they enjoy). In winter the lower creek gardens are emphasized with the deep greens of a large collection of mainly hybrid rhododendrons which thread the valley in the light shade provided by magnolias and maples. Through spring and early summer this lower part of the valley is rich with the pinks and mauves of the rhododendrons. Deep in the valley the creek divides and rejoins, flowing through a series of man-made ponds and channels. A serpentine pathway (this part of the garden is called the Serpentine Garden) crisscrosses the creek, leading along the banks, over small bridges

Dr Laurie designed this pool, surrounded by slate and softened by various heights, colours and textures of foliage.

and through dense foliage. Pink and white dogwoods (*Cornus*) are well grouped with the rhododendrons in similar shades. Today most of the watercourse that existed in the early garden has been restored, the creeks cleaned and rebridged, and ponds relined. In one case, where pond restoration proved impossible, a bog garden was established; ferns now fringe a planting of hostas, rodgersias and irises. The water features now look, possibly for the first time, as the Victorians planned them; their 'naturalness' is of a distinctly European character. In a sheltered dell the rare Japanese *Pterostyrax hispidus* bears its scented panicles of white flower in the company of the more tender large-leaved rhododendrons and the Chinese *Clethra delavayi.*

At one point the path leaves the dark shrubbery and opens into an open bowl of grassy meadow, bordered with self-sown trees through which mossy steps can be seen climbing the hill into the bush beyond. On one side stands a single rhododendron, planted in isolation so that its perfectly balanced shape can be appreciated. On the side rimmed by the creek, a large willow weeps with elegance over an impressive Victorian fountain. There is an element of gothic romanticism in the siting of an imposing two-tiered fountain in the middle of a wilderness-water garden. It is only today, with the stonework looking mellow and mossed with age and well-grown trees and shrubs surrounding it, that the original intention can be enjoyed. There is an odd but pleasingly effective contrast between the formality of the fountain and the informality of the setting. Adding charm and perhaps a little impudence to the scene is a quaint thatched circular structure, formerly an aviary.

To the other side of the house more impressive steps lead downward to an open glade where native trees have been retained. Trees mark the edges of the glade and are densely underplanted with native shrubs. A carpet of mint bushes (*Prostanthera*) also provides a dramatic mist of blue-mauve below the trees in early spring. The trees and underplantings screen the garden from the quiet road which winds along the valley.

It is the preservation of the traces of the old garden, especially the stonework, which, together with impressive plant collections give the garden of Panmure much of its strong personality. The garden is a well-coordinated mixture of modern formality near the house and swimming pool (which at present contains fat healthy-looking trout), and Victorian garden conceits. This difficult mixture succeeds largely because of the skilful planting. It is a garden of strong contrasts and steep slopes, but above all it is a plantsman's garden. The garden today owes as much to the vision and plantsmanship of its present owner as it does to its first architect. It owes little to its many and varied incarnations in the intervening period.

Cordyline australis and *Phormium tenax* are prominent in this view of the bridge and steps from the lower garden.

WESTERN AUSTRALIA

Tipperary Church

YORK

Tedye & Bryant McDiven

*I*N 1835 THE BURGES FAMILY estab-lished a large property 'Tipperary' some miles to the north of Perth where the trunks of the wandoo gums (*Eucalyptus wandoo*, also known as *E. redunca* var. *elata*) match the burnt sienna of the roadside dirt. The area proved productive of wheat and sheep. York, the nearby township, developed into one of Western Australia's first rural settlements and today is noted for its early Australian architecture, as a centre of rural activity and for its cultural life. Cut into the bark of a tree in the garden at Tipperary church, the original survey marks remain clearly visible today.

The property thrived and in 1892 Mona Mary Sophia Burges erected the small brick Church of St Paul to serve the religious needs of those working on the property and nearby. The church was typical of many to be found in the Australian countryside, standing isolated by the roadside and con-sisting of a single but spacious room with pointed windows and doors and high pitched roof in a loosely gothic style. The Meckering earthquake in 1968 damaged the church and it subsequently passed into private hands, being bought by the artists Tedye and Bryant McDiven in 1978.

Today the restored church has been exten-ded and makes a comfortable and elegant house. A lodge for visitors with classic Aus-tralian cross-banded verandahs has been erected nearby and, a third building, known as The Salek Minc Gallery, displays an art collection. The late Dr Salek Minc's extensive and eclectic collection passed into the McDiven's care at his death. The little settle-ment is set in open farming country, where the pastures of the Avon valley are dotted with massive gnarled wandoo and York gums and the horizon swells with a roll of

Left   Eucalyptus wandoo is a strong feature on the edge of the garden. *Rosa* 'Lorraine Lee' grows on the left.

At the beginning of a walk dedicated to the film producer Sydney Box, a large vase provides an effective link between the garden and the dry Western Australia landscape.

tree-clad hills. The boundary with the road is now planted with a row of bushy yate (*Eucalyptus lehmannii*), whose winter and spring flowers vary from pale yellow to a greenish white. The greens in this countryside are the muted dusty sage-greens of an Australian landscape. The climate is mild but the drying winds which ripen the crops parch the gardens too. The rainfall only averages an annual total of 10–12 inches (250–300 mm) and, for 90 per cent of the year, there is an almost total lack of humidity. The earth is a warm burnt-sienna clay lying over rock and can only be cultivated easily when soft after wet weather. The settlement's connection to a main water supply is only recent and yet this garden thrives, adding its soft greens to a soft green landscape and its misty blues to a huge span of sky. The sky over Australia appears bigger than other skies. At Tipperary Church the sky curves away to infinity.

The garden falls into two distinct geometric forms and two distinct colour groups. Close to the rectangular buildings the garden is walled into rectangular garden rooms which provide sheltered links between the three buildings. These garden rooms overflow with colourful flowers and are bright with the green foliage one associates with well-watered ornamental plants. Beyond the buildings the garden slopes gently towards the open shallow valley and the rolling hills which surround it. Here the garden is segmented with deep curving, sometimes circular lines, which echo the curved lines of the countryside and the great curving span of the open sky. The colours in this section are largely confined to the smoky blues and sage greens of the natural landscape. The two areas are well integrated and linked by the use of the warm brick tones which originate in the church's brickwork and the garden's clay base. The shade is used extensively to give the garden form in both areas.

Leading to the front door is an enclosed rose walk. The layout is formal and a simple bird bath stands at its centre. This garden makes ample provision for local birds and their baths are often scented with a floating rose or a sprig of rosemary. The beds are bordered with the prostrate rosemary 'Blue Lagoon', with clear blue winter-borne flowers which reflect the unusual blue, almost navy, of thriving clumps of *Osteospermum ecklonis*. In one corner the softer misty blue flowers of the upright form of rosemary complete the winter picture. Over the kitchen window *Eucalyptus leucoxylon megalocarpa* hangs its silvery blue-grey branches and displays its rose-pink flowers for long periods. The birds play and feed here throughout the year and can be seen standing on their heads in the curious manner of all honey-eaters as they swing from the twigs in this tree.

All birds are made welcome here with the exception of the fabulous Port Lincoln ringed neck parrot, *Barnardius zonarius*, whose bright green, blue and yellow plumage has caught the attention of generations of artists but whose destructive habits have infuriated an equal number of gardeners and wheat growers. Nevertheless their constant noisy presence, together with black cockatoos, white cockatoos, pink and grey galahs and brilliant blue kingfishers, gives the garden an exotic touch and displays colours rarely found in the local vegetation. In summer this walled area, like the other walled garden rooms, glows with roses, which bloom with vigour in the dry clay soil. The area is reserved for picking roses. The soft creamy pink shades of 'Champagner' are a particular favourite as it never drops, in spite of scorching heat, and it lasts well when cut.

Beyond the paved reception area immediately in front of the church door the garden divides. Paths branch off leading to the lodge, through walled gardens in the direction of the gallery and at an angle down into the lower garden. This area, which has a lot of foot traffic, is held together with refreshing greens, interesting leaf contrasts and sculptural forms. The cabbage tree (*Cordyline australis*) is used to give height and strong lines which are then softened with clouds of feathery fennel – a dramatic, unusual and successful combination. On the ground the spider plant (*Chlorophytum elatum* 'Variegatum') and a variegated westringia are used to bring light to the ground beneath. Stars of flower are added from clumps of blue *Ipheion uniflorum*.

One path leads invitingly through a gap in a wall and into two small linked and enclosed courtyards. The walls afford wind protection

Early morning in one of the walled rose gardens with *Rosa* 'Penelope' flourishing on the right.

Left A view from one of the two circular walled gardens towards the church.

199

to the rose bushes which billow from every corner, bed and wall. Water is provided lavishly and the walls ensure that some humidity remains in the air. Many of the roses retain their leaves in winter and bloom spasmodically throughout the year. In spring and summer the wealth of flower is magnificent. In the first courtyard 'Black Boy' (an Australian rose bred by Alister Clark) clothes one wall in abundant deep red flowers. The eglantine or sweetbriar perfumes the air and 'Mutabilis' flowers for 365 days of the year.

The next courtyard, which is shielded on one side by the lodge, contains the water tank, the symbol of country life in Australia. The crude lines of this feature have created a visual challenge to many Australian gardeners, but here the high stilts are completely lost in a torrent of the rose 'Kiftsgate', jasmine and wisteria. The colours are quieter in this courtyard, there are 'Iceberg' roses, a gardenia tree and an elderberry bush, and the gate is guarded by a white butterfly tree (*Bauhinia*).

Beyond lies a large severely formal courtyard. At one end stands a large wandoo gum, at the other the peaceful countryside unfolds between the tree trunks in the lower section of the garden. One side is bounded by the gallery which is entered from this court-

Framed by the *Eucalyptus* 'Wandoo', *Rosa* 'Lorraine Lee' flourishes in front of the octagonal tea house.

yard. The ground is flat and apart from one bed (in which foliage is as important as flowers) is covered by long geometrical strips of mown grass and severely raked gravel. Nothing distracts the eye from the tree and the tranquil countryside beyond. The simple elongated shapes of grass and gravel lead the eye naturally from one to the other. The visual excitement and colour in the romantic little courtyards are left behind, the eye is rested and the brain cleared. The courtyard provides the perfect preparation for inspecting the art collection.

The buildings and walled gardens lie in a row parallel to and adjacent to the road. The second part of the garden lies on the far side of these rectangles and leads the eye to embrace the valley, the hills and sky. The area is shaded by groups of native trees: some like the wandoo gums have been there for many years; others like the jam trees (*Acacia acuminata*) are more recent, but well grown. (When the trees become infested with mistletoe it is shot down using a .22 rifle.) A large circle of mown grass opens below the front door – a circle of cool refreshing green bordered by low walls. The changing shadow patterns from the overhang of 'cathedral-cut' trees play on the grass and the sun intermittently flickers on the bark. It would be dark and perhaps at times too dark if it were not for the extensive use of the almost luminous plantings of the large-leaved succulent *Cotyledon orbiculata* which line the low walls. This lower section of the garden is magical when moonlight falls on mist in the valley and gleams on the tree trunks. The leaves of the succulents add curves of light at all times. In moonlight they seem to glow and when they flower an apricot-pink radiance emphasizes the curves of the garden. On either side of this circular garden great wings, like the wings of a Chagall angel, of smoky blue cypress trees (*Cupressus glabra*) open their span to the world beyond.

The garden is rich in religious symbolism. Below the central circle of grass lies the Trinity garden, composed of three circular gardens. The central circle is a simple raked surface with a strongly designed raised central pond. On either side are two matching circles of hip-high brick containing small

chosen so that the sitter, surrounded by flower and scent, automatically takes in the view to the hills or lies back and gazes upwards into the light foliage high above. Protection from the wind and the world outside are afforded to the sitter and plants alike. It is an ingenious solution to a climatic problem which enhances the enjoyment of the garden, extends the range of plants which can be grown in the drying winds, and lends a pleasing originality to the total design. It also forces the viewer to see the garden from a different and important angle.

In the lower part of the garden much attention has been given to gentle colour and strong form. Swirling rows of smoky feathery cypress, native rosemary, both the lavender and the white forms, several junipers and plumbago are used to give the design movement and to relate it to the world beyond. One long curved wall of the blue-grey deliciously scented *Acacia meisneri* has been laid out in memory of the late Sidney Box, the noted British film producer, who retired to Western Australia and was a close friend of the McDivens. Balancing the walk on the other side of the garden, a path leads under an arbour to an octagonal teahouse, where once more the garden can be enjoyed without wind and, in this case, without the company of the ubiquitous bush fly. The arbour is clothed with honeysuckles and roses, including *Rosa banksiae* 'Lutea', and the hybrid roses 'Sea Foam' and 'Lorraine Lee'. The last of these is another Alister Clark rose and is constantly in flower even in winter. Under the trees Spanish shawl (*Schizocentron elegans*) and babies' tears (*Erigeron karvinskianus*) make good ground-cover plants. Somewhat surprisingly Canterbury bells (*Campanula medium*) do well in this climate.

The key to this garden's success lies in the artistry of its creators but of great importance also is the knowledge, some of it gleaned the hard way, of what will grow well in this climate. The garden is, according to its owners, immature, although that is not the impression it gives: it conveys a feeling of tranquil antiquity. The more exuberant exotic plants are hidden behind walls and the lower garden enhances and enjoys the serenity of the ancient continent beyond.

A late November evening view towards the strongly-designed central garden, where wide bands of newly-planted grey-leaved succulents (*Cotyledon orbiculata*) soften the curve of the low brick walls.

gardens each entered by way of a narrow flowering arch. These matched gardens are unusual in design but look right in their surroundings, where their circular shapes reflect the curve of the world around them. One is densely planted with scented-leaved pelargoniums, which in this climate winter outside. They display their interesting leaf shapes and colours throughout the year and carry decorative flower through most of the warmer months. The scents include rose, lemon, spice, apple and peppermint. In summer this garden is thick with the native bees which swarm in the gums above. The other circle is planted with a low inner lining of cypress and bordered with the flowers of an English cottage garden such as forget-me-nots, daisies and violets.

Each walled circle contains two chairs and as the horizon levels vary slightly the chairs are of different designs. They are carefully

A Suburban Garden

PERTH

Tania Young

*T*HE CLIMATE IN PERTH is hot with drying winds. The annual rainfall of 35 inches (900 mm) is received mainly in the winter months. Twenty years ago Tania Young, who had never lived with a garden before, began to make her garden on a site whose only adornment was four, well-grown trees. In the front garden, taking up an important position, stood a splendid, old, white gum (*Eucalyptus rossii*) and a Norfolk Island pine (*Araucaria heterophylla*), which holds its horizontal branches, tier above tier, in a perfectly symmetrical form. Behind the house stood a large, spreading plane tree (*Platanus orientalis*) and a magnificent Moreton Bay fig (*Ficus macrophylla*) an evergreen species with thick glossy laurel-like leaves that can measure up to 10 inches (25 cm) in length. These figs make excellent shade trees and at the time of settlement were regarded as Australia's finest avenue tree. Today they are rarely planted because of the water and space they consume and the mess made by their falling figs. Happily, the garden designed and planted by Tania Young was planned to incorporate these impressive trees.

The house is set back from the street and today is shielded from the road by a wall of greenery. Seen through the trees, the house looks as if it had been there for over a century, with large well-spaced trees overhanging the lawn and evergreen shrubs planted with low-growing trees bordering the house and garden walls. The wall separating the street from the garden is planted with a mixture of exotic and native plants. *Melaleuca hypericifolia*, from New South Wales, with its dramatic summer-borne red bottlebrushes, and the indigenous west Aus-

tralian green honey myrtle (*Melaleuca diosmifolia*), which bears unusual yellowish-green dense bottlebrushes in late summer, grow in the company of the fragrant glossy-leaved Japanese *Viburnum suspensum*. The South African *Bauhinia galpinii*, which carries rich red nasturtium-like flowers, and double pink oleanders are used to give the plantings a dense feeling – a feeling which is enhanced by the lustrous, rich-green leaves of kangaroo vine (*Cissus antarctica*), which winds through the oleanders. A Siberian elm (*Ulmus pumila*) has been planted to remind Tania Young of her Russian heritage. A camellia stands by the front door with an

Left The house seen through tropical foliage from the sunken garden.

Right A eucalyptus shades the brick-paved picking garden where roses, including *Rosa* 'Iceberg', foxgloves (*Digitalis purpurea f. alba*) and *Anthriscus sylvestris* flower.

Right   The purple bracts of *Bougainvillea* 'Mrs Butt' and the scented flowers of *Trachelospermum jasminoides* fall from the wooden pergola by the back door.

A shady waterfall and pool lie beneath the fan palms in the sunken garden, with *Agave attenuata* in the foreground.

underplanting of ferns. On the other side of the door a bed contains the evergreen palmate glossy leaves of *Fatsia japonica* and several extremely elegant pigmy date palms (*Phoenix roebelenii*), with graceful deep green leaves that arch almost to the ground. The formal front garden, with its emphasis on interesting leaf shapes and cool greenery, and the symmetrical sweep of the drive add great elegance to an already elegant house.

A simple iron gate, set to one side of the house, gives access to the garden at the rear. Beyond the gate a paved area is shaded by the fan-like leaves of the Chinese fan palm (*Livistona chinensis*). Beneath its huge fans of leaf are ferns mixed with the strap-like leaves and soft-orange blooms of clivias and the glossy deep green lobed leaves of *Acanthus mollis*, a plant that produces impressive spikes of soft mauve flowers. Three Bangalow palms (*Archontophoenix cunninghamiana*) hang their graceful fern-like leaves over the area. In autumn these palms produce lovely shell-pink flowers from beneath their softly arching leaves. Behind the house the magnificent plane tree is used to mark the division between the central open lawn and the sunken shady garden which lies to one side. To the other side of the lawn lies a covered area which is used for evening meals.

A deep shady patio looks into the sunlight of the open lawn with its fringe of thick vegetation. The patio forms a garden room in itself and is embellished with a selection of well-trimmed container-grown plants. Here the particular emphasis is on scented plants and the flowers of Yeddo hawthorn (*Raphiolepis umbellata*) and *Murraya exotica* provide their heady scent for many months. Perfectly shaped cumquats (*Fortunella japonica*), with flowers strongly smelling of orange blossom and highly decorative fruits resembling miniature oranges, give the area a feeling of eighteenth-century formality. The flowering plants have been chosen to give a display over several months but they must be able to withstand the close trimming needed to give the area its tidy, formal appearance. Neatly shaped tubs of yesterday-today-and-tomorrow (*Brunfelsia pauciflora*) display glossy leaves and their blue-purple flowers. White daisy bushes (*Chrysanthemum frutescens*) are planted at the edge of the patio and display their white flowers for most of the year. Camellias lend their formal shapes to the scene and decorate the winter with their bloom. Pink and white impatiens are tucked into the containers and bloom on the patio and throughout the shady parts of the garden for many months.

From the shade of the patio one looks out into the light of the open lawn. Bordering the right side of the lawn lies the dense plantation which separates the sunny lawn from the shady sunken garden. Under the huge plane tree hangs a group of Kentia or thatch palms (*Howeia forsterana*), and tall tree ferns. A large pink-flowering hibiscus provides summer colour and is set off by the pendulous creamy-white flowers of *Datura suaveolens*. *Philodendron domesticum* is used as a

The stone-paved area at the side of the house is shaded with a mixture of exotic and tropical trees. A combination of perennials like *Acanthus spinosus* and *Clivia miniata* are planted beneath the trees.

glossy ground-cover. Opposite the patio stands an impressive weeping mulberry (*Morus alba* 'Pendula') displaying glossy green leaves in summer which turn to a golden yellow in autumn. To the left, dominating the scene with its overhanging branches and numerous graceful light-green leaflets, stands the tree known as the pride of Bolivia (*Tipuana tipu*). In late spring the sprays of apricot to yellow pea-shaped flowers add drama to this tree-lined lawn. Beside the house and rising to the full height of its two storeys stands a golden shower tree (*Cassia fistula*), which displays long drooping sprays of fragrant yellow flowers and, later in the season, conspicuous brown cylindrical pods. Beneath the trees the blue form of *Campanula poscharskyana* displays its bell-like flowers and pots containing hippeastrums and bromeliads are moved through the garden as they raise their eye-catching blooms. A central back lawn is traditional in Australian gardens but this one has distinctive character. It has the feeling of an open cool green glade surrounded by lush vegetation and overhung with light foliage and flower. Nothing here reminds one of the essential dryness of the climate or of the sparse vegetation which surrounds many houses in dry climates.

The sunken garden has an even more lush atmosphere. It is approached through plantings of ginger plants, with the lemon-yellow spikes of *Hedychium gardnerianum* and the white spikes of *H. coronarium* scenting the

air. Goldstripe bamboo and the spectacular black-stemmed bamboo border the path which leads to a shadowy paved area. A waterfall plays over rocks and into a small pond and fills the air with the sound of falling water. Pacific irises bloom from the water. To one side and bearing a curious similarity to the fall of water, stands the rare, variegated form of the bird-lime tree (*Heimerliodendron brunonianum*). It carries tricolour leaves (two greens with cream edges) and pale pink new growth. A pair of brolgas, the creations of the South Australian sculptor Cecil Norris, dance under a fan of palm leaves. At their feet are asparagus ferns (*Asparagus plumosus*) and sword ferns (*Nephrolepis cordifolia*). The great Moreton Bay fig stands at the far end of this area with an equally impressive *Magnolia grandiflora*, which displays its huge saucers of creamy white scented blooms throughout the summer months. The two great trees are underplanted with the wispy forms of variegated spider plant (*Chlorophytum comosum*) and the contrasting tufted leathery forms of bird's nest ferns (*Asplenium nidus*).

On the left side of the open lawn is the covered area which is used for evening meals. The area is sheltered by the branches of the tipuana tree and shaded by the scented star-like flowers of *Trachelospermum jasminoides* and the free-flowering purple-bracted bougainvillea hybrid 'Mrs Butt', which are supported by a wooden pergola. Growing from a hanging pot the large-flowered *Hoya carnosa* covers one wall with its waxy, scented pink blooms. An old wooden wheelbarrow holds containers filled with *Spathiphyllum* 'Mauna Loa' whose white spikes of flower are freely borne in the shade of the vines. The whole shady area is greened with the decorative glowing leaves of the root climber *Epipremnum aureum* 'Marble Queen', and the glossy leaves of syngoniums. The area gives an impression of shady greenery and the foliage is so lush that the flickering light from above seems to have a cool greenish glow.

The shadows open to the bright light which surrounds the swimming pool. To one side is a magnificent stand of palm-like *Strelitzia nicolai*. The huge spath-shaped leaves which can exceed 6 feet (1.8 m) in

Right Brolgas, the creations of Cecil Norris, dance in the dense vegetation.

White camellias and ferns lead into the deep-shaded patio, paved with brick in a herring-bone pattern.

length add their sculptural forms to the area and the plants produce an intermittent supply of dramatic beak-like flowers which are made all the brighter by the constant attendance of nectar-feeding birds. The wall behind the pool is covered with neatly clipped ivy and in two recesses variegated New Zealand Christmas trees (*Metrosideros robusta*) are clipped into formal shapes. On the opposite side of the pool a formal seat is placed beside a raised urn and the small statue of a lady stands in a recess above the seat. In summer two huge matching urns are filled with a torrent of sky-blue plumbago and a froth of white petunias. Container-grown cabbage palms (*Cordyline australis*) add their sparse rosettes of strap-like leaves

and angular forms to the area. Tania Young had always wanted a place where she could pick flowers for the house in the early mornings and behind the pool lies a walled picking garden. Some shade is provided with a *Cassia fistula* and the spectacular form of the African tulip tree (*Spathodea campanulata*). A lemon tree and passionfruit vine (*Passiflora edulis*) provide their exquisite flowers and fruits for the house and abundant roses are there for the picking. 'Iceberg', 'Fragrant Cloud', 'Queen Elizabeth' and 'Just Joey' bloom well in the sunlight and Tania Young has established that 'Julia's Rose' will bloom equally well in half shade. Growing with the roses are foxgloves, forget-me-nots and, later in the year, lots of self-sown pink and white cosmos.

Tania Young has divided her garden into garden-rooms, giving each area a distinct character. The garden is given cohesion with the lavish use of tropical greenery and contrasting leaf shapes and patterns. Perhaps the most interesting aspect in this garden is the way in which the strong sometimes harsh light has been used to enhance the garden's atmosphere. Shadowy and shady areas filled with a magical tracery of flickering light are contrasted with areas of open sunlight or areas where there is only a frail lace of leaves between the sun and the ground. This attention to the use and enjoyment of light is hardly surprising as Tania Young is also a photographer and well-known for her environmental portraiture.

Bishop's House

PERTH

Lord & Lady McAlpine

B*ISHOP HALE*, Perth's first Anglican bishop and a man of independent means, commissioned the building of what is known today as Bishop's House in 1859. The house, of classic Georgian design (with the addition of heavy open verandahs suitable to a hot climate), is largely faced in brick and tile. After many vicissitudes and extensive restoration by Lord and Lady McAlpine, the house now looks much as it did when the bishop built it: an imposing glowing terracotta structure trimmed with

gleaming white paint and set in a leafy garden. But some things have changed dramatically since Bishop Hale's time and the house and garden now sit in the central Perth business district and are hemmed in by swirling traffic and imposing modern buildings. The strong lines of soaring skyscrapers pierce the sky and the roar of traffic and noise from the building sites nearby is continuous.

Doubtless the bishop was attracted to the site by the presence of water but whether he intended to place the house right on top of a spring so pure that a brewery was established next door is, today, unclear. The spring, now rising in the wine cellar, flows through the garden by way of a series of ponds, streams and falls, providing the water and humidity so important to a garden in this arid windy climate.

On the bishop's long journey to Australia the clipper stopped, as most did in those days, to replenish at the island of St Helena. There the travellers visited the Emperor Napoleon's temporary resting place and cuttings were taken from the great willow (*Salix babylonica*) which overhung the grave site. The cuttings took well and the surviving trees, with massive trunks, thick branches and furrowed bark now weep from a great height over the garden. At some stage one has fallen across the bottom of the garden and the huge trunk still lies a few feet from the lower boundary, forming a natural ha-ha or sunken wall. At either end of the trunk, some 20 feet (6 m) apart, the willow has sent up suckers and these, now imposing trees, form a curtain between the garden (most of which lies to the rear of the house) and the city beyond. In this climate willows hold their leaves through the winter, dropping them in

Left The house seen against a backdrop of city buildings. The amphitheatre is in the foreground.

The parterre garden in front of the house.

with their irregular shapes and soft lines.

The past few years have seen considerable replanning and replanting in the garden, which might be better described as a series of gardens within one space. As the land slopes away from the rear of the house the central section has been subdivided into smaller gardens or garden rooms, each with a particular theme. Immediately below the house is a parterre and beyond that a citrus grove. The fall of the land is then supported by a sunken wall, below which lies a sculpture lawn planted with fruiting trees. Large trees stand at the far end but others, dispersed throughout the block, provide a harmonious link between the various garden themes within the one garden. The well-treed area at the end of the block was, until recently, the rubbish dump. Today it has been given dramatic sculptural form with underplantings of tree ferns (*Cyathea australis*), ginger plants (*Hedychium densiflorum*) and bird's nest ferns (*A. nidus*). On occasion, when a tree fern has failed to establish, the dark trunk has been left in place and the crown planted with *Nephrolepis exaltata* 'Bostoniensis' – a cunning way of maintaining the natural sculpture created by these ancient plants.

To one side of this central series of gardens lies a wide bricked driveway, which leads from the road up the side of the garden and to the rear of the house. Much of this driveway is spanned by a strong metal frame which has been planted with golden-shower senna trees (*Cassia fistula*). These trees are to be trained over the arbour-like structure. The other side of this giant arbour is planted with white wisteria so that the wisteria will wreathe the arbour with its dramatic bloom during the brief spring period when the senna trees are without leaf. The senna's yellow flowers are borne in the height of summer, when many gardens here are dry and rather bare.

The narrow strip of garden which separates the covered driveway from the heavy building on the boundary is dressed with a row of native trees which soften its outline. The strip is heavily underplanted with camellias and evergreen Kurume azaleas. There are also extensive plantings of camellias and azaleas elsewhere in the garden, which is bright with cerise, pink, carmine,

Above A view along the verandah.

Top A view of the cottage garden at one side of the house. Notice the brick tubs.

the gales of spring and bursting back into leaf about six weeks later.

By 1895 Bishop Riley, later to become Archbishop Riley, and his wife were ensconced at Bishop's House and under their aegis English oaks were established in the garden. Today these early plantings in the company of a large palm (*Phoenix canariensis*), an equally impressive gum (*Eucalyptus botryoides*) and huge plane trees hang over the garden, providing shade and breaking up the hard lines of the man-made landscape

scarlet and white flowers throughout the cooler months.

The driveway, which is wide enough for two cars to pass, leads to a side door. Here the verandah rails are twined with roses and honeysuckles (*R. bracteata* and *Lonicera* sp.) and the ground below is densely planted with flowering annuals and perennials. Like a cottage garden, this area is informal and richly embroidered with flowers. Pink obedient plant (*Physostegia* 'Rose Bouquet'), *Salvia farinacea* 'Alba' and *Phygelius capensis*

combine to make a striking summer display which survives for several months and stands up to the summer heat. Two brick barrels (brewery barrels were placed either side of the path and the tubs bricked-in) guard this entry and complete the cottage atmosphere. The cumquats planted within the barrels add their orange glow to that of the bricks.

On the other side of the central line of gardens is a stretch of wilderness which merges at its far end into the large trees at the

The view from the verandah over the parterre garden, looking down through citrus trees towards Napoleonic willows at the far end.

lower boundary. Narrow paths lead through thick vegetation. Banana palms and bamboos, including those with black or thick chinese-yellow stems, have been used to create thickets of jungle. One path follows closely a small but fast-flowing stream, bridging it and circling the still ponds which lie, hidden from the open garden, in the shady woodland glades. Here, under the trees the noise of the surrounding city fades and one can clearly hear the sound of a small waterfall and feel the peaceful atmosphere created by the still water in the two ponds. In this relatively small space in the shadowy light one can feel alone and removed from the busy world beyond. It is an area of dark mystery. One pond includes huge sculptured stepping stones, created by William Turnbull, and is edged with the luminous pale green foliage of *Syngonium hoffmannii*. Eventually the path winds back into the light, the open garden and the sounds of the city.

To the side of the house and above the wilderness, half-moon turfed steps have been cut into a steep lawn providing a small but serviceable amphitheatre. The theatre is backed with curves of port-wine magnolia

(*Michelia figo*) and a hedge of evergreen jasmine (*Jasminum nitidum*), which in this climate blooms and scents the garden throughout the year. Above and to one side of the amphitheatre stand an orchid house and an old beaver house from the zoo which is now the gardener's shed.

A herb garden has been established at a still higher level bordering the side of the house. Narrow strings of box pick out the simple geometric design and outline the beds. In the centre a great urn planted with *Lavandula dentata* adds its formal presence to the design. Its height is balanced with standards of honeysuckle.

At the front entrance to the house a narrow strip of lawn is bordered with a neat row of white roses grown as standards. In this climate 'Iceberg' flowers freely in summer and also has the happy habit of holding its glossy leaves through the winter and producing odd flowers in this season. The doorway is flanked by two old wooden grain bins, their scale in perfect proportion to the imposing architecture of the porchway.

Broken shade in the wilderness garden. Note the play of strong light on the different leaf shapes and textures.

Left A circle of huge sculptured stepping stones, created by William Turnbull, break the surface of a shady pond.

The parterre garden, here planted with standard roses and under-planted with white petunias, was planted earlier in the season with white ranunculus. A rustic summerhouse stands at one end of the central path.

They are filled with flowering plants throughout the year. In summer they foam with jasmines, welcoming the visitor with their froth of scented white flower and displaying their glossy green leaves against the rich terracotta of the house. Large camellias stand in pots along this front section of the verandah; their leaves also gleam richly against the brick and their pink winter-borne flowers lend an exotic touch to a formal setting.

The fairly new parterre is of particular interest. An oblong of level ground immediately below the symmetrical house is divided into quarters which are curved on their inmost corner to allow for a central circular bed. It is the treatment of this fairly standard design which is of interest.

The beds are edged with parallel lines of box and flowers are planted between these hedges. White *Primula malacoides*, white petunias and white salvias are used alternately for these ribbons of flower. The simple geometric layout becomes more emphatic with this bold treatment and balances the strong geometry of the heavy verandah which stands above the parterre (and might hang somewhat oppressively if it were not for this impressive forecourt). The bright whites of the lines of flower match the paintwork on the lines of the house. The parterre is given height in the traditional way with standard rose bushes but once again they have been placed in an unusual way. Instead of occupying the centre of each bed they are placed within the ribbon plantings, one at each corner of the four large beds and one in the centre of the circular bed, giving further emphasis to an already strong design. These large standards are in a variety of shades; the combination of pink and white is used extensively in this part of the garden. The roses are given uniformity and the design given winter leaf and flower by grafting 'Iceberg' into the multi-coloured heads of each rose bush. The four large compartments are plain green, with smooth grass, while the rose in the central circular bed rises from a crown of clipped honeysuckle, which has been trained round a wire frame. The wide central pathway running parallel to the house is planted with topiary – cypresses have been persuaded to grow into amusing bobbles, alternating bare trunk with green bobble as they reach upward. This central path terminates at one end in a rustic brush-thatched summerhouse and at the other in a neat barricade of box hedging. The pathway at right angles to the house leads into the neat rows or citrus trees (rows which do not precisely align with the axis of the parterre) and, to one side of these higher garden rooms, a pleasing archway, planted with a banksian rose and *Trachelospermum jasminoides* leads to the amphitheatre and wilderness. The basement of the house adjacent to the parterre is screened by open lines of *Camellia sasanqua* underplanted with white impatiens.

Each element within this garden falls into a recognized category, such as parterre, wilderness or herb garden. But this garden is not mere pastiche or an exercise in period reproduction to match an important and historic piece of architecture. Each garden bears the strong characteristics of its type but, above all, it is the personal garden of individuals who enjoy style but are not afraid to break with conventions. The owners' enthusiasm for topiary means that clipped specimens may be found in the less formal parts of the garden. The wilderness is not just an artful reproduction of untamed nature but contains part of an extensive collection of modern sculpture and examples of topiary.

Right William Turnbull's sculpture 'Metamorphic Venus' stands under the leaves of a weeping willow.

The rustic summerhouse is not placed in the cottage garden but in the formal parterre to one side of the imposing and symmetrical house. And, when the local zoo disposes of a superannuated beaver house, it is added to the lively mix of styles and given prominence by being placed near some important old aloe trees. The axis established by the parterre does not correspond with the axis in the citrus grove, a treatment which, while it does not extend the vista in the conventional way, is certainly not boring.

Many unusual touches make this an exciting garden in which one senses both the enthusiasm and enjoyment of the present owners and the significance of its important past.

'Circling Birds', the sculpture by David Wynne, is set amongst banana trees.

Biographical Notes

JOCELYN BROWN. 1890–1971, garden designer whose strongly designed gardens derive from the neo-Georgian mode of the thirties and forties. The structured architectural elements in her designs were softened by lavish planting. She was a noted draftsman, painter of flowers and flower-arranger. 'The successful and satisfying planting scheme will embody good proportion, scale, line, contrast and unity.'

ALISTER CLARK. 1864–1949, noted plantsman who specialized in the breeding of daffodils and roses. His roses, bred for Australian conditions, tolerate considerable neglect.

WILLIAM GUILFOYLE. 1840–1912, Director of Melbourne Botanic Gardens, 1873–1909. He designed numerous private gardens, favouring the sweeping lawns and bold curves which he described as the English landscape style. His work represents a well-controlled rationalization of Victorian garden ideals. 'At every step, the visitor finds some new view – something fresh, lively and striking.'

ELLIS STONES. 1896–1975, garden designer and landscape artist who was noted for his sense of, scale, his reverence for the natural landscape and his ability to model his arrangements of bluestone (basalt) on the formations found in the bush. '... more can be learnt by observing nature than through any other form of teaching.'

EDNA WALLING. 1896–1973, garden designer who, through her designs, use of plants and writing, was the leading exponent of the naturalistic style which replaced the geometric formality that epitomized much Edwardian garden design. Her surviving gardens are noted for their stonework, harmonious planting and elegant proportions. 'Who shall say this tree must be so far from its fellow, and that shrub so remote from its neighbours, for is not the joyous garden the one in which the happy association of plants is largely accidental?'

PROFESSOR LESLIE WILKINSON. 1882–1973, architect whose public and private buildings are characterized by their classic proportions, elegant finish, sense of style and climatic suitability. 'It is not so important to be in style, as to have a sense of style.'

The avenue of fastigiate poplars, entered through a long adjacent hedge of purple lilac (*Syringa vulgaris*), creates one of many vistas at Bolobek, Victoria.

Select Bibliography

BLIGH, Beatrice, *Cherish the Earth: The Story of Gardening in Australia* (Ure Smith. Pty Ltd: National Trust of Australia, 1973)

CUFFLEY, Peter, *Cottage Gardens in Australia* (Five Mile Press, Australia, 1983)

DIXON, Trisha & CHURCHILL, Jennie, *Gardens in Time* (Angus & Robertson, 1988)

ELLIOT, Gwen, *The Gardener's Guide to Australian Plants* (Hyland House Publishing, Australia, 1985)

ELLIOT, Gwen, *New Australian Plants for Small Gardens and Containers*, 2nd rev. edt. of *Gardener's Guide to Australian Plants* (Hyland House Publishing, Australia, 1989)

GRIFFITHS, Trevor, *My World of Old Roses* (Whitcoulls, New Zealand & London, 1983)

HITCHMOUGH, James, *Garden Bulbs from Australia & New Zealand* (Viking O'Neil, 1989)

LORD, E. Ernest, *Shrubs and Trees for Australian Gardens* (Lothian, 1948)

MCLEOD, A. Judyth, *Our Heritage of Old Roses* (Kangaroo Press Pty, 1987)

MCLEOD, A. Judyth, *Lavender Sweet Lavender* (Kangaroo Press Pty, 1989)

MACOBOY, Stirling, *What Flower is that?* (Hamlyn, Sydney 1969, London 1974; Omega, London 1984)

PESCOTT, R. T. M., *W. R. Guilfoyle: The Master of Landscaping* (Oxford University Press, Melbourne 1974, London 1975)

PROUDFOOT, Helen, *Gardens in Bloom: Jocelyn Brown and Her Sydney Gardens of the 30's and 40's* (Kangaroo Press Pty, 1989)

STONES, Ellis, *Australian Garden Design* (Macmillan Company of Australia, 1971)

WALLING, Edna Margaret, *A Gardener's Log* (First pub. Oxford University Press, Melbourne 1948; Macmillan, London 1969)

WATTS, Peter, *Historic Gardens of Victoria: a Reconnaissance*, from a report of the National Trust of Australia, ed. Margaret Barrett, (Oxford University Press, Melbourne & Oxford, England 1983)

WATTS, Peter, *The Gardens of Edna Walling* (The Women's Committee of the National Trust of Australia, 1981)

WOODWARD, Penny, *An Australian Herbal: A Practical Guide to Growing and Using Herbs in Temperate Australia and New Zealand* (Hyland House Publishing, Australia, 1988)

Converting The Wilderness: The Art of Gardening in Colonial Australia (Australian Gallery Directors Council, and Howard Tanner, 1979)

Index